THE OLD FRENCH FABLIAUX

The Old French Fabliaux

CHARLES MUSCATINE

YALE UNIVERSITY PRESS

NEW HAVEN AND LONDON

Parts of chapters II and V first appeared
in *Genre,* 9 (1976) and in *Court and Poet,*
ed. Glyn S. Burgess (Liverpool: Francis Cairns,
1981), respectively, and are reprinted here
with the kind permission of the publishers.

Designed by Sally Harris
and set in Garamond type, by
David E. Seham Assoc., Inc.
Printed in the United States of America by
Halliday Lithograph, West Hanover, Mass.

Library of Congress Cataloging-in-Publication Data

Muscatine, Charles.
    The Old French fabliaux.

    "Bibliography of fabliaux": p.
    Bibliography: p.
    Includes index.
    1. Fabliaux—History and criticism.   2. French
poetry—To 1500—History and criticism.   3. Humorous
poetry, French—History and criticism.   4. Sex in
literature.   I. Title.
PQ207.M87   1986   841'.03'09   85–17992
ISBN 0–300–03527–6

The paper in this book meets the guidelines for
permanence and durability of the Committee on
Production Guidelines for Book Longevity
of the Council on Library Resources.

10   9   8   7   6   5   4   3   2   1

*Title page illustration: Scene from "The Three Canon-
esses of Cologne." Bibliothèque de l'Arsenal MS 3525,
fol. 84vo. Courtesy of the Bibliothèque Nationale,
Paris.*

To Richard Benson Sewall

. . . first he wroghte, and afterward he taughte.

Contents

Acknowledgments   ix

Abbreviations   xi

CHAPTER I   The Genre and Its Literary Background   1

CHAPTER II   The Social Background   24

CHAPTER III   Plot and Style   47

CHAPTER IV   The Fabliau Ethos   73

CHAPTER V   Sexuality and Obscenity   105

CHAPTER VI   The Fabliaux in Medieval French Culture   152

Notes   171

List and Index of Fabliaux   201

General Index   215

Acknowledgments

Many friends, students, and colleagues have helped with this work, and I am grateful to all of them. For guidance in reading, particular thanks are due John Benton, Thomas N. Bisson, Carlo Cipolla, Natalie Z. Davis, Alan Dundes, Jean-Louis Flandrin, Erik Kooper, Gershon Legman, Jacques Le Goff, Steven Hirsch, Helen Rodnite Lemay, Bryce Lyon, Willem Noomen, and Richard Shapiro. I have had the privilege of long conversations with Per Nykrog and Jean Rychner, and of seeing in manuscript work in progress by Elisabeth Schulze-Busacker, Laura Kendrick, and Carter Revard. Susan Dannenbaum and Sarah Schumacher Page helped expertly with bibliographic problems. Grace O'Connell and Sylvia Brown prepared the typescript with unfailing serenity and good humor. Nancy R. Woodington edited it with a keen eye and a mercifully light touch. Howard Bloch, Christine R. Hilary, Roy J. Pearcy, and Eric Rutledge made valuable comments on the text, but have no responsibility for its remaining deficiencies. The early stages of the work were supported by a Fulbright grant for study in France, and by a fellowship from the John Simon Guggenheim Memorial Foundation.

Abbreviations

While there are many more recent editions of individual poems, and the new collected edition *(NRCF)* is still in progress, for brevity in identifying fabliau passages I usually refer to volume and page (e.g., II, 195) of the collection of Montaiglon and Raynaud *(MR)*.

Béd   Joseph Bédier, *Les Fabliaux* (1893), 5th ed. (Paris: Champion, 1925).

BM   E. Barbazon and M. Méon, *Fabliaux et contes des poètes françois,* III (Paris, 1808).

CH   Thomas D. Cooke and Benjamin L. Honeycutt, eds., *The Humor of the Fabliaux* (Columbia, Mo.: University of Missouri Press, 1974).

CFMA   Classiques Français du Moyen Age.

Goug   Georges Gougenheim, ed., *Cortebarbe: Les Trois Aveugles de Compiègne,* CFMA (Paris: Champion, 1932).

JO   R. C. Johnston and D. D. R. Owen, eds., *Fabliaux* (Oxford: Blackwell, 1957).

Liv   Charles H. Livingston, ed., *Le Jongleur Gautier le Leu, Etude sur les fabliaux* (Cambridge: Harvard University Press, 1951).

MR   Anatole de Montaiglon and Gaston Raynaud, *Recueil général et complet des fabliaux des XIIIe et XIVe siècles,* 6 vols. (Paris, 1872–1890).

Nar   Pierre Nardin, ed., *Jean Bodel: Fabliaux,* 2d ed. (Paris: Nizet, 1965).

NRCF   Willem Noomen and Nico van den Boogaard, eds., *Nouveau Recueil complet des fabliaux,* 10 vols. (Assen: Van Gorcum, 1983–).

Nyk   Per Nykrog, *Les Fabliaux* (Copenhagen: Ejnar Munksgaard, 1957).

Reid   T. B. W. Reid, ed., *Twelve Fabliaux* (Manchester: Manchester University Press, 1958).

Ren   (by volume and page) *Le Roman de Renart,* ed. Mario Roques, *CFMA,* 6 vols. (Paris: Champion, 1948–1963). Vol. I contains Branche i; vol. II, Br. ii–vi; vol. III, Br. vii–ix; vol. IV, Br. x–xi; vol. V, Br. xii–xvii; vol. VI, Br. xviii–xix.

Rich   *Richeut,* ed. and trans. Donald Eugene Ker, "The Twelfth-Century French Poem of Richeut," Ph.D. diss., Ohio State University, 1976 (Ann Arbor: University Microfilms, 1978).

Rom   (by volume and page) *Romania.*

Rom Rev   (by volume and page) *Romanic Review.*

Ros   C. Rostaing, ed., *Constant du Hamel* ([Paris]: Gap, 1953).

Rych   (by volume and page) Jean Rychner, *Contribution à l'étude des fabliaux,* 2 vols. (Neuchatel: Faculté des Lettres, 1960).

Warnke   Karl Warnke, ed., *Die Fabeln der Marie de France* (Halle: Niemeyer, 1898).

WG   Martha Walters-Gehrig, *Trois fabliaux* (Tübingen: Niemeyer, 1961).

Bibliographical Note

In the second and subsequent citations of most books and articles, I use an abbreviated title; the first citation can be located by referring to the Index, under the author's name. Translations are mine unless otherwise noted.

CHAPTER I

The Genre and Its Literary Background

WE KNOW A GREAT DEAL MORE OF THE LEARNED Middle Ages than of the unlearned, more of official medieval attitudes than of actual ones, more about the formal and ceremonial, the legal, ecclesiastical, and military life of the times than about the daily, informal, domestic experience of ordinary people. This is a natural result of the superior survival of the written part of the culture, and of the preservation of some documents and not others. The documents we have today, the intonations we hear, are mainly those of the important, official voices. The great exceptions of course are the voices we hear incidentally, often only implicitly, in the crevices and at the edges of officialdom and in imaginative literature. But the imaginative literature of the Middle Ages has its own limitations in this regard. It is for the most part highly formal, ceremonial, and official, and its greatest strength is in its imaginative idealism. The Middle Ages is the period par excellence of lyric, of epic and romance, not of realism; and its characteristic "realism" is run through with caricature and comedy, as if in literature nothing but high life could be taken very seriously.

Medieval comedy, however, should be taken more seriously than it is. The Middle Ages imagined by the average educated person today is still rather archaic, more one-sided even than our actual knowledge should permit. The knights go forth on their quests; the monks copy manuscripts; the philosophers debate the freedom of the will; the peasants till fields, some people go on pilgrimages; and all of them huddle in the shadow of a monolithic establishment known as The Church, being careful to do nothing that The Church frowns upon. No one, in this picture, has fun or misbehaves, or moves his bowels.

If it were only to add some color and variety, a deeper study of medieval comic writings would be justified. The present work aims, however, a little further, to ask whether the comic writings—in this case a coherent body of Old French poems known as fabliaux—should not be taken much more importantly into account than they have been, as evidence for the history of medieval sensibility.

In the scheme of all of extant medieval literature, the Old French fabliaux seem relatively unimportant; they are certainly unpretentious. Some of them are narratives so slight as to raise the question why they were written down at all. They have further tended to repel interest, or at least public discussion, by their frequent prurience. Some of them are no more than extended "dirty jokes." Nevertheless, serious interest in the fabliaux has lately been steadily increasing. This is partly because times have changed, the boundaries of prurience have shrunk, and we have learned to regard racy stories with more honest attention and less embarrassment; coincidentally, Per Nykrog's fundamental critique in 1957 of Joseph Bédier's classic work on the fabliaux has initiated a worldwide revival of scholarly attention to the genre.[1] It is time to raise new questions about the cultural bearings of the fabliaux.

Perhaps just because of their unpretentiousness and candor, the fabliaux can be trusted to reveal genuine features of medieval sensibility that other genres tend to conceal. They show us medieval culture unembarrassedly in the midst of its everyday pleasures and transgressions. The transgressions, we are made to feel, are mainly those of a minor sort, those that go counter to medieval notions of purity in matters of personal conduct, of money, and especially of sex.

Few medieval moralists would have considered the sexual activities depicted in the fabliaux acceptable. But even Dante places illicit sex farther from the center of Hell than do some current evaluations of medieval sensibility. There is a modern school of critics who would have us believe that any depiction of sexual transgression in medieval imaginative literature is "exegetical" or symbolical, and that its main drift is to cast direct scorn or indirect mockery on the sin of concupiscence. A more sophisticated and more prevalent but equally misguided view is that the espousal of sexual and other "forbidden" pleasures in medieval culture is only temporary and fugitive truancy—holiday license—from the teachings of the Church; it represents the last vestiges of pre-Christian primitivism. This book tests this kind of judgment, taking sexual attitudes as part of a larger cultural pattern with possible connections to the patterns of later cultures, including our own.

The fabliaux make up a distinct literary genre, but like the other genres, it was not created by nature but by people. The poems did not reproduce themselves genetically, like rabbits or robins, but only by tradition, with its looser and more complex lines of kinship. So we cannot describe the genre with scientific precision nor determine once and for all which of the eligible works are truly fabliaux and which are not. Those who have tried to do so disagree, and their differences of opinion show just the indistinctness and gradualness that we might expect in the emergence of a new genre and in the establishing of a name for it.[2]

Almost all scholars agree that the fabliau is well established as a genre at the beginning of the thirteenth century. Most of the 150-odd poems[3] that we have were composed between 1200 and 1340, though almost none can be dated precisely. Among the few of their authors whose names have survived, the earliest identifiable one is Jean Bodel, very likely the well-known poet of Arras who composed the *Jeu de Saint Nicolas* and the *Chanson des Saisnes*. Bodel died in 1210; there are good reasons to regard him as the father of the genre.[4] The last identifiable author of fabliaux, Jean de Condé, died in 1346.

The fabliaux have come down to us in forty-three manuscripts or fragments of manuscripts, most of them made in the thirteenth and fourteenth centuries. The five most important contain 59, 42, 30, 27, and 23 fabliaux respectively, along with a variety of pieces of other kinds. Individual fabliaux often reappear in different manuscripts: *Auberee* and the *Sacristain* fabliau eight times each; *La Couille noir* and *Le Chevalier qui fist parler les cons* seven times each; *La Dame escoillee* six times. At least thirty texts appear in three or more manuscripts and have thus been dubbed by Nykrog the "classics" of the genre.[5] Rychner's painstaking comparisons of different copies of the fabliaux give us a good idea of the variety of ways in which they were transmitted. Many, of course, are simply scribal copies, more or less faithfully taken from another written text. But many texts were obviously changed in the course of their transmission, some unintentionally but no less radically by having been written down from memory. Others show a wide range of conscious alteration—by people of very unequal talents—from minor editing to full-scale rehandling for another set of tastes, another audience. In the process many fabliaux were damaged from an artistic standpoint, and many acquired incoherencies in language and even in plot. Inept and battered rehandlings circulated alongside polished "originals" all through the period, however, and then as now were accepted as authentic fabliaux.[6] At the end of *Les Deus Vilains* Gautier le Leu, one of the most prolific of fabliau writers, gives us a glimpse of a fabliau changing hands:

> Saciés de fit que Li Goulius
> Le raconta en tamains lius
> A Saint Amant et a Marcienes.
> Uns bacelers de Valencienes,
> Qui avoit esté ens el leu,
> Le raconta Gautier Le Leu
> Et il mist le fablel en rime.
> Dix en a fait, ves ci l'onsime.   [*Liv*, 206]

[Take note that Li Goulius (another jongleur?) told this story in many places around Saint-Amand and Marchiennes. A young fellow from Valenciennes who was right there told it to Gautier le Leu, and he put the fabliau into verse. He has done ten of them, and here is the eleventh.]

Most of the fabliaux were professional compositions produced by jongleurs like Gautier le Leu. The title *jongleur* embraces in this period the whole range of professional entertainers from well-endowed composers of poetry to the humblest of itinerant jugglers, fiddlers, and acrobats.[7] Though comparatively few of the jongleurs could have been talented enough to compose poetry, many were professional reciters of the poetry of others, and we must assume that they did much of the recitation which was the principal mode of fabliau performance. *Les Deux Bordeors ribauz*, which presents a comic interchange of boasts and insults between two jongleurs, shows the fabliaux firmly in the jongleur repertoire along with other literary genres, lyric, romance, and epic:

> Ge sai contes, ge sai flabeax;
> Ge sai conter beax diz noveax,
> Rotruenges viez et noveles,
> Et sirventois et pastoreles.
> Ge sai le flabel du Denier,
> Et du Fouteor à loier,
> Et de Gobert et de dame Erme,
> Qui ainz des elz ne plora lerme,
> Et si sai de la Coille noire;
> Si sai de Parceval l'estoire,
> Et si sai du Provoire taint
> Qui o les crucefiz fu painz;
> Du Prestre qui menja les meures
> Quant il devoit dire ses heures;
> Si sai Richalt, si sai Renart . . .
> De Charlemaine et de Roulant
> Et d'Olivier le conbatant.   [I, 11]

[I know stories, I know fabliaux. I can tell fine new tales, *rotrouenges* old and new, and *sirventois* and *pastourelles*. I know the story of the Penny (not a fabliau), and of the Fucker for hire, and Gombert, and about Dame Erme who never shed a tear, and the one about the Black Balls. I know the story of Percival, and the dyed Priest who was painted along with the crucifixes, and the Priest who ate mulberries when he was supposed to be saying his hours. I know about Richeut and Renart . . . Charlemagne and Roland and Oliver the fighter.]

The fabliaux were recited in public places and in private residences, wherever the performer could find an audience in the mood for entertainment. A text of the mid-thirteenth century finds the fabliaux a profitable and flourishing business:

> Fableaus sunt or molt encorsé;
> Meint denier en ont enboursé
> Cil qui les content et les portent
> Car grant confortement aportent
> As envoisiez et as oiseus.   [Rych II, 38]

[Fabliaux are much on the increase these days, and those who recite and circulate them have made a pretty penny at it. For they are a great comfort to the gay and idle.]

In Le Vilain au buffet a group of minstrels compete for a new scarlet robe at a courtly feast; among the entertainments they offer are fabliaux (I, 204). The fabliau Boivin de Provins reports that its hero was also its composer, and that he received three nights' lodging and ten sous for reciting it to the family and friends of the provost of Provins, "qui mout ama la lecherie" (V, 64). In one of its uses fabliau may in fact mean an ordinary after-dinner anecdote rather than a specific literary composition:

> Et, quant ce vint après souper,
> Si commencierent à border
> Et contoient de lor aviaus,
> Lor aventures, lor fabliaus.
>   [MR III, 81–82; cf. Nyk, 8]

[And when it came time, after supper, they began to crack jokes and told about their amusements, their escapades, their stories.]

But a passage in the thirteenth-century romance *Les Merveilles de Rigomer* seems to point unambiguously to recited fabliaux as an accepted after-dinner genre:

> Puis le souper qui mout fu biaus
> Dient et content des fabliaus
> La u estoient a sejor.[8]

[After supper, which was very fine, they recited fabliaux there where they were resting.]

The setting is the house of a very rich *vilain*.

The endings of a few of the fabliaux show the reciter calling for a share in the drinking as recompense (*Nyk,* 28; *Liv,* 311), and the beginnings of others testify to the noisy and convivial atmosphere that was the setting for much recited poetry in the Middle Ages:

> Or fetes pais, si m'entendez.   [III, 58]
>
> Or escoutez, laissiez moi dire.   [V, 179]
>
> Or oés, mai que nus ne tence!   [VI, 54]

The height of comically exaggerated conviviality is depicted by Watriquet de Couvin, one of the three fourteenth-century court minstrels whose fabliaux seem to end the tradition. He represents himself as a character in his own fabliau *Les Trois Chanoinesses de Couloigne.* Once met, the three canonesses invite the minstrel to a private dinner; he recites to them an Art of Love and a requisitely spicy fabliau while they all eat and drink, each of the ladies sitting quite naked in her bathtub (III, 137–142).

As might be expected, poets other than jongleurs occasionally tried their hands at composing fabliaux. Bédier (p. 387) cites the high-society clergyman Henri d'Andeli, who wrote the *Lai d'Aristote* alongside a number of more serious works, and the noble Philippe de Rémi, sire de Beaumanoir, author of romances and a prominent jurist as well. The fabliau *Sacristain III* reports that its author, named Sire Jehan le Chapelain, recited it to his host in recompense for hospitality, according to "the custom in Normandy" (VI, 117). Nykrog (p. 29) notes a fragment of a fabliau written by "the young magistrate of Hamiel." Though many a professional *fableor* begins by announcing his disinterested pleasure in telling stories, occasionally we hear a more self-consciously amateur note:

> Ma paine metrai et m'entente,
> Tant com je sui en ma jovente,
> A conter .I. fabliau par rime
> Sanz colour et sans leonime;
> Mais s'il i a consonancie,
> Il ne m'en chaut qui mal en die,
> Car ne puet pas plaisir à touz
> Consonancie sanz bons moz.   [V, 32]

[Since I am young I am going to devote myself to telling a fabliau in verse, without any fancy rhyming or rhetoric. But if my rhymes are simple, I don't care whether anyone speaks ill of them. Rhyming without fine words can't please everybody.]

There is perhaps an academic or clerical note to these lines as well: it is reinforced by the ending of the poem (*Les Trois Dames qui troverent un vit*) which is more sententious than it need be.

The beginnings of *Le Povre Mercier* (*JO*, 44) and *Les Trois Dames qui troverent l'anel II* (I, 168), and the ending of *Le Meunier d'Arleux* (II, 44) identify their authors as *clers*, "clerks," that is, as church-educated scholars; and in *Le Povre Clerc* a well-to-do peasant takes advantage of the visit of a clerk to ask for a story (V, 196). This clerk's refusal to tell a fabliau does not invalidate what must have been a normal expectation. Indeed, recent study of the fabliaux has tended more and more to stress their clerical connections. The more we appreciate the sophisticated and learned elements in their background and composition, the more we must impute to them an authorship involving clerks. Clerks are, interestingly, the only class of people uniformly admired in the fabliaux, and they must obviously have shared with the jongleurs not only the labor of composing the fabliaux but even of reciting them. It has long been appreciated that the line between clerk and jongleur was readily and often crossed in this period. Poor, unbeneficed clerks, *vagantes*—wandering scholars—easily turned their Latin literary training and their talent for disrespect into semi-professional vernacular entertainment.[9] They came even to share with the professionals some of the bad reputation already characteristic of show business. In *Un Chivalier et sa dame et un clerk,* an outraged lady summoning her servants to attack a supposedly lecherous clerk expresses it in clear synonymy; she calls him *un clerjastre, un menestrauz*—"a false clerk, a minstrel" (II, 232).

While for the most part the fabliaux were conveyed to their audiences by being recited aloud, they were recited from the written text as well as from memory. Nykrog (pp. 37–38) cites half a dozen fabliau passages which allude to the presence of a book or piece of writing, as "Ensi nus raconte cis livres," "ce dit l'escriture," and the like.[10] The verb *dire*, which suggests unaided recitation, is commonly used in the fabliaux to refer to their presentation:

> Por ce que fabliaus dire sueil,
> En lieu de fable dire vueil
> Une aventure qui est vraie.   [I, 188]

[Because I'm in the habit of telling fabliaux, instead of a fable I'd like to tell a true story.]

But in at least one text there seems to be a direct allusion to hearing fabliaux read—"Quant il oent bons fableaus *lire*"— though in another copy of the poem the same line reads "Quant il oient un biau mot *dire*" (*Rych* II, 38).

However frequently or infrequently medieval oral performance may have depended on the written texts, it is of course to the latter that we owe the preservation of the fabliaux. Performers and revisers made written copies for professional use, and wealthy amateurs caused individual copies to be made— from written text or from recitation—for their private collections. Random, piece-by-piece acquisition by individuals with a taste for fabliaux is the most plausible explanation of the character of the major fabliau manuscripts that have come down to us. The pieces are in no discernable order and at no consistent state in age or quality. They are mixed indiscriminately with pieces of every other kind: "popular proverbs and translations from the Latin . . . courtly tales, moral poems and comical recitations."[11] The manuscripts are, in short, private libraries, originally collections of unbound individual pieces which were recopied on parchment and bound together in the relatively uniform and sumptuous condition to which they owe their preservation.[12]

On the level of their bare themes or motifs, the fabliaux are directly related to the continuous worldwide tradition of telling funny stories. Most of the tradition is oral: an Indianapolis friend recently told me a joke that had a motif—the obscene marketplace—very similar to that of the fabliau *Le Sohait desvé*. From time to time these stories are written down in literary form or are collected by folklorists in the field, and it is possible to trace many of them from place to place and from period to period. With the aid of modern indexes of folklore motifs, any number of fabliaux can be found to share motifs with other stories recorded in oriental and classical antiquity, in the Middle Ages, and ever since. For instance, the three motifs of *Le Vilain mire* have been variously identified in a second-century Indian collection, in thirteenth-century French sermons, in fourteenth- and fifteenth-century moral tales, in Basque folklore, German jestbook, Italian farce, and of course in the Molière comedy *Le Médecin malgré lui*.[13] But given the predominance of oral transmission in this kind of diffusion, we cannot assume direct influence of one literary text on another unless they show convincing similarities of detail. In the case of the fabliaux they generally do not. Very few of the fabliaux can be traced back directly to a known literary source. In the course of discrediting the old theory of the Indian origin of the fabliaux, Bédier (1893) shows that, of the eleven fabliaux having motifs that could conceivably have been derived directly from oriental sources, none were actually so derived. And he could find only six or seven fabliaux which even share their motifs with what scanty remains we have of the comic literature of Greece, Rome, and the early Middle Ages.[14]

The texts that we have seem mainly to have been elaborated and written down from oral tradition. We can take quite literally the report of Garin, the author of *La Grue*:

> Voudré je un fabliau ja fere
> Dom la matiere oï retrere
> A Vercelai devant les changes.   [V, 151]

[I'd like to do a fabliau on a subject I heard tell about at Vézelay in front of the Exchange.]

—and of the clerk Engerrand d'Oisi, who put *Le Meunier d'Arleux* down in writing, he says, because he didn't want such a story to perish (II, 44).[15]

Derived from oral tradition, these poems were nevertheless created in a literary milieu by men of a rich literary culture. The fabliaux thus show relationships to a variety of other literary genres, and in sketching these relationships we will come to a fuller understanding of the emergence of the fabliau itself. The attitudes and sensibility which finally called forth the new genre were already beginning to be expressed in a number of mixed and provisional forms in the twelfth century. There is, for instance, a well-documented element of comedy and "realism" threaded through early Old French romance. With few exceptions, twelfth-century romance is elevated and courtly. Yet if only to provide a measurement of the height of their idealism, or to acknowledge their own mature awareness that their narratives are indeed romances, poets like Chrétien de Troyes, Gautier d'Arras, and Hue de Rotelande variously admit scenes of everyday realism and moods and characterizations of comic disenchantment that prefigure the later fabliau spirit.[16]

In similar mood the twelfth-century courtly *lai*, or shorter tale, coexists with a genre which burlesques it gently, and in so doing subjects courtly characters in Breton-Arthurian settings to fabliau moods or incidents. In the *Mantel mautaillée* and the *Lai du cor,* King Arthur's court is put into confusion by a magic test of fidelity that only one of the ladies can pass. The *Chevalier à l'espee* is a courtly adventure with an uncourtly ending; the lady rejects Gawain for an unknown knight whose sexual prowess, the author suggests, may be greater than the hero's. The *Lai d'Ignaurès* is a strange, part courtly, part brutal, priapic version of the "eaten heart" motif of romance. The *Lai du lecheor* (euphemistically so called) shows a group of ladies composing a Breton lai in honor of the female part toward which, they say, the entire institution of masculine lovemaking and chivalry aims. The *Lai d'Aristote* shows the dour philosopher made to fall in love with his pupil, King Alexander's beautiful mistress. The triumph of sexuality over philosophy is celebrated by her saddling and riding him through a garden. If this poem is a fabliau, as many critics have it, then it is surely the most refined and elegant of all. In an entirely different mood, the tradition of the *chanson de geste* produced a mock epic poem, *Audigier,* which shares vocabulary and motifs with the most scatological of the fabliaux, and the *Une Seule Fame qui servoit cent chevaliers,* which is generally included among the fabliaux themselves. [17]

Also suggestively related to the fabliaux are some twenty short Latin "comedies," written mostly in the region of the Loire in the second half of the twelfth century. [18] The earliest of these, the *Geta* and *Aulularia* of one Vital de Blois, clearly relate the genre, through intermediary texts, to the ancient comedy of Plautus, but although all of them are predominantly in the form of direct discourse, and two of them are entirely so, they were not necessarily intended for the stage. They are short comic narratives comparable to fabliaux in their emphasis on intrigue, wit, and a not-too-delicate sexuality. Fabliau character types—the sensual young women, the rascally servants, the tricked husbands—seem to be prefigured in the Latin comedy, as do several fabliau themes.

But the Latin poems, written in elegiac distichs, are a purely clerical production for a purely clerical audience. They are closely related to the contemporary emergence of a school of rhetoric in this same region; the comedy *Milo* was written by the Loire scholar Matthew of Vendôme, also author of a rhetorical handbook in which he refers to his poem. The *De clericis et rustico* is praised as a comic model in the *Documentum de arte versificandi* attributed to the rhetorician Geoffrey of Vinsauf. The style of the comedies is marked by rhetorical sophistication of all sorts, and by humorous references to such learned subjects as dialectic, platonic epistemology, and astronomy. The texts themselves were widely circulated in the later Middle Ages— the comedy *Pamphilus* has given us our word "pamphlet"; they were admired, studied, glossed, and extracted in many a school. But their relationship to the vernacular fabliaux does not seem to have been one of direct adaptation. The fabliau authors do not refer to them, and fail to imitate them in fundamental traits. What the Latin comedies show us, however, is a stratum of comic sensibility, incorporating a goodly portion of irreverence and obsceneness, that existed in clerical circles before the fabliaux began to emerge, and that could be drawn upon in the creation of the newer genre.

The Latin comedies are themselves part of that wider current of secular humor in Latin that also includes the variety of songs, anecdotes, confessions, and debates produced by clerics, including the goliards and vagantes, wandering scholars, who seem to have reached the peak of their activity in the twelfth century. These productions, too, must in the widest sense be counted within the fabliau background,[19] as must the plentiful touches of realism and even of humor in the traditions of the pious legends and lives of the saints and of the sermon.[20]

But clerical humor was not limited to Latin, and its most celebrated vernacular production, the *Roman de Renart,*[21] must be taken very seriously into account here. The *Renart* is a great series—a cycle—of twenty-odd narrative poems begun by Pierre de Saint-Cloud in the last quarter of the twelfth century and continued by other poets well into the thirteenth. It chronicles the adventures of the tricky Renard the fox, his enemy Ysengrin the wolf, and a miscellany of other characters, mostly animal. Nine or ten of the tales (or "branches") can safely be dated before or about 1200, and many of the impulses attendant on the creation of the fabliaux are to be found in this beast epic as well. The *Renart* action often transpires in the same locus of town, village, and farm, among the same peasants, minor clergy, and officialdom, and has much of the same style and ethos. The affinity between the two genres was apparently felt by poets who soon introduced human characters into the cycle, and by the thirteenth-century collectors and editors who did not hesitate to incorporate into it a number of tales which are in everything but their animal characters pure fabliaux.

Thus Branche VI [XXI] (which has nothing to do with Renard) turns on the finding of a *bacon,* a side of pork—one of the most familiar objects in the fabliaux—by a peasant. He is persuaded to divide his find with Ysengrin the wolf and Patou the bear. The division of the find, a fabliau theme, is proposed in typically outrageous fashion by the bear. They will hide the pork in the woods overnight. The next morning they will return and show their respective behinds; whoever has the biggest *cul* will win the whole pork. The contest is won, in an exhibition of female ingenuity typical of fabliaux, by the peasant's wife, who competes in a disguise and posture strongly reminiscent of the fabliau *Berengier au lonc cul.* The episode of Renart as dyer (*teinturier*) in branche IB is likewise substantially a fabliau, as are the tale of Isengrin and the rams, branche V [XX], and the tale of the peasant Lietart, Renart, and the death of Brun the bear, branche X [IX]. Correspondingly, a certain malicious intelligence is several times referred to as *renart* in the fabliaux; and the beleaguered husband in the fabliau *Le Sacristain I* suggests to his wife that they foil their enemy by behaving like the clever fox: "ouvrons du sens Renart" (V, 118).

Related as they are, the two genres are, however, not quite the same. The *Renart*, particularly in its earlier branches, relates to an earlier period and ranges higher in its social reference than the fabliau, dealing comically with the twelfth-century baronial circle, referring to the royal court, the upper nobility, and to some levels of high feudal justice that scarcely appear in the fabliaux. Both genres contain some parody of courtly literature, but the parody in the *Renart* is more consistent and more often parody of epic, while the occasional parody in the fabliaux is almost exclusively of romance. The *Renart,* unlike the fabliau, has important models in Latin, notably the mock-epic *Ysengrinus* by the Flemish cleric Nivard. Both genres are anticlerical, but the *Renart* poets far exceed the fabliaux in the self-conscious impudence of their obsceneness, the thorough-goingness of their satire of religious hypocrisy, of their parody of monastic life, and of such clerically based humor as the burlesque of the Mass in branche XIV and of the Office of Vespers in branche XII.[22]

The animal characters in the *Renart* of course make a difference, but it is easy to overestimate. While the substitution of animals for humans might promise a greater degree of abstraction in the beast epic, the fabliau's use of type characters nearly approaches this kind of abstraction. The collectedness of the *Renart*, its having a single "epic" hero for a group of tales, also makes it different from the fabliaux; but here again the difference can be overestimated. We have, in fact, two works roughly contemporary with the *Renart* which seem to be examples of an intermediate genre, the comic cycle with human characters.

Trubert (thirteenth century) chronicles in almost 3,000 verses five consecutive adventures of the same hero, who first appears to be a stupid country lout but soon becomes, by dint of outrageous and obscene devices in the fabliau manner, the bête noire of the local duke and duchess. He succeeds repeatedly in seducing the duchess, torturing the duke, and ends up by impregnating their daughter. With the possible exception of the fourth adventure, which carefully and elaborately burlesques the chivalric tradition of the champion, all of these are fabliaux, though the tireless malignity with which the nobles are pursued is not characteristic of the genre.[23]

If its traditional dating (ca. 1170) were correct, *Richeut* would be one of the earliest vernacular texts closely related to the fabliaux. It contains several distinguishable episodes, and some allusions which suggest that others may have been lost. Unlike most of the other French texts we have mentioned, it is not written in the standard octosyllabic couplets, but in a tail-rhyme strophe derived from Latin liturgical chants and most commonly found in the vernacular in satirical works of the thirteenth century. The existence of allusions to its heroine, Richeut, and her servant Hersent in texts from ca. 1155 makes it likely that a Richeut tradition, possibly a cycle, antedates the present poem.[24] In the opening episode of this narrative of some 1,300 verses, the prostitute Richeut makes herself pregnant so as to become rich collecting hush money from her clients, including a priest, a knight, a *borjois,* and many others. There follows a rambling chronicle of the birth of her son,

Samson, and his remarkable education, which comically reflects the breadth of his possible parentage: among other things he is a dialectician, can compose Breton lais, and shoot dice. But mainly, under his mother's tutelage, he is a corrupter of women, king of the *lechëors*. We can faintly distinguish three or four divisions in this account: Samson's youth (554ff.); his behavior at court and beyond (756ff.); his swindling of a monastery, corrupting of a nunnery, and general sexual prowess (892ff.). At verse 985 begins a fabliau which terminates the work. Returning after a dozen years, Samson fails to recognize Richeut, who then conducts a test to see which of them is the greater at the art of deceiving the other sex. She wins by tricking Samson into an ardent candlelight conquest of old Hersent, who has been disguised with cosmetics as a noble young maiden.

Whether or not we admit separate episodes of the *Renart, Trubert,* and *Richeut* into the canon of true fabliaux, it is clear that something like the genre was emerging in the vernacular in a number of variant forms, propelled by attitudes and motives—comic, satiric, or if not satiric, then disrespectful—that we find in the fabliau proper.

Something like the fabliau in form was also emerging in didactic literature, in the moral fable and exemplary tale. The period knew a great number of these tales, both in Latin and in the vernacular, with animal or with human characters. They were widely circulated in collections designed for preachers, for use as illustrations in sermons. Most of the fable collections descend from ancient pseudo-Aesopic sources, often enlarged, in successive adaptations, from oral tradition. The earliest such collection in French is the *Fables* (ca. 1180–90) of the Anglo-Norman poet Marie de France.[25] Six of them, with human characters, are so much like fabliaux that Nykrog (p. 16) includes them as "fabliaux avant la lettre" in his list.

Nykrog (appendix, part iv) rightly rejects the notion that the fabliau was simply derived from the fable, but the relationship between the two genres remains interestingly close, if difficult. The contemporary taste for fablelike fiction is already well attested by the *Roman de Renart* and by such a tale as *Dou lou et de l'oue* (Of the Wolf and the Goose), included in the list of his own fabliaux by Jean Bodel.[26] The captive goose complains that whereas she is about to be consumed unceremoniously, all her companions will have the happier fate of being well roasted, spiced, and downed to the sound of music. The wolf tries to oblige by providing some singing, whereupon the goose escapes. After pronouncing the moral— eat first and sing afterwards, "Mal chanter fet devant mangier"—the author rather tediously prolongs the tale, having the wolf hunt another goose and eat it on the spot. Then the lesson is drawn two or three times more. This is a conventional enough piece of medieval moralizing; what is piquant is that Bodel's *Le Vilain de Farbu* and *Le Vilain de Bailluel,* his ribald *Gombert et les deus clers* and *Barat et Haimet,* along with a great many other unmoral or immoral fabliaux, also contain the same kind of moralizing. As several critics have observed, about two-thirds of the fabliaux either end with an explicit moral in the manner of fables or offer an analogous moral teaching in the course of the narrative.[27]

Whatever it means, the phenomenon cannot be dismissed as a mere "vestigial survival" (*Reid,* p. x), though it may represent a variety of intentions. Some fabliaux offer perfunctory lessons that either have little to do with the story being told or refer to only a trivial aspect of it, and some can be suspected of parody or burlesque. But some are actually called *essemples;* and conversely, when the *Disciplina Clericalis,* an early twelfth-century Latin compilation of moral tales by Petrus Alphonsus, was translated and expanded in French about 1200, the translator-adapter could call a number of the tales fabliaux. The frame of this collection is a conversation between a wise man and his son, in which the former tells the latter morally instructive stories. At one point the question before us is actually raised, for when the son asks to be told stories about women and their tricks—"aucun fablel, aucun rien" (v. 1147), the father hesitates. He fears that once they are written down by the son, they may fall into hands that will use them for evil purposes. The son reassures him, pointing out that many—including Solomon—have blamelessly told such stories for instructional purposes in the past.[28]

By some such principle the ancient story of the Matron of Ephesus, who allows herself to be seduced on her husband's grave, could be transmitted to the Middle Ages as a moral exemplum, retold both by Marie de France in her *Fables* and by the anonymous author of the racy fabliau *Cele qui se fist foutre sur la fosse de son mari.* Marie concludes:

> Par iceste signefiance
> poum entendre quel creance
> deivent aveir li mort es vis.
> Tant est li munz fals e jolis. [*Warnke,* no. 25]

[By the meaning of this we can appreciate how much faith the dead can have in the living—so false and frivolous is this world.]

The fabliau author concludes his version with seven verses on the utter unreliability of woman (III, 122). In both of these cases, as in many other fabliaux, the lesson drawn is apt but too general; it fails to articulate the full moral import of the tale. To this problem we shall have to return in chapter four. Meanwhile, it is to be expected that if the most bawdy of the fabliaux can pretend to the status of moral fables, the least bawdy fabliaux are almost indistinguishable from such fables. The difference, in fabliaux such as *La Housse partie, Fole Larguesce, Le Preudome qui rescolt son compere de noier,* and *La Bourse pleine de sens,* is rather a matter of tone and intention than of literary form.

This survey of its literary settings brings us back to the question of the distinctness of the fabliau as a genre. We have seen that at the edges it becomes indistinguishable from a variety of other literary kinds. There are, we might add, a number of other variations: there are very long fabliaux, of over a thousand verses, and short ones, of a few dozen;[29] there are polite ones and unpleasantly crude ones; there are skillful works of art and amateurish scribblings. But the notion of the genre itself is firm. In the medieval use of the term *fabliau* we do find a certain amount of ambiguity and overlapping. The term—in modern usage, from the common Picard dialect form of the Old French word for *fable,* plus a diminutive ending— was on a few occasions applied to other genres: fables, debates, *dits,* allegories. The name *fable,* and those of other genres (*lai, chanson, dit, essample*) and such general terms as *conte* and *aventure* were occasionally applied to undoubted fabliaux. Often two or more different terms are used in different places in the text, or in different copies, to describe the same piece.[30] This much ambiguity is perhaps no more than we might expect to find surrounding a new literary term; on the other hand, although there was no compulsion for the authors of fabliaux to use the term, over sixty of the fabliaux are actually so called in medieval texts, and another ninety unlabeled poems can be admitted to the list without controversy.

Bédier's definition of the genre: "Les fabliaux sont des contes à rire en vers" (p. 30)—the fabliaux are funny stories in verse—is substantially accepted by Nykrog and has the virtue of being handily uncomplicated.[31] Were we compelled to refine this definition further, we would move in the direction, already marked out by recent critics, of taking more centrally into account the fabliau's typical style and attitude. As Pierre Le Gentil once remarked: "The fabliau has its roots in the real."[32]

CHAPTER II

The Social Background

T WAS JOSEPH BÉDIER'S IDEA IN *LES FABLIAUX* (*1893*)
that the fabliaux were by origin "bourgeois"; his
theory held the field until 1957, when it was severely shaken
by Per Nykrog, whose entire work is marshalled around a contrary notion: that the fabliau is essentially a courtly genre.
Both of these positions now appear too simple and too extreme;
we cannot attribute either the origin or the fundamental attitudes of the fabliaux to a single social class. Yet there remain
rich and suggestive connections between the genre and its
background in thirteenth-century society.

Bédier's view was based on a modest estimate of the literary
value of the fabliaux and on the assumption of a neat correspondence between social class and literary taste. Struck by
the remarkable contrast between groups of genres and styles
in the French literature of the time—romance and fabliau,
imaginative elevation and disenchanted comedy—he aligns
(p. 369) with it a corresponding contrast between conceptions
of life (which is fair enough), and then between public and
social classes:

> On the one hand the courtly world, and on the other the
> world of the bourgeois and the peasant. The fabliaux are
> . . . the poetry of the little people. Down to earth realism,
> a merry and ironic conception of life, all the distinctive
> traits of the fabliaux, of the *Roman de la Rose* [of Jean de
> Meun], of the *Roman de Renart,* show likewise the features
> of the bourgeois. On the other hand, the worship of
> woman, dreams of fairyland, idealism, all the traits that

distinguish the lyric poetry and the romances of the Round
Table, also mark out the features of the knightly class.
There is the same distance from a bourgeois of the thirteenth century to a baron as from a fabliau to a noble tale
of adventure. To each his own literature: here the poetry
of the chateaux, there the poetry of the town square
(p. 371).

It must be said in his defense that Bédier recognizes the
simplicity of this formulation. But it seems to him to be supported by chronology: the fabliaux come into being with *Richeut*
(dated by Bédier 1159) at just the time of the formation of an
urban middle class. Although he does not press the geographical point, he observes early in his book that of the seventy-
two localizable fabliaux, over half originate in the northern
provinces—Picardy, Artois, Ponthieu, Flanders, Hainaut
(p. 43). These are the very regions in which the great commercial towns flourish. Later he imagines for us a merchant
of one of these towns bringing into being his own literature;
and he evokes the well-documented literary life of thirteenth-
century Arras, with such accomplished bourgeois poets as Jean
Bodel and Adam de la Halle and crowds of lesser rhymesters,
including the literary confreries formed by prominent bourgeois
(pp. 374–375).

Bédier's coupling of social class and literary genre for the
bourgeoisie is silently supported by the already well accepted
and far less challengeable coupling of "courtly" society and
literature. But while he seems to insist on the social origins
of the genres and on the social basis of their attitudes, he readily
points out that genres and social classes were in fact not kept
in segregation. He cites evidence to show that fabliaux were

recited and enjoyed in high society, and that the courtly genres can be found to contain plentiful infection by the fabliau spirit. Conversely the most aristocratic genres flourished in bourgeois society—as in Arras, for instance, where noblemen mingled with bourgeois patricians. "It seems, then," he concludes, "that there was in the thirteenth century, up to a certain point, a confusion of genres and promiscuity of audiences" (p. 385).

This important qualification of his theory was largely lost sight of in the ensuing decades, and the fabliaux came generally to be accepted as a "bourgeois" genre; they appear under "La Littérature bourgeoise" in Bossuat's bibliography of Old French.[1] Meanwhile there were a few dissenting voices, notably that of Edmond Faral, who in *Les Jongleurs en France au Moyen Age* (1910) tacitly opposed Bédier by remarking that since the fabliaux pleased both commoners and persons of rank, and since the same society listened to a dirty story and to a moral one with equal interest, it is not easy to assign a given social origin to a fabliau just because it has this or that character (p. 207). Later in the book (pp. 217–218) he apparently modifies his position by attributing to two different classes of jongleurs two different sets of tastes and genres, with social distinctions similar to Bédier's. "There were," he says, "with certain reservations, popular genres and aristocratic genres." Faral came later to see the fabliaux as closely related to the Latin comedies mentioned in chapter 1; he emphasizes, then, their clerical connections, and comes in a 1924 encyclopedia article to a more emphatic position on their social origins:

> The fabliaux are neither the creation nor the property of a particular social class, but represent rather a propensity [*tendance d'esprit*] which was that of an entire epoch. A

taste for coarse joking seems indeed to have cohabited in the same breasts with more subtle and refined tastes. This is why it is an historical error to say that the fabliaux belong to "bourgeois" literature: it is advisable to say simply that they belong to "realistic" literature.[2]

A view much like Faral's is found in a few pages of Leonardo Olschki's *Die romanischen Literaturen des Mittelalters* (1932). Olschki likewise explicitly denies the bourgeois origin of the fabliaux, arguing that they appear before there is any sign of a firmly established bourgeois self-consciousness, lifestyle, or set of tastes. The fabliau audience was a mixed one and certainly included the upper classes. He recalls the *Heptameron* of Marguerite of Navarre, the *novelle* of Bandello, and the *Contes* of La Fontaine, remarking that a taste that we can attribute to this queen, this bishop, and this poet cannot justly be denied their distant and much less sensitive predecessors. Olschki takes the fabliaux somewhat more seriously than does Bédier, finding in them a range of life experience, a depth of irony and of resignation underlying a sense of humor that is not simple or trivial but "diverse, bittersweet, and above all, honest."[3]

There was no important adjunct to these views until the Danish scholar Nykrog published his now celebrated and widely influential dissertation. Nykrog stays as aloof as does Bédier from the particular details of thirteenth-century economic and social life. Like Bédier he assumes a roughly three-level hierarchy: nobles, bourgeois, and peasants; but while he indicates occasionally (e.g., pp. 27, 136) that the nobles and "grands bourgeois" shared the same tastes, recognizes the same mixture of genres that Bédier had noted, and announces that "there are no absolute social distinctions in the literature of the thir-

teenth century" (p. 27), the thrust of his argument—and its
net effect on the reader—is as extreme as Bédier's:

> When a jongleur, or any other poet, composes a fabliau,
> he addresses it in the first place to those who are his
> principal clients: the rich, nobles or patricians [grands
> bourgeois] (p. 27).

> [The fabliaux] were not only read and appreciated in
> courtly circles, but . . . are so profoundly penetrated by
> the manner of thinking of these circles that to understand
> them well it is necessary to consider them a sort of courtly
> genre (p. 18).

Nykrog reviews and augments Bédier's study of the actual
composition and performance of the fabliaux. However, this
"external" evidence remains inconclusive. There is as much to
indicate a popular audience as an aristocratic one.[4] But most
of Nykrog's argument is "internal," based on the texts, their
subjects, characters, plots, and style. Its burden is that in all
major respects the fabliaux have a kind of symbiotic relationship
with courtly literature: they either imitate it, parody it, or
stand in a position so pointedly opposed that the one can hardly
be conceived without the other. The argument ends with the
paradoxical suggestion (p. 262) that the fabliaux may even
have been the conduit by which courtly ideas were fed into
the popular literature of Europe.

The greatest merit of Nykrog's work, apart from the richness
of its texture, is the verve and psychological sophistication
with which he takes up and elaborates Faral's perception that
"fabliau" tastes and attitudes must have coexisted, in the same

circles and in the same people, with "courtly" tastes and attitudes. The main weakness of his work is the single-mindedness with which it pursues Bédier, perpetuating Bédier's presumed preoccupation with the class origins of the fabliaux at the expense of serious attention to the range and quality of fabliau attitudes themselves. By presenting the fabliau as a "courtly burlesque" (p. 71), as simply an appanage of courtly literature, Nykrog diverts our attention from what Faral and Olschki rightly perceived, that the fabliau attitudes belong to the whole culture. Their social significance is much greater than what would be suggested by a mere comic opposition to "courtly" attitudes. Even were we to accept Nykrog's thesis we should have to look more carefully at the condition of those courtly *seigneurs* and *grands bourgeois* to whom the fabliaux were presumably addressed. For if the fabliaux are not bourgeois in origin, they are manifestly impregnated with attitudes that in modern times we have come to think of in part as "bourgeois" and worse; the fabliau audience must be seen as living in an environment in which these attitudes possess an extraordinary interest and validity.

It is in this sense that Bédier's thesis, untenable as to fabliau origins, retains a measure of truth. The view to be presented here is that the flourishing of the fabliaux, the rise of the cities, and the emergence of an urban middle class are equally visible symptoms of the same social and spiritual climate. Some phases of fabliau mentality seem more characteristic of rural society than of urban; but it is a rural society that is being transformed by essentially the same forces that are creating a bourgeoisie.

Fabliau attitudes, then, are deeply related to those of medieval town and commercial life, but they do not depend on

them. Of course, many fabliaux are set in substantial towns—
Compiègne, Provins, Arras, Abbeville, Orléans, Amiens, Valenciennes—and some of their plots actually depend on a town
economy. Thus pieces like *Auberee, La Veuve,* and *Le Foteor* deal
with a population that includes well-to-do merchant families,
and their action takes place in a locus of some geographical
complexity. Nevertheless it is curious that apart from the ordinary generic "merchant" (who often has business abroad and
thus by his absences contributes vitally to triangle plots), the
fabliaux deal with very few of the typically urban occupations.
There are spice-merchants (V, 40), a master carver (I, 194),
a dyer (*Liv,* 261), some money-changers (I, 245, V, 215),
town prostitutes (V, 52), a tinker (V, 181), and not many more.

Quite a few fabliaux, like *Le Chevalier a la corbeille, L'Espervier, Guillaume au faucon,* and *La Gageure,* suggest a milieu
of nobles or gentry who live in chateaux or in country houses
with extensive gardens. But the greatest number of fabliaux
are not specifically set in towns or in chateaux at all, but must
be imagined taking place in smaller rural communities, in a
population of peasants, a few artisans—a miller, a smith, a
carpenter—perhaps the local seigneur, his officers and chaplain,
a knight or two, a priest, with a church and perhaps a tavern
and a larger religious establishment nearby.

If these poems are not distinctively "bourgeois" in their
characters and setting, neither are they notably marked by an
urban texture of expression. Later on we shall have to examine
in some detail the quality of the things they deal with directly.
What concerns us at the moment are the more habitually and
unconsciously used images that turn up in their proverbs, their
similes and metaphors, their habitual expressions of quantity

and of worth. These are remarkably concrete and material, but insofar as they can be localized as between town and country, the country expressions by far predominate.

Leaning over backward to include in the class of town expressions the metaphors and similes based on commerce, we find them surprisingly few: "He examined it inside and out as if he were buying it" (*Auberee*, in *Reid*, 59); "Was it by the day or by the piece that you work?" the lady asks in *Le Foteor* (I, 310); "I'm not so drunk you can sell me a bladder for a lantern," says the innkeeper in *Le Prestre comporté* (IV, 23). The city itself and its characteristic trades turn up only occasionally. One mistress in *Le Prestre pelé* "has more creases and wrinkles than Rouen has streets and alleys" (*Rom* 55: 546). Gombert and the clerk "held each other by the hair so tight you could have carried them slung over a pole from one end of town to another" (*Nar*, 92). The expression "Worth more than ginger or zedoary" in *Le Vilain mire* (*JO*, 65) may reflect the town-based spice trade. The expression "fautré son fautre" describing the beating of the husband in *La Dame qui fist batre* (IV, 140) may mean "fulled (or beat) his felt." If so it is the second metaphor from textile-manufacturing in this poem (cf. IV, 139). There are surely more of these (e.g., *Nar*, 93; *Reid*, 25) and of other "town" expressions to be found in the fabliaux; but they are still rare—extraordinarily rare for the literature of a time and a region in which commerce and manufacture, of textiles particularly, were flourishing.

There is of course a whole class of expressions turning on domestic economy, on parts of the body, on everyday living that do not arise from a particular ecology: "spit . . . as if he had swallowed a fly" (V, 27); "quivered like a hotcake in the

pan" (VI, 262); "took his ass by the ears" ([i.e., "got going"]
II, 72; I, 308); " 'now I've baked me my bread' " ([i.e., "now
I've done it"] I, 214); "before someone could change the dice
on them" (*Nar*, 141); " 'I'm nothing to her but a raincoat' "
(VI, 98); "had no ulcer on his legs" ([i.e., "was quick and
agile"] *JO*, 82). But there are many expressions based on rural
life, on farming and sheep-raising, on animals, vegetables,
grains, and fruits. The figuration of fabliau poetry, though it
is not very rich, gives the overall impression of having sprung
from the country life of its time. Things in the fabliaux are
worth or not worth "three nuts," "two garlics," "a scallion,"
"a quail's egg," "an almond," "a rotten apple," "a leek," "two
rotten pears," and the like.[5] The butcher in *Les Braies le prestre*
is "more frightened than a sheep among ten wolves" (VI, 260).
The old woman in *Le Chevalier a la corbeille* goes "trembling
like a little leaf in the north wind" (II, 191). The maid in
Constant du Hamel runs faster than "a cow pricked by a gadfly"
(*Ros*, 87). Others, variously, are "happy as a rat in a haystack"
(I, 295), "quieter than a water rat (*Nar*, 122), or beaten "like
an ass at a bridge" (*Nar*, 117).[6]

Sexual metaphors and similes in the fabliaux are heavily rural.
The task of describing the epic genitalia of Gautier in *Le Fevre
de Creil* involves comparisons with "a monk reaching for pears,"
"an onion of Corbueil," "a Lombard bean," and "a goose swallowing . . . a grain of barley" (I, 232).[7] The same sexual-rural
motif is apparent in the titles of fabliaux like *La Dame qui
aveine demandoit pour Morel sa provende avoir* (*The Lady Who Asked
for Blackie to Be Fed His Oats*), *L'Esquiriel* (*The Squirrel*); and
Porcelet (*Piggy*), and it forms the basis of the various tales on
the theme of *La Damoisele qui ne pooit oïr parler de foutre*, where
the young lady who can't stand to hear blunt expressions for

intercourse is led to lovemaking with the aid of a whole series of rural circumlocutions. The lover in one version tells her father that he "knows well how to plow and sow, thresh and winnow" (V, 26), with evident double entendre, and intercourse in the fabliaux is described, among other ways, as trampling the grapes (VI, 150), drawing in the shafts (III, 269), harrowing land (*Rom* 26:90), exercising the right of pasturage (*Liv*, 221), and hunting rabbits (with a favorite pun on *con/ connin*) or hares (II, 239). A highborn lady insults a knight whose beard is sparse with a proverb: "it is easy to judge from the straw that the ear of grain [*espis,* with pun on *espi,* lance] is no good" (III, 248).

Other fabliau proverbs follow the same rural tendency: "The bad herder feeds the wolf" (V, 156); "the driver thinks one thing and the donkey thinks another" (*JO*, 23); "with a mild shepherd, the wolf shits wool" (*Rych* II, 109). All in all it is striking how much in their habitual turns of expression the fabliaux, no matter where they are set, hold to this substratum of rural imagery. In the expressions that have caught my eye, it is the experience of the rural lower classes, indeed, that seems most to be reflected. Figures of speech reflecting exclusively courtly and chivalric activity (cf. II, 189–190; III, 65; *JO*, 26) are as rare as those from typically urban life.

This does not mean, however, that the fabliaux are country literature any more than "hard rows to hoe" and "telling sheep from goats" in modern American means that we are still on the farm. But it does show that city experience has not yet penetrated very deeply into the habitual modes of expression; and it confirms the historical observation that city and country, aristocratic and peasant mentalities can still be expected to take much in common from their common rural-agricultural

background. Except perhaps for two or three of the largest
cities, urban life and country life were not nearly so remote
from each other in the thirteenth century as they are now.[8] In
the first place the populations of new or newly grown towns
were necessarily drawn from the country; in the twelfth and
thirteenth centuries new immigration to towns in the northern,
"fabliau" regions of France seems to have come mainly from
the surrounding countryside, within a day's journey.[9] The assumption of urban rights and protections was easy for im-
migrant freedmen, and even a runaway serf, if not claimed by
his master within a year and a day, could in many towns be
received and defended as a "bourgeois."[10] So we must imagine
the lower classes in the towns, the *varlets* and the petite
bourgeoisie of artisans and small merchants, to have been
drawn, often recently, from a rural setting, and to have
preserved a good deal of rural sympathy and mentality. Furthermore, some of them—perhaps many—continued to have
kinsmen, property, or legal ties in the country. It was possible
for a peasant living in a town as large as Metz to remain a
legal dependent of a rural abbot or seigneur, or to be mayor
of an outlying village.[11]

The urban upper class had similarly close ties with the
country. The lesser among them might occasionally be owners
of land, particularly in the areas near town where supervision
would be easy, or more often might have made loans with
agricultural income as security. They were occasionally retained
to run the country business affairs of larger landowners, who
were themselves often members of the highest circles of the
city bourgeoisie.[12] The history of the latter group in the thirteenth century furnishes generous instances of progressive "en-
noblement" and of a consequent movement back to the rural

locale typical of seigneurial life. Beginning as wealthy industrialists, merchants, and investors in houses and land, they developed close cultural ties with the aristocracy, aped their tastes and manners, and set themselves up with many of the outward appurtenances of the old feudal aristocracy—including country estates.[13] A related segment of the urban upper classes is composed of individuals who had moved in the reverse direction. Younger sons of seigneurial families, or men of families unable to maintain their landed fortunes in a complex and changing economic situation, filled ministerial positions in the urban centers of political power, and associated themselves with and perhaps helped make up the class of city patricians.[14]

A powerful source of contact between town and country was the increase of economic exchange characteristic of the time. The beginnings of industry in towns meant that some things formerly manufactured in rural households for local consumption, especially textiles, were now better purchased in the town market. Correspondingly, there was a greater movement of the raw materials of industry—vegetable, animal, and mineral— from country to town, along with the grain, wine, fruits, vegetables and other foodstuffs necessary for the support of growing urban populations.[15]

If economic circumstances help explain the preservation of a country mentality in the city, the reverse is also true. The commercial revolution of the thirteenth century touched the country, seigneur and peasant alike, as much as it did the city. In the rural areas of the region that concerns us, the century can be generally described as a period of economic expansion and social change. For the serfs the terms of forced labor were constantly liberalized, and in many areas by the end of the century serfage was virtually eliminated. The population was expanding, newly mobile, and people readily went to seek their fortunes in the towns or formed smaller rural communities of a new cohesiveness and independence. The money economy that made it possible for people to buy their freedom also made possible a new rural commerce. Production for financial profit replaced the closed economy of local consumption characteristic of feudal times. For the seigneur, rents, tolls, agricultural and juridical income, and other sources of money had to be increased if he was to preserve his estate in the face of dwindling returns from forced labor. For the smaller farmer—freedman or one whose feudal obligations claimed only a part of his energy— there was the opportunity to acquire land and a team to work it, to hire laborers from among less fortunate or less capable neighbors, and to turn a profit that would finally make of him a *prodom,* a respected leader of the rural community, and perhaps ultimately a member of the country middle class, the gentry.

This economic expansion was accompanied, then, by a marked social mobility on all levels of society. In some cases it meant social regression: the destruction of old feudal fortunes, and the exploitation and degradation of workers and peasants by those richer and cleverer, whether in town or country. The end of the thirteenth century saw a deeper division between rich and poor than did the beginning. The position of the poorest peasant, who had if anything lost ground in a period of economic expansion, became more desperate than ever. But at the same time opportunity had presented itself; new social illusions, if not expectations, had been set in motion. Where wealth begins to replace hereditary privilege as the primary source of power, anyone can hope to rise.

This is precisely the condition of the society represented in the fabliaux. Though social mobility is not one of their primary topics, it is importantly evident in them, and they show it putting a certain strain on the traditional feudal idea of the social structure, which provides for three God-given and immutable estates. As the fabliau *Les Putains et les lecheors* puts it, possibly with irony:

> Quant Dieus ot estoré lo monde
> Si con il est à la reonde,
> Et quanque il convi[n]t dedanz,
> Trois ordres establi de genz,
> Et fist el siecle demoranz,
> Chevaliers, clers et laboranz.
> Les chevaliers toz asena
> As terres, et as clers dona
> Les aumosnes et les dimages;
> Puis asena les laborages
> As laboranz, por laborer.   [III, 175]

[When God had made the world, just as it is all around, and as much as was fitting therein, he established three orders of people to be settled in society: knights, clergy, and workers. He assigned all the knights to owning the land, and to the clergy he gave the alms and tithes. Then he gave the workers the work that there was to do.]

To appreciate the fabliau representation of society, it is necessary to make a distinction between conventionally accepted social ideas and actual social behavior. Nykrog reads the fabliau treatment of the estates—their ample respect for the aristocracy and contempt for the peasant—as evidence that the fabliaux must represent the aristocratic point of view. But the point,

as Alberto Vàrvaro has said, is that a hierarchical view of society, with nobles on top and peasants on bottom, is shared
generally by all levels of society, and cannot be used as an
index of the social origin of a work.[16] If Vàrvaro is right—
and I think he is—we must also call into question Nykrog's
related assumption (p. 109) that in fictional conflicts the social
standing of the victor must be that of the audience. Indeed,
we know that as audiences we are not necessarily ourselves.
The servant-girl will readily identify with the princess, the
bourgeois youth with the gentle knight, and the peasant will
no doubt be only too ready, as in *Le Prestre et le chevalier,* to
join in the general contempt for his own class:

> . . . sont li vilain
> Felon, quivert, failli, et vain,
> Maléureus de toute part,
> Hideus comme leu ou lupart
> Qui ne sevent entre gent estre.   [II, 49–50]

[. . . the peasants are mean, vile, false, and weak, altogether
wicked, and ugly as wolves or leopards that don't know how
to behave among people.]

But general acceptance of social hierarchy does not alter the
fact of social mobility. Social thought was much slower than
social evolution in the Middle Ages, and the fabliaux suggest
that many people, while they must have accepted in principle
the clear, simple, traditional system, were actually responding
to a newly ambiguous atmosphere of social change, competition, and social hostility.

The social dynamism that the fabliaux bring into some
prominence is by no means always regarded adversely; one may
accept the hierarchy but have ceased to accept one's own place

in it. So there is no simple formula by which we can describe fabliau social attitudes, and it is sometimes difficult to tell precisely what attitude is being evoked by a given poem. For instance, acceptance of the hierarchy at face value, as in the various anti-vilain fabliaux, may be accompanied by an excessiveness of feeling that compromises the picture. Thus while such fabliaux as *La Crote, Le Pet au vilain,* and *Le Vilain asnier* seem to accept the natural baseness of vilains with more or less good humor, the virulent hatred of them in *Le Vilain qui n'iert pas de son hostel sire* and *Les Chevaliers, les clers et les vilains* suggests fear, insecurity, and, however remotely, the threat of social mobility. The tone of the latter poem is complicated, but not redeemed, by the last six lines (*BM,* 29) containing the sentiment that a vilain is he who does *vilonie,* even if he is of high lineage. Correspondingly, a pro-vilain piece such as *La Vieille qui oint la palme au chevalier* cannot be counted as anti-hierarchical, even though it ends with a condemnation of the corrupt rich. In the fabliaux there is plenty of affection, both sympathetic and patronizing, for members of the lower classes who are not socially threatening. As Vàrvaro ("Società," p. 295n.) remarks, *Le Vilain qui conquist paradis par plait,* which celebrates traditional peasant ingenuity, ends nevertheless with a denunciation of success by cleverness:

> Li vileins dit en son proverbe
> Que mains hom a le tort requis
> Qui par plaidier aura conquis;
> Engiens a fauxée droiture,
> Fauxers a veincue nature;
> Torz vait avant et droiz à orce:
> Mielz valt engiens que ne fait force. [III, 214;
> cf. *Rich,* 183; *Reid,* 22]

[There is a peasant proverb that says that many a man brings
false suit in court who will win it by arguments; cleverness
has corrupted justice, and falsehood conquered the natural
order. Wrong goes forward and right turns awry. Cleverness
counts for more than strength.]

If this commentator is not merely being the conventional mor-
alist, he thus recognizes the emergence of a new order while
remaining hostile to it. This is the stated position, with different degrees of good humor, of some of the fabliaux that
poke fun at social climbing.

The social mobility experienced in the culture is an important source of the conflicts, contrasts, and productive tensions that make many fabliaux go. The fabliaux represent in
some detail, for instance, the element of newly rich peasants
that we find in the historical records.[17] Introduce "uns vilains
riches" into a story, and you create at once a circle of dramatic
and psychological possibilities. For instance, Aloul is excep-
tionally well off. He has a large house, a garden, a maidservant
and a substantial meinie. He owns a sword and has married
the daughter of a *vavassour*. His avariciousness and his social
inferiority to his wife support his role as the typical jealous
husband (I, 255) and provide the initial sympathy for her de-
termination to be unfaithful. The malicious description of his
epic campaigns against her priest-lover seem to be fueled by
the author's equal hostility toward both sides. Similarly, in
La Couille noir, Jouglet, and *Le Vilain mire,* the marriage of the
vilain to someone of higher station provides some motivation
or tone for the action, with a variety of possible attitudes toward
the vilain-hero. In *Boivin de Provins,* the impersonation of a
typical well-to-do vilain newly come to town is the main vehicle
of the plot. In both *Estormi* and *Le Sacristain III* the financial

reverses of a wealthy villager motivate the local priest's mer-
cenary offer to the wife, and provide some of the sympathy for
her in her self-defense. *La Male Honte* turns entirely on the
disposal of the estate of a *vilain-preudom*.

In a group of fabliaux—including *Le Provost a l'aumuche, La
Vieille qui oint la palme au chevalier*, and *Le Vilain au buffet*—
we see members of the lowest classes, servants or peasants,
quite successfully competing with hostile manorial officers.
The rich peasant Constant du Hamel (whose wife is a "cortoise
dame . . . preus et gente et avenant" [*Ros*, 71]) is more than
a match for a provost, a forester, and a priest. The peasant-
hero in *Trubert* conducts a Robin Hood campaign of terror
against a ducal family.

The outrageously overbearing conduct of the tavern keeper
in *La Plantez* (III, 170–171) is more than a matter of temperament. His victim is an impecunious *gentil ome*, and spilling
the poor man's wine is an act of social aggression. The bourgeois
in the fabliaux, as we should expect, are amply concerned with
their status and its maintenance. *Le Vallet qui d'aise a malaise
se met* is a dissertation against the premature marriage that
leads to financial (and thus social) ruin. The audience's sympathy in *Auberee*, on the other hand, is marshalled in favor of
the reckless young lover whose rich father—characterized as
"sages et cortois"—opposes his marriage to the beautiful
daughter of a poor neighbor. The father's declaration (*Reid*,
54–55) is a compendium of the upper-bourgeois position:

> "Beax filz," fait il, "de ceste chose
> Te deüsses tu molt bien taire;
> Cele n'est pas de ton affaire
> Ne digne de toi deschaucier.
> Ge te vorrai plus sozhaucier,

Que que il me doive couster;
Que ge te vorrai ajoster
As meillors genz de cest païs.
De ta folie m'esbahis
Qui tel garce vels espouser."

["Fair son," he said, "you had better not talk about this;
she isn't your kind, or even fit to take off your shoes. I want
to raise you higher, no matter what it may cost me. I want
you to associate with the best people in this country. I'm
amazed at your foolishness, wanting to marry such a
wench."]

To make matters worse, the girl is virtually bought in marriage
by another rich bourgeois; it is then he who becomes the butt
of the comedy. A similar mobility or tension within the town
middle class seems to be implied in *Les Trois Boçus,* which
opens with the marriage between the beautiful daughter of an
honored bourgeois of modest fortune and a hideous but very
rich hunchback. One of the most delicious satires of bourgeois
pretension in the fabliaux is prepared by the description of the
excessively beautiful young man in *La Vieille truande:* messenger
to a knight, master of courtly speech, he is attacked by a deformed old hag who first tries to seduce him, then has the
insupportable presumption to claim him as her son:

"Vos fius!" fait il, "vielle brehaigne!
Li passions ançois vous pregne
Que ja me mere soit si faite,
Si clope ne si contrefaite,
Car me mere est haute borgoise."   [V, 175]

["Your son!" he said. "You barren old thing! May the colic carry you off sooner than my mother could be so crippled and lame. *My* mother is upper class."]

In the period we are studying, noble status and knighthood were just merging; it was becoming more and more common for aristocrats to be dubbed *chevalier* and to take chivalric vows.[18] Knightly status, however, did not correspondingly mean either the possession or the assumption of wealth and power, and the existence of a class of impoverished knights is well recorded in the fabliaux. Thus in *Le Chevalier qui fist parler les cons I* the poverty of the young knight who owns neither land nor vines but spends all his time and substance tourneying motivates his squire's theft of the clothes of three bathing maidens. The knight forces the squire to return this treasure— even though the clothes are worth a hundred pounds, and their cash reserve is down to twelvepence. This knightly act leads to the rather remarkable gifts, the first one designed to make him rich, which each of the maidens confers on him in turn (*Rych,* II, 38–48). Much of the incidental humor of *Le Prestre et le chevalier* similarly turns on the contrast between the attitudes of the knight and his squire regarding the former's lack of money (II, 54, 65, 85). *Le Vilain mire* records the unhappy beginnings of a marriage between the daughter of one of these poor knights and a rich peasant.

The denouement of *Le Chevalier a la robe vermeille* is based on a vavassour's sense of his social status. A vavassour is one of the lesser degrees of feudal aristocracy, and this one (an arriviste, we may suspect) is tricked by allowing his wife to persuade him that a man of his importance should wear only custom-tailored clothes (III, 42–43).

Berengier au lonc cul, in both versions, turns on social pretension and social decline in an aristocratic milieu. Version II (MS A) simply couples a lady of high birth (*haute parage*) with a husband of vilain origin whose knighthood is a matter of boasting and pretense. In Version I (MS D) the social commentary is much more ample. The wife is the daughter of a chatelain who goes deeply into debt to a rich vilain-usurer.

> Et li chastelains li devoit
> Tant que paier ne pooit,
> Ainz dona a son filz sa fille;
> Ainsi bons lignaiges aville,
> Et li chastelain et li conte
> Declinent tuit et vont a honte;
> Se marient bas por avoir,
> Si en doivent grant honte avoir
> Et grant domaige si ont il.
> Li chevalier mauvais et vill
> Et coart issent de tel gent,
> Qui covoitent or et argent
> Plus qu'il ne font chevalerie:
> Ainsi est noblece perie.   [*Rych* II, 100–101]

[The chatelain owed him so much that he could not pay up; so he gave his daughter to the vilain's son. This is how good families are degraded, and chatelains and counts decline and bring shame on themselves. They marry below themselves for money and ought to be greatly ashamed at the harm they do themselves. From this sort of people, who love gold and silver more than chivalry, you get the base, wretched, cowardly sort of knights: and that is how nobility perishes.]

The girl's father dubs his son-in-law, and toward this pre-
posterous upstart chevalier the author is merciless:

> Il ne prisoit ne pris ne los
> Ne chevalerie .II. auz;
> Tartes amoit et flaons chauz
> Et molt despisoit gent menue. . . .
> Mielz amast estrain enpaillier
> Que manoier escu ne lance. . . . [*Rych* II, 101]

[He wouldn't give two cloves of garlic for fame, glory, or
chivalry. What he loved was tarts and baked custards, and
he hated the common people. . . . He would rather pitch
hay than handle a shield or lance. . . .]

Apt social retribution, in fabliau terms, calls for his kissing
of his wife's behind, an action that is also proposed in *La Gageure* to symbolize the superiority of an upper-class lady's family
over that of her lower-class husband (II, 194).

As I have said above, this ample evidence of social interplay
and social tension in the fabliaux does not mean that social
issues, however important, are the central topic of these poems.
I have dealt with the topic at some length partly to support
the argument that we cannot speak of simple, homogeneous
social classes or of simple social attitudes in discussing fabliau
origins or audiences. Partly, too, I have wished to show how
an examination of this topic begins to suggest the value of the
fabliaux as evidence for the history of the culture. The fabliaux
have long been mined for realistic details of daily living in
thirteenth-century France,[19] but they can be seen as a source
of much broader historical insight. The mixed, ambiguous,
and finally ironic treatment of society in the fabliaux not only
confirms the outline derived by social historians from archival

statistics; it gives it shading, tone, and attitudinal color. It
has, in short, its own validity as history.

In dealing with the ethical and cultural import of the fabliaux, we need to keep in mind, then, a socially heterogeneous
and mobile audience, and to hold in abeyance the notion (common to both Bédier's and Nykrog's theories) that the fabliau
is somehow more natural and congenial to one social group
than to another. We have seen that even the rural aristocracy
were deeply implicated in the same web of materialism, of
interest in money and profit and new opportunity, that accompanied the creation of the urban commercial classes.[20] And
in city and country there are substantial groups, newly mobile,
perhaps the gentry and aristocracy of the future, for whom the
status and special attitudes of the courtly circle can only be
assumed—paradoxically enough—after successful application
of the fabliau ethic. So that if for a narrow circle this ethic
may ultimately have become of dubious respectability, it was
nowhere of dubious interest or power. There is indeed something ethically serious and defensible woven into these frivolous
and often indefensible tales. The fabliaux in the thirteenth
century were not quite so vulgar as they were later to be made.

CHAPTER III

Plot and Style

HEIR STORY IS SO OBVIOUSLY IMPORTANT A FEA-
ture of so many fabliaux that we would not be
far wrong in attributing much of their meaning and power to
their narrative interest. Bédier's definition of fabliaux as *"contes
à rire"* seems properly to make story an essential part of the
genre. Some pieces propel us into the story with a minimum
of preliminaries:

> Oiez, seignor, un bon fablel.
> Uns clers le fist por un anel
> Que .III. dames .I. main trovèrent.
> Entre eles .III. Jhesu jurèrent
> Que icele l'anel auroit
> Qui son mari mieux guileroit
> Por fère à son ami son buen.   [I, 168]

[Listen, lords, to a good story. A clerk made it about a ring
that three ladies found one morning. Among the three of
them they swore by Jesus that whichever fooled her husband
best to give her favors to her lover would get the ring.]

There follow the three economically told episodes of *Les Trois
Dames qui troverent l'anel*. The triangle of peasant, wife, and
priest is introduced in *Le Prestre qui abevete* with as little cer-
emony:

> Ichi après vous voel conter,
> Se vous me volés escouter,
> I. flablel courtois et petit,
> Si com GARIS le conte et dit

47

> D'un vilain qui ot femme prise
> Sage, courtoise et bien aprise;
> Biele ert et de grant parenté.
> Mout le tenoit en grant certé
> Li vilains et bien le servoit,
> Et icele le prestre aimoit. [III, 54; cf. I, 194]

[In what follows I want to tell you, if you want to listen
to me, a courtly little tale as Garin tells it about a peasant
who took a wise, polite, and well-bred wife; she was beautiful, and from an important family. The peasant kept her
in fine style and served her well, and she was in love with
the priest.]

There follow a brief three pages of bawdy action after which
the epically gullible peasant is persuaded that his witnessing
of his wife in sexual intercourse with the priest is an optical
illusion. This taste for incident is continuous through most of
the fabliaux, whatever their quality; and the most artistic of
them, granting the other literary strengths that they may have,
leave us with a sense that the narrative is still a major source
of their interest. Thomas D. Cooke, in the principal study of
fabliau plots, has argued that a feature of plot, the comic climax, is "the most important single feature" of fabliau comedy.[1]
It is certainly true that when we think of such fabliau "classics"
as *Auberee, Le Bouchier d'Abeville, La Borgoi .l'Orliens, Le Chevalier qui fist parler les cons, Saint Pierre et le jongleur, Boivin de
Provins, La Gageure,* and many others, we think of their well-
made plots, developed and well-motivated actions that come
to a satisfying climax and denouement. Similar success in plotting can be credited to *Un Chivalier et sa dame et un clerk* and
Le Sacristain II for their unusual psychological consistency; to

La Dame qui fist batre son mari for its rapid tempo and consecutive narration; and to *Le Pescheor de Pont seur Saine* for its good proportions.

Having noted this much about fabliau plots, which is perhaps no more than what we should expect from a narrative genre, we are free to remark the surprising extent to which plot in the fabliau is, conversely, neglected. Plot interest is so often muted, or suspended, or abandoned as to suggest that while it is admittedly a major source of interest in the genre, it is not an exclusive one nor, ultimately, an essential one.

Fabliaux that fall short of having satisfactory plots in our classical sense can be placed in half a dozen categories, ranging from those having, if anything, too much plot, to those having virtually no plot at all. I would classify as overcontrived and overcomplex those, for instance, of *Aloul, Brifaut,* and *Le Prestre teint,* where, although the narrative is well supplied with incidents, the succession of incidents lacks shape, and the denouement—such as it is—is rather trivial and disappointing in proportion to all that has gone before. Similar are the related *Les Tresces* and *La Dame qui fist entendant son mari qu'il sonjoit,* which combine a low level of verisimilitude with lack of proportion, in stories that are nevertheless rich enough in sheer incident.

Gautier le Leu, one of the most memorable of fabliau poets, seems curiously uninterested in his plots. He spends the first thirty lines of *Le Prestre teint* delivering a tirade on a certain inn at Orléans where he paid the bill with his clothes. It has nothing to do with the plot. The tale turns importantly on the priest's hiding in a tub of dye, but we are not told that the husband is a dyer for almost two hundred verses (*Liv,* 261). Later, when the husband outlines to his wife the plot laid to

entrap the priest in a tub, the audience is not informed that
the tub will be one full of dye (*Liv*, 264). In Gautier's *Les Deus
Vilains,* which is little more than a series of scatological jokes,
fifty verses worth of action transpire at an inn, and the Host's
wife is grotesquely involved in it, by the time that we learn
that the Host has a wife at all (*Liv*, 203). Another example of
his defective sequencing is the indefinite timing in *Connebert*
(*Liv,* 227–228) of the cuckold's discovery of his wife in the
act of sinning with the priest.

Other fabliaux show similar carelessness that muffles plot
effect. In *Estormi* the narrator at one point (I, 202) tells us
unembarrassedly, and just in time, that he has forgotten to
mention an essential point: Dame Yfame has told the priests
that her husband will be out of town that night. The author
of *L'Oue au chapelain* fails to explain—considering the rich,
conventional presence of sensualist clergymen in the fabliaux—
why his roast goose and his mistress need to be hidden at the
mere approach of a messenger; and he delays until his effect
is lost the news that the messenger is knocking loudly at the
door with a message from another priest (VI, 47–48).

A surprising number of fabliau narratives have weak endings.
Le Chevalier qui fist sa fame confesse, which in its middle spends
some effort on physical and psychological verisimilitude and
contains some charmingly realistic speeches by the wife, trails
off at its end. The denouement, in which the wife supposedly
convinces her husband that she had penetrated his disguise
from the first (I, 186–187), is unpersuasive. The rendering of
the wife's alibi at the end of Rutebeuf's *La Dame qui fist trois
tors entor le moustier* is similarly weak (III, 197). In Rutebeuf's
Frere Denise, about a Friar Minor who smuggles a girl into the
order, the plot is underdone throughout. At the denouement

the invective aimed at the friar clearly claimed more of the author's interest than did the easy opportunity for dramatics (III, 269–272). The finale of *La Dame qui se venja du chevalier* is likewise slack; the concluding gambit is followed by a long spate of moralizing about women that rehashes some of the plot in a way that further dulls its edge (VI, 31–33).

Jean de Condé shows remarkable sangfroid when confronted with problems of plotting. In *Le Clerc qui fu repus derriere l'escrin,* when the husband is confronted with not one hidden lover but two, Jean simply dispenses with any resolution. The husband remains silent, the lovers depart, and the narrator tells us that he won't say what happened next (IV, 51–52), simply assuring us that the wife knew well how to get herself out of difficulty. The wordplay and misunderstanding that uncovers the lovers is the point of the piece; the rest of the plot is left to go begging. Similarly in *Le Pliçon,* when the guilty squire escapes but leaves his clothes behind, Jean says that he can tell us nothing about this incriminating evidence. If the lady could conceal the squire from her husband so well, disposing of his clothes would surely not have given her much trouble. Jean's *Sentier battu* has at its center not so much a plot as a spate of wordplay: a brief dialogue involving a cruelly witty rejoinder to an insult. If the rejoinder is taken as a comic climax, it is well-enough told, but Jean follows it with fifty verses that do not cut off a denouement so much as drown it in repetitive sententiousness (III, 250–251).

Certainly a part of the defectiveness of fabliau plotting results from faulty recollection of originally competent plots recited from memory. There are, doubtless, versions of fabliaux having plot defects not found in other versions of the same tales; and we may at many points be dealing with an original attempt at plot-interest damaged by rehandlers or by scribes.[2] But conscious disregard for pure plot-interest is clearly evident in quite a few fabliaux which exhibit a preference for other literary values.

There is a group of poems in which the authors seem content to trade suspense for irony by giving away the plot, or at least the essential parts of it, in advance. Gautier le Leu tells at the beginning of *Connebert* that the outcome will be a self-castration by a priest (*Liv,* 223). The announcement has something of the character of an advertisement for the remainder of the story, but it also creates irony at the expense of the victim—along with the grisly process of his punishment—that the audience is expected to enjoy more than it would a surprise at the plot's climax. There is some of the same grim preference for irony in the premature revelation that the son will not return home with the father in *L'Enfant qui fu remis au soleil* (I, 165), and that the priests will die in *Estormi* (I, 202). In the excellent *Prestre et Alison* we are several times virtually given the denouement before it occurs (II, 12, 14). The ironic pleasure of watching the trickster be tricked is set up in *Le Meunier d'Arleux* by the early revelation that the miller will fail in his designs on Maroie (II, 32). In *Le Prestre et le chevalier* a considerable capital of surprise and suspense is traded away for the pleasure of following the knight's stratagems after they have been revealed in advance (II, 60–61). Perhaps the same sort of ironic satisfaction is sought in the several fabliaux in which the joke, or the whole plot, is related more than once.[3]

Even farther from a primary interest in plot are the considerable pieces in which, on balance, the story line and its manipulation are clearly felt to be less important than other elements—which I shall lump here under the term *texture.*

Some fabliaux have such substantial portions of comic characterization, of extended description either satiric or just lov-
ingly familiar, of exhibitionistic dialogue savored mostly for
its own sake, of sententious editorializing, of autobiographical
rambling, or of any combination of these, that plot seems to
get lost. Thus, determining the winner of the epic duel in *Sire
Hain et Dame Anieuse* is not nearly so important as savoring
the interchange of assault and insults along the way. Here is
the climactic moment:

> Tant ont feru et escremi
> Cil qui se combatent ensamble,
> Que li contes dit, ce me samble,
> Qu'Anieuse le pis en ot;
> Quar sire Hains à force l'ot
> Reculée encontre un treille.
> En coste avoit une corbeille;
> Anieuse i chéi arrière,
> Quar à ses talons par derrière
> Estoit, si ne s'en donoit garde;
> Et quant sire Hains la regarde,
> S'en a .I. poi ris de mal cuer.[4]

[They exchanged blows and battled so—these two who were
fighting each other—that the story is, as it seems to me,
that Scold had the worst of it. For Sir Hate had backed her
up by force against a trellis. Beside it was a big basket.
Scold fell backwards into it, for she was back on her heels
and didn't notice it. When Sir Hate looked at her, he
laughed at her maliciously a little.]

The plot movement here is slack and uninspired as compared
to the lively dialogue that surrounds it.

Le Fevre de Creil has a plot and climax notably weak in interest in comparison to its virtuoso phallic description and its pre-liminary characterization of the smith's nymphomaniac wife. In *La Saineresse* the plotlike cuckolding of the husband is far overshadowed in interest by the sustained double entendre with which the wife afterwards describes the event to him.

Les Trois Chanoinesses de Couloigne dawdles comfortably through its scene-setting and through a variety of interesting subjects before arriving at the wishing contest, barely a fifth of its length, that provides what climax it has. Even if we had not lost the fifty verses describing the daring wishes of the canonesses, they would hardly overbalance the amplified and relaxed treatment of the preliminaries that seems to be the central impulse of the piece. Similarly, *L'Oue au chapelain, Le Prestre et Alison, Le Provost a l'aumuche, Le Prestre et les deux ribaus, Le Prestre qui dist la Passion, Le Vilain qui n'iert pas de son hostel sire, Les Deus Chevaus,* and *Les Trois Dames de Paris,* among others, all seem to use their sometimes mediocre plots as a pretext for revelling in the sensory quality, in the feel and texture, of the life they describe.

We come, finally, to a group of fabliaux which seem to contradict Bédier's definition of them as "stories." They have hardly any plot at all. One could, of course, exclude them from the genre for this reason, but two of them call themselves fabliaux, and each is accepted as such by some of the author-ities.[5] In this group we have the great *La Veuve* of Gautier le Leu, with its dense dramatic monologues; *Le Vallet qui d'aise a malaise se met,* an account of the transition of a young married man from good estate to bad; *Le Roy d'Angleterre et le jongleur d'Ely,* an exhibition of sustained wordplay; and *Les Putains et les lecheors,* a satirical contrasting of the clerks' good treatment of whores with the nobles' bad treatment of jongleurs.

The import of these observations on fabliau plot is that we must be careful where we locate the genre's center of gravity. The fabliaux seen as a whole make very important use of plot, but show also very surprising neglect. Their values can be powerfully expressed through plot, but they do not need to be. Whether the pleasurable suspense and surprise of great narrative are accidentally or willfully neglected, whether they are slighted through mischance or design, it is clear that the fabliau audience could nevertheless be satisfied by other, compensating values: irony, satire, verbal wit, and the appreciative and telling description or characterization which convey pleasure in the shared recognition of the felt texture of life.

Recognition of the felt texture of life is powerfully conveyed by fabliau style. As has been widely observed, while fabliau authors freely take excursions into fantasies of various sorts, they largely deal with a world that is seen realistically, and they speak of that world with a colloquial, everyday voice.[6] So, while some authors are quite capable of lyric, epic, and romantic notes, and while virtually every stylistic trait of Old French poetry could be found somewhere in the fabliaux, the typical style of the corpus is a plain style and, in a limited sense of the term, a realistic one.

There is a certain scholarly temptation to attribute this plain, realistic style to rhetorical theory, to equate it with the *stilus humilis* recommended by medieval textbooks on the art of poetry.[7] These texts generally divide styles into the high, the middle, and the low, a classification taken from classical theory and first expressed in the *Rhetorica ad Herennium* (ca. 86–82 B.C.).

> Sunt igitur tria genera . . . in quibus omnis oratio non vitiosa consumitur: unam gravem, alteram mediocrem, tertiam extenuatam vocamus. Gravis est quae constat ex verborum gravium levi et ornata constructione. Mediocris est quae constat ex humiliore neque tamen ex infima et pervulgatissima verborum dignitate. Adtenuata est quae demissa est usque ad usitatissimam puri consuetudinem sermonis.

> [There are, then, three kinds of style . . . to which discourse, if faultless, confines itself: the first we call the Grand; the second, the Middle; the third, the Simple. The Grand type consists of a smooth and ornate arrangement of impressive words. The Middle type consists of words of a lower, yet not of the lowest and most colloquial, class of words. The Simple type is brought down even to the most current idiom of standard speech.][8]

The division of oratorical styles in the *Ad Herennium* is thus mostly a matter of levels of diction, and the use of figures appropriate to those levels. The low style is elsewhere in the text defined in terms of "the most ordinary and everyday speech."[9]

In its medieval application to the composition of poetry, this doctrine was interpreted as applying not simply to levels of diction, but rather to the social levels of the subject matter. Thus the early thirteenth-century *Documentum de Modo et Arte Dictandi et Versificandi* attributed to Geoffrey of Vinsauf:

Sunt igitur tres styli, humilis, mediocris, grandiloquus.
Et tales recipiunt appellationes styli rationi personarum
vel rerum de quibus fit tractatus.   [II, 3, 145][10]

[There are, then, three styles, low, middle, grand. And
they get such names because of the persons or things dealt
with.]

John of Garland, in his *Poetria* written for instruction at Paris
in the 1220s or 1230s, follows Geoffrey:

Pastorali uite conuenit stilus humilis, agricolis mediocris,
grauis grauibus personis, que presunt pastoribus et agricolis.

[The low style suits the pastoral life; the middle style, farmers; the high style eminent personages, who are set over
shepherds and farmers.]

He gives two illustrative examples of the low style which, as
Nykrog (*Nyk,* 223) notes, are suggestive of fabliau plots. The
"good" example:

> In tergo clauam pastor portat; ferit inde
> Presbiterum cum quo ludere sponsa solet.

[The shepherd carries his club over his shoulder; he uses it
to beat the priest his wife has been playing with.]

The "bad" example:

> Rusticus a tergo clauam trahit et ter tonse
> Testiculos aufert; prandia leta facit.

[The peasant draws the club from his shoulder, and in three strokes removes that shorn sheep's testicles; he has a happy supper.][11]

The fact that this sort of textbook was designed for Latin composition did not necessarily prevent its influencing vernacular poetry; the fabliaux are not free of the traces of rhetorical school doctrine in any case. But it is still not very helpful to think of fabliau style as the result of this theory. In its medieval version the theory's boundaries are vague (the middle style is particularly indistinct), and although the fabliaux manifestly deal sufficiently with "low" characters and subjects, they by no means limit themselves to the low. Indeed, the fabliaux deal very seldom with shepherds, the social class ideally treated in the low style, but pay considerable attention to the class of farmers which rhetorical tradition, following the model of Virgil's *Eclogues, Georgics,* and *Aeneid,* assigned the middle style. Moreover, they do not much smell of the lamp, do not, except for the occasional use of rhetoric for parodic effect, feel as if their stylistic procedure had a strong theoretical base.

It is more likely the practical decorum of traditional storytelling that produces the plain style of the fabliaux. Should we insist on medieval doctrine as a source for this style, a more plausible one is that comic stories generally take colloquial diction:

> Attamen est quandoque color vitare colores,
> Exceptis quos sermo capit vulgaris et usus
> Offert communis. Res comica namque recusat
> Arte laboratos sermones: sola requirit
> Plana. . . .[12]

[Yet it is sometimes a color to avoid colors, except those afforded by ordinary speech and common usage. A comic subject rejects artfully labored diction. It requires plain words only.]

This is no more than experience and common sense would derive from the telling of funny stories, and no doubt the classical tradition of style theory itself, more descriptive and less prescriptive than its medieval version, is ultimately derived from some such practical base.

Beneath this use of colloquial diction and of a limited rhetorical palette in comedy and in the fabliaux there lies of course the inherent capacity of a particular style to convey a particular range of feeling and attitude. The basic, plain style of the fabliaux, their "realism," is a style called up to support the attitudes and ethos characteristic of the genre, and it fits the atmosphere of familiarity, of easy intimacy and confidence, that seems to have been a condition of fabliau performance.

A determining trait of fabliau style, and a major vehicle of its meaning, is its imagery. The quality of this imagery is made evident in dozens of the fabliau titles: *L'Anel qui fesoit les vis grans et roids; Berengier au lonc cul; Les Braies au cordelier; Brunain, la vache au prestre; Le Chevalier a la corbeille; Le Chevalier a la robe vermeille; La Couille noir; La Crote; Le Cuvier.* . . . I have made a selection only through the Cs, and it is already apparent that we are dealing with a literature preoccupied with *things,* with parts of the body, articles of clothing, farm animals, baskets, turds, tubs. But the titles, often fortuitously chosen, do not tell the whole story. There are at least fifty fabliaux in which the plot depends upon such close attention to quite particular things that without the things there would be no

plot at all. In *Auberee* our attention is importantly concentrated
on a sewing needle; in *Boivin de Provins* on a purse and strings;
in *Dame Jouenne* on three sharp awls; in *Le Maignien qui foti la
dame* on a three-legged stool; in *Les Trois Meschines* on some
face-powder; in *La Nonete* on the abbot's pants. The plot of *Le
Provost a l'aumuche* depends on the hiding of a piece of meat
under a furred hood; that of *Le Vilain de Farbu* on hot iron and
hot porridge. A well-larded bacon with a cord through it becomes at one point the principal character in *Barat et Haimet*
(cf. *Nar,* 23).

In addition there is in the fabliaux a large category of other
things which, precisely because they are *not* central to the plots,
inescapably denote the texture of the world that is being depicted. For, it might be argued, things centrally required in
plots might exist in worlds of very different kinds: for instance,
the cups, rings, and horses, the iron bars, mirrors, beds, and
garments of romance. In the fabliaux, however, the secondary
detail, the incidental texture, is of a piece with the primary.
Much of this detail, of course, is brought in ad hoc, as incidental support of the plot. For an iron to be heated, a hot fire
is provided in advance (I, 226); for three hunchbacks to be
hidden, a lady is given a box-bed having three compartments
(I, 17); a gamester leaves the tavern owing five sous, and his
sister puts up her surcoat as security (I, 208). It is commonplace
in the fabliau for necessary details to be brought into the setting
or action at the last moment, as the upstairs room *(solier)* in
La Borgoise d'Orliens (I, 120) and the secret exit in *Estormi*
(I, 209).

This sort of imagery, its contribution to verisimilitude, is
itself a large factor in the realistic effect of the style. However,
there are many instances in which concrete detail seems more

gratuitous, in excess of the demands of the bare story, and we begin to get a fabliau poetics of texture. In *Aloul* the priest projects a foray into the peasant's house and bed. In his way is placed not only a watchdog, but a door with a squeaky hinge, on which he urinates to make it quiet (I, 262). Another lover-priest, coming to arrange a tryst with his mistress, leaves his vestments off to be pressed (*Dame qui fist trois tors,* III, 193). A *borgois* concealing the murder of a monk by setting the corpse up in the abbey privy puts a twist of hay in its hand (*Sacristain* I [V, 122]). The wife of the vilain of Bailluel makes a cake for her lover, and covers it with a towel. For her husband she makes a bed out of straw and dried pea-stalks, covered with hempcloth (*Nar,* 78, 80). A lady on the way to bed with her lover takes up a pasty and some wine, a white linen towel, and a fat wax candle (*Dame qui fist batre,* IV, 141). The widow in *Jouglet* goes matchmaking for her son dressed in the better of the two mantles that she has, the one of badger, the other of catskin (IV, 113). A priest sets his pretty "godmother" on a cushion by the fire but drawn back a little the better to see her face (*Oue au chapelain,* VI, 47). In *Le Prestre et Alison* we are told of the good *bourgeoise,* who

> Maintes foiz avoit vendu auz
> A sa fenestre et oignons,
> Et chapeax bien ouvrez de jons.   [II, 8]

[had often sold garlic and onions at her window (stall), and hats well made of rushes.]

A monk imagines in bed how much he would enjoy making love with one of the girls he has seen that day: "If I might hold the plumpest and the softest in my arms . . ."

En ce lit et en ces blans dras,
Qui souef flairent la buee.   [*Rom,* 44: 561]

[in this bed, between these white sheets that smell so sweetly
of fresh laundry.]

It should be apparent that in the hands of skilled and in-
ventive poets fabliau descriptive imagery can be deployed in
the interest of literary effects—emotional tone, psychological
or social comment—well in excess of the demands of plot.
Although many fabliau settings are spare, if not bare, some
leave us with an impression of dense physical reality through
the use of details that accumulate in the course of the narrative:
thus the castration scene in *Connebert,* with its forge, anvil,
nails, razor, hammer, and fire (*Liv* 229–230); the inn of *Sacristain II,* with its wooden spits, bowls, firewood, axe, pan,
and sack (*Reid,* 48); the house of Travers in *Barat et Haimet,*
with its post and beam, wall and sill (*Nar,* 130–131).[13]

More sustained and elaborate description, suggesting the
catalogues and the rhetorical *descriptio* of learned or courtly literature, is rare enough to be noticeable. It can be used either
to emphasize and deepen the everyday texture, or conversely,
with courtly formality and courtly images, for parody or irony.
The catalogue of worldly goods advertising the widow's wealth
in *La Veuve* suggests a gratuitous pleasure in material texture:

J'ai assés caudieres et pos
Et blanques quieltes et bons lis,
Huges, sieges et caelis,
Et bons manteals et peliçons
Qui furent fait a esliçons,
S'ai asés dras lignes et lagnes,

> Et s'ai encore de deus lagnes,
> De le grosse et de le menue.
> Ma maisons n'est mie trop nue,
> Ains i a certes bials harnas,
> Car j'ai encore deus hanas:
> Li uns en est fais al viés tor,
> A l'eur reverset tot entor;
> Mes sire l'avoit forment cier. [14]

[I have plenty of kettles and pots, and white mattresses and
good beds, chests, chairs, and bedsteads, and good cloaks
and furred wraps made from the best materials, and I have
lots of cloth of linen and wool and two kinds of firewood,
big and small. My house isn't at all empty; there are plenty
of fine furnishings, like my two tankards. One is made in
the old style, with the border decorated all around. My husband was very fond of it.]

The outrageous bill for the first night's hospitality in *Le Prestre
et le chevalier,* which primarily illustrates the priest's avarice,
is totted up in such detail as to suggest also a certain pleasure
in the list for its own sake:

> Vous conterai .v. saus au pain,
> Et .v. au vin, plaisant et sain,
> Et .v. à le char de porc saine;
> Autrestant a valut la laine.
> S'en a .v. as gelines crasses,
> .V. as capons et .v. as hastes,
> .V. as pastés, .v. as gastiaus,
> Que nous aussmes boins et biaus,
> .V. as aus et .v. as oissnions,

.V. au poivre et .v. as poissons,
Et si ara .v. saus au feu,
.V. au serjant et .v. au keu,
.V. pour l'avaine. Or sont .c. saus,
Que je ne soie au conte faus.
S'en ara .v. as napes beles,
.V. as pos et .v. as paieles,
.V. as tables, .v. as plouviers
Que nous euismes boins et chiers;
Les gyngembras, les ricolisses,
.XXX. sous coustent les espises;
Que je n'oubli .v. saus au sel,
Et .v. au lit, .v. à l'ostel,
Et .v. au fain, tout sans l'avaine,
Et .v. à la litière sainne,
C'on mist desous vos .ii. chevaus;
Si sera li contes ingaus.   [II, 58–59]

[I'll count five sous for the bread, and five for the fine, sound wine, and five for the good pork; the wood came to that much too. And there's five for the fat hens, five for the capons and five for the roast meats, five for the pies, five for the good and fine cakes we had, five for the garlic and five for the onions, five for the pepper and five for the fish, and then there'll be five sous for the fire, five for the servant, five for the cook, and five for the oats. Now that makes a hundred sous if my count is not wrong[!]. Then there's five for the pretty tablecloths, five for the pots and five for the pans, five for backgammon, five for the good, expensive plovers we had; the ginger and the licorice—the spices cost thirty sous; let me not forget five sous for salt, five for bed,

five for shelter, and five for the hay, besides the oats, and
five for the good bedding we put under your two horses;
that makes up the bill.]

Many of these items have already been listed in the tale once
before (II, 55–57).

In their occasional excursions into courtly style, the fabliau
poets use very rarely the conventional spring landscape description familiar in romance and lyric. Indeed, they rarely
describe any natural or seasonal settings at all. The description
of night in *Le Prestre et le chevalier* is unique:

> Quant là vinrent, si estoit nuis
> Et si estoient clos li huis,
> Et les bestes èrent venues,
> Et les estoilles par les rues
> Luisoient, qui clartet donnoient
> A chiaus qui les chemins aloient.   [II, 49]

[When they got there it was night, the doors were closed,
and the animals had come home, and the stars were shining
along the streets, giving light to those who were making
their way.]

The April garden description in *Aloul* (I, 756–757), cited by
Nykrog (*Nyk,* 72–73) as a prime example of parody, comes
near the opening of a long series of bawdy incidents occasionally
punctuated by reminiscences of courtly or epic style.

The courtly portrait appears full-fledged with the conventional set of ideal traits in one version of *Le Chevalier qui fist
parler les cons I* (VI, 180–181), and in *Guillaume au faucon* (*Reid,*
84–85), a predominantly courtly poem that barely qualifies as
a fabliau by virtue of tonal irregularities at its very end (see

below, chap. 5). A shorter portrait, but still courtly and conventional, is that of the maiden Gille in *Le Prestre et le chevalier*
(II, 48).[15] For the most part, fragments of courtly portraiture
are used for local effects, sometimes, as Nykrog has brilliantly
pointed out, supported by comic reminiscences of romance
themes.[16]

There are, however, a few descriptions that seem to transcend
the limits of both realism and romance to produce not parody
or comedy but a convincing if unconventional charm. Such,
for instance, is the scene in *L'Espervier* in which the young
squire carries a message to his lord's mistress. He is kneeling,
holding her mirror so that she can tie her wimple, when her
beauty overcomes him (V, 46–47). Similarly both realistic and
charming are the picture of the pretty "wife" of the priest in
Le Bouchier d'Abeville, dressed in her green robe with its great
pleats set off by her belt worn tight about her waist (III, 237–
238), and that of the blond-haired young gallant in *Le Foteor,*
sitting on a bench with one leg crossed over the other, "turning
in his hands a pair of white gloves that he was putting on"
(I, 307–308). But the ultimate in this genre is Henri d'Andeli's
description of the young Indian mistress of Alexander in the
Lai d'Aristote as she walks in her nightgown in the garden on
a warm morning,

> Nuz piez, desloiee, desçainte,
> S'en vait escorçant son bliaut,
> Chantant basset . . .   [*Reid,* 77]

[Barefoot, her hair down, ungirdled, tucking up her gown
she goes, singing in a low voice . . .]

As exceptional as the sustained courtly portrait is the sustained "realistic" one. One of the longest is that of the lecheor

Boivin de Provins disguised as a rich peasant to trick Mabile the whore:

> Vestuz se fu d'un burel gris,
> Cote, et sorcot, et chape ensamble,
> Qui tout fu d'un . . .
> Et si ot coiffe de borras;
> Ses sollers ne sont mie à las,
> Ainz sont de vache dur et fort;
> Et cil, qui mout de barat sot,
> .I. mois et plus estoit remese
> Sa barbe qu'ele ne fu rese;
> .I. aguillon prist en sa main,
> Por ce que mieus samblast vilain:
> Une borse grant acheta,
> .XII. deniers dedenz mis a,
> Que il n'avoit ne plus ne mains;
> Et vint en la rue aus putains
> Tout droit devant l'ostel Mabile.   [V, 52]

[He was dressed in gray homespun, gown and jacket and cloak all of the same . . . and he had a hood of rough wool. His shoes are not laced (i.e., not elegant), but are of hard, strong cowhide; and he, who knew plenty about trickery, had left his beard unshaven for a month and more; the better to resemble a peasant he carried a stick in his hand; he bought a big purse, put twelve pennies in it—he had no more nor less—and came into the street of the whores, right in front of Mabile's house.]

In *Le Prestre et les deux ribaus* there is a comic "portrait" of a vagabond gamester trying for the first time to ride a horse:

Mès trop li sont cort li estrier,
Quar il ot une longue jambe
Plus noire que forniaus de chambe;
Plas piez avoit et agalis,
Grans estoit, haingres et alis,
Et deschirez de chief en chief,
Et li huvès c'ot en son chief
Sambloit miex de cuir que de toile;
Dès la cuisse jusqu'en l'ortoile
N'ot fil de drap, ce vous tesmoing,
Ne dès le coute jusqu'au poing.   [III, 65]

[But the stirrups are too short, for he has a long leg, blacker than a cookstove; he had flat feet, he was tall, lean, and lanky, and ragged from end to end, and the cap he had on his head seemed more of hide than of cloth; from his thigh to his toe there wasn't a thread of clothing, I assure you, nor from his elbow down.]

Evident here are elements of caricature and of the grotesque that creep also into the long description of the old beggar woman in *La Vieille Truande* (V, 172–173), that of the hostile, piggish seneschal in *Le Vilain au buffet* (III, 200–201), and into some of the briefer descriptions, especially of the aged and the crippled.[17]

Descriptions of characters in the fabliaux are for the most part brief and direct, and realistic when not merely formulary. Priests are lecherous, clerks clever or debonair, wives amorous, husbands jealous, and peasants rich or stupid; but some characters are described with a unique trait or two, occupational, physical, or psychological, that will have a quite practical bearing on the action. Thus the appearance of a carver (I, 194), a dyer (*Liv,* 261), a smith (I, 231), a manure-carter (V, 40), a provost with "a big square head" (I, 113), a girl who faints if she hears mention of intercourse (III, 81), a young servant lad with a huge penis (I, 231–232), a knight's wife who doesn't respect his family (II, 193), a tavern keeper who is outrageously proud (III, 170). Character development—such as it is in the fabliaux—is done mostly through action and speech.

Fabliau action is seen through shrewd eyes that notice and appreciate small expressive detail. They catch a good amount of realistic gesture: a wink, or a glare, a stare, a fearful look, a look of disappointment, of consternation, a conciliatory embrace, a propitiatory one, and a consoling one, a congratulatory handshake, a hand taken to draw an interlocutor aside, and one taken to make him sit down; a vilain on a straw pillow by the fire scratches himself in comfort, and a squire scratches himself first with joy, then with terror.[18]

Some scenes are caught with particular acuteness: a monk handling both circumspectly and possessively a forbidden purchase at a market (*Rom* 44: 562); a corruptible bishop in close parley "mouth-to-mouth" with a rich priest (*JO* 42); a peasant woman licking her fingers after snacking on a roast partridge (I, 189); a lecherous priest beckoning with a finger to the church charwoman, and embracing her while keeping an eye on the street (VI, 11); a maid inspecting the unusual wound suffered by her mistress (V, 180); a husband contemplating with remarkable deliberateness a strange young man in his wife's bathtub (I, 305); a provost bending down behind his table companion "as if to wipe his nose" in order to hide a piece of pork under his furred hood (I, 114); a fisherman's wife awakened too early, dressing in her sleep (VI, 246).

Except for an occasional excursion into courtly monologue

or dialogue,[19] speech in the fabliau is realistic and dramatic. *La Veuve* contains some of the best dramatic monlogue before Chaucer, and the long speech of Boivin de Provins in front of the whore's house (*Rych* II, 111–112; see below, chap. 4) is in the same class. But long speeches are otherwise rare; the fabliau greatly prefers dialogue, and some pieces, as *Dame Jouenne* and *Le Bouchier d'Abeville,* are composed predominantly of direct discourse. Expectedly, the fabliau poets are good at rendering blunt diction and all of the shriller and more pointed sounds of everyday life: oaths, exclamations, curses, arguments, the language of the tavern and of dicing.[20] But the sensitive reader will come now and again upon dialogue that is more nuanced, more delicately revelatory of motive and character, which in another period might well have been written for theatric social comedy or farce:

> "Maroie," fait ele, "que dist
> Li valléz, qui tant a là sis?"
> "Dame, ne me chalt de ses dis;
> Jà est .I. gloz, .I. mal lechière."
> "Ne t'a mie fait bele chière,
> Quant si t'en revienz esmarie:
> Que dist-il? Nel' me cele mie."
> "Jà me dit quil est .I. fouterre."
> "Dit il ce, par l'âme ton père?"
> "Oïl, Dame, foi que vos doi."
> "Tu me gabes, ge cuit, par foi."
> "Non faz, Dame, foi que doi vos."
> "Maroie, alom i anbedox."
> "Dame, alez i trestote soule;
> Il n'i a mie trop grand foule;

> Ge n'ai cure de ses paroles,
> Trop sont anuieuses et foles."
> "Maroie, ge i vois savoir."
> "En non Dieu, vos faites savoir;
> Jà en revenrez tote saige."   . [I, 309]

["Mary," said she, "what did he say—the young man who's
sat out there so long?" "Lady, I don't care for his talk; he's
a scoundrel, a wicked lecher." "He certainly didn't welcome
you if you come back so angry. Don't hide it; what did he
say?" "Well, he said to me he's a—fucker." "By your father's
soul, is *that* what he said?" "Yes, Lady, by my faith." "In
faith, I think you're kidding me." "No I'm not, Lady, by
my faith." "Mary, let's both go over there." "Lady, go by
yourself. There isn't a big crowd. I don't like his talk; it's
very disagreeable and stupid." "Mary, I'm going over to
investigate." "In God's name, that's a wise move; you'll
come back very well-informed."]

The scene, from *Le Foteor,* is among the favorites of both Bédier
and Nykrog, each of whom has his own list.[21] To theirs I
would surely add the scene of the peasant-husband in *La Sorisete
des estopes* trying to recapture a mouse in the dark, then reporting
its loss to his wife (IV, 162–164), and the shrewdly caught
dialogues of the mother in *Le Vallet qui d'aise a malaise se met,*
first in bed with her husband, then in bargaining with her
intended son-in-law (II, 160–163).

The fabliau style, then, supports a characterization that is
neither detailed nor profound: few complex individuals emerge
from these texts. But it is a characterization that is nonetheless
realistic. It is very much the characterization of experienced

observation, of practical insight. It is full of stereotyping, to
be sure; but these are the quick provisional judgments, the
shorthand notations, that people use in the practical conduct
of life. Beneath the occasionally fantastic action, beneath the
caricature, as Bédier rightly observed, there is something natural. Vàrvaro calls it a realism more hidden and more genuine
than surface reporting.[22] Fabliau characters act according to an
ethos, explicit or implicit, that is rooted in the everyday life
of the culture.

CHAPTER IV

The Fabliau Ethos

S WE HAVE SEEN IN OUR EXAMINATION OF THE imagery, the essential traits of concrete things are the central data of so many fabliaux that we can readily identify the fabliau "cosmos" as a particularly material one. The appreciation of things takes so great a place in the value system of the poems, dominates so much their thought, feeling, and attitude, as to imply a deep materialism of outlook. This is in turn coupled so frequently with a high valuing of sensory pleasure that we might call the resultant "philosophy"—the ethos of the fabliaux—a sort of hedonistic materialism.[1]

The attitude is manifest at once in the remarkable interest the fabliaux have in food and eating.[2] Whole fabliau plots turn on the possession or non-possession of a crane *(La Grue),* a heron *(Le Heron),* or a piece of fat meat *(Le Provost a l'aumuche).* *Le Prestre qui manja mores* involves eating ripe berries; *Le Vilain de Farbu,* a bowl of hot gruel. *L'Oue au chapelain* deals with a clerk who can't resist roast goose, and *Les Perdris* with a woman who can't resist roast partridge. Eating habits are a trait of characterization in the fabliau. The rich peasant's despicable son in *Berengier* ignored chivalry but "loved tarts and baked custards" (III, 253). Of the mean seneschal in *Vilain au buffet* it is said,

> . . . comme porciaus,
> S'encressoit, et plains ses bouciaus
> Bevoit de vin en larrecin,
> Maint cras chapon et maint poucin
> Menja toz seus en sa despensse. [III, 200–201]

[He fattened himself like a pig, drank his bellyful of wine on the sly, and ate many a fat capon and many a spring chicken all alone in his larder.]

This seneschal insults a desperately hungry peasant:

> "Veez quel louceor de pois . . .
> Il covient mainte escuelete
> De porée à farsir son ventre."   [III, 202]

[Look at that gulper of peas! It would take many a bowl of leek-soup to stuff his gut!"]

The Bishop's Chamberlain in *Le Prestre comporté* "loved the back of a salt herring much better than a good pike" (IV, 26). The dietary habits of Gautier le Leu's *Fol vilain* are tinged with satire. He puts away at a sitting, and at ruinous expense, white breads, some custards and cakes, a great salt mackerel, and twelve pints of spiced wine (*Liv,* 150). At his wedding celebration, his bride is described:

> Qui la veïst sopes mollier
> En une caudiere bolant
> O avoit car de truie olant
> C'on diut le nuit mangier al poivre;
> S'i fist on savor de genoivre.   [*Liv,* 154]

[You should have seen her dipping bread in a pot where there was boiling some smelly sow-meat that they were going to eat that night with pepper; they made the sauce with juniper.]

The contrariness of a wife is no better described than through her cooking. If Sire Hain asks for peas, Dame Anieuse produces soup, and vice versa. When he asks for stew, she makes a roast,

and burns it. When he asks for saltwater fish, expecting bone-
less ray or shark, she brings home spiny, freshwater sticklebacks
(I, 97–98).³ For his wedding feast the Count in *La Dame escoillee*
orders his chef to prepare sauces with special seasonings; but
his new bride commands that nothing be used but garlic (VI,
106). Conversely, conjugal felicity in *Le Sacristain II* is expressed
by Guillaume's shopping for bread and meat while Ydoine
makes the sauce herself with wine, pepper, and cumin
(*Reid,* 39).

The quality of being hospitable, one of the few unchallenged
virtues in the fabliaux, is regularly exemplified and measured
by the kind of food and drink provided one's friends and guests.
The rich hunchback in *Les Trois Boçus* provides peas in lard
and capons for his Christmas visitors (I, 15). The rascals en-
tertaining Boivin de Provins pledge their garments to buy capons and geese; the ensuing dinner in one version also involves
wine, chicken stew, pâtés, and pastries (*Rych* II, 114–115).
In *Le Sot chevalier* the guests who come in from the storm are
fed peas, wild duck, meat roasted and larded, rich pasties, and
wine (*Liv,* 193). The widow of *La Veuve* invites her friend over
on Sunday, promising "apples and nuts and Laonnois wine"
(*Liv,* 177). The Miller of Arleux promises a pretty customer
bread and tart, meat, fish, and lots of wine if she will come
home with him (II, 33). Clever Auberee begs some food from
a lady—a jug of wine, a loaf of bread, part of a side of bacon,
and a big potful of peas—in order to be obliged to repay her
hospitality (*Reid,* 59).⁴ For their lovers, women of the fabliaux
provide various menus (sometimes along with a hot bath), as
"pot roast, pasties with peppers, and good wine" (II, 236);
wine, a pancake made with eggs, and some fat pork (II, 193–
199); or wine in the cask, a roast capon, and cake (*Nar,* 78).⁵

Food, then, is a ready index of general pleasure in the fabliaux. It is sometimes described so particularly as to suggest an inherent value—appreciation of gastronomical detail for its own sake. In the related tales of *Le Heron* and *La Grue,* the plot requires the Duenna to leave the bird in the kitchen awhile. In *Le Heron* she admires the fat heron, then goes out to buy pepper to cook it with, and wine (*Rom* 2: 6, 90). In *La Grue* she goes out to find a knife for carving the well-prepared crane; but before she does so we are told that it wasn't cooked in garlic sauce but with pepper (V, 155). In *Les Trois Dames qui troverent l'anel I* we are gratuitously informed that the dish to be roasted for dinner is "six eels, salted and dried and smoked" (I, 172). A brief stage exit of the wife in *Le Prestre comporté* is motivated by her going for eggs to decorate the tart (IV, 3). The stupid peasant of Farbu is sent to market to buy a fresh cake ("tout tendre") and comes back with one that is terrible, full of bad dough (*Nar,* 72). Martin the peddler in *Le Sacristain II* resents not having been invited to share in the bones and chitterlings when a peasant's pig was slaughtered; but he is bribed to go on an errand nevertheless with the promise of some bacon broiled over charcoal, and bread to go with it (*Reid,* 50). In *Le Bouchier d'Abeville* the preparation of the sheep is told with a gusto well beyond the demands of plot:

> "Veez comme est cras et refais,
> . . . . . .
> Cuisiez les espaules en rost;
> S'en fetes metre plain un pot
> En essau avoec la mesnie,
> . . . . . .

>Ainz mès plus bele char ne fu,
>Metez le cuire sor le fu;
>Veez comme est tendre et refete:
>Ainçois que la saveur soit fete
>Ert ele cuite voirement."   [III, 232–233]

["See how fine and fat it is. . . . Make a roast of the shoulders and have a potful put on to stew for the servants. . . . There was never such beautiful meat; put it on the fire to cook. See how tender and succulent it is. It will be well done before the sauce is ready."]

The irresistible quality of the roast partridges in *Les Perdris* is partly conveyed by the gradualness of the feast, partly by specific details:

>S'en pinça une peléure,
>. . . . . . .
>Andeus les eles en menjue;
>. . . . . . .
>Le col en tret tout souavet,
>Si le menja par grant douçor;
>Ses dois en lèche tout entor.   [I, 188–189]

[She took a pinch of the skin . . . ate both of the wings . . . pulled off the neck very gently, and ate it with sweet satisfaction. She licked her fingers all over.]

In *L'Oue au chapelain* the goose is cooked very slowly, very well done, and its sauce, "thick, white, [the spices] well ground" makes the clerk sweat all over (VI, 46–47). The exemplary meal in the fabliau is the one found in *Le Prestre et le chevalier*. The plot requires it to be an expensive one, and it is described

in enthusiastic detail, along with the linens and candelabra
and the ritual of washing from bright and shining basins:

> Fu premiers li pains et li vins.
> Li chars de porc et li connins
> Aporta on, pour .II. mès faire;
> Celle viande doit bien plaire.
> Après orent oisiaus nouviaus;
> Puis fu aportés li gastiaus,
> Et li capon furent au soivre,
> Et li poisson à le fort poivre,
> Et les pastés à déerains
> Fait aporter li Capelains,
> Por ce qu'il èrent biel et chier.
> Por mieus séoir le Chevalier,
> Et à toute l'autre maisnie
> Dame Avinée, qui fu lie,
> Aporta nois et autre fruit,
> Et kanièle, si com je cuit,
> Et gyngembras et recolisse;
> Mainte boine herbe et mainte espise
> Lors aporta dame Avinée.   [II, 56–57]

[First came the bread and wine. For the second course they
brought the pork and the rabbit, very good meats indeed.
After that they had young birds, then the cakes, and the
capons done in a spicy sauce and the fish in a hot pepper;
and the Chaplain had the pasties served last, for they were
fine and expensive. To please the knight and the rest of the
company even better, the happy Dame Avinee brought out
nuts and other fruit, and cinnamon bark, I think, and ginger
and licorice. Dame Avinee brought out many a good herb
and many a spice.]

"They drank," the same account adds, "wine, red and white,
clear as tears and pure and fresh, plenty, and in great draughts"
(II, 57). Fabliau characters drink virtually no water, and little
mead or beer.[6] They overwhelmingly drink wine, not only in
quantity but, as the passage above indicates, with pleasure and
appreciation. The stakes of the wager in *La Gageure* is a barrel
of wine. In *La Borgoise d'Orliens* the servants are rewarded with
"a measure of the best wine in the house" (*JO*, 25). The three
blind men who enter Compiègne hear a hawker lauding the
local inn:

> "Ci a bon vin fres e novel,
> Ça d'Auçoirre, ça de Soissons."   [*Goug, 3*]

The new wines of Auxerre and Soissons are indeed pleasing to
the feasters, who pour for each other with hearty ceremoni-
ousness:

> "Tien, je t'en doing, aprés m'en done;
> Cis crut sor une vingne bone."   [*Goug, 4*]

> ["Here, I'll pour some for you, then you pour for me. This
> grew on a good vine."]

Long before the use of bottles and corks, keeping wine was an
uncertain matter, and it is no wonder that new wine comes in
for its share of praise. Yet the fabliau world knows and appreciates old wine too; in *Le Vescie a prestre* it is distinguished
from ordinary wine ("vin de despense," III, 112).

In *Le Prestre comporté* the innkeeper gives a purely gratuitous
description in praise of wine from mountain vineyards:

> ". . . dou vin froit et cler et pur
> Vous donrai, sans longe bargainne,
> Qui crut en crume de montaigne

Si haus com li solaus i lieve,
.II. liues ains ke l'aube crieve."   [IV, 21]

["Without a lot of bargaining, I'll give you wine that's cool
and clear and pure, grown on a mountain slope as high as
the sunlight gets two hours before daybreak."]

Wine with dinner is just one manifestation of the wife's
pleasure at the return of her husband after a three-month absence in Jean Bodel's *Le Sohait desvé:*

Qant l'ot acolé et baisié,
Un siege bas et aaisié
Por lui aaisier li apreste,
Et la vïande refu preste,
Si mangierent qant bon lor fu,
Sor un coisin, delez lo fu
Qui ardoit cler et sans fumiere.
Mout i ot clarté et lumiere;
Deus mes orent, char et poissons,
Et vin d'Aucerre et de Soissons,
Blanche nape, saine vïande.
De servir fu la dame engrande:
Son seignor donoit dou plus bel
Et le vin a chascun morsel
Por ce que plus li atalant.   [*Nar,* 100]

[When she had hugged and kissed him, she prepared a deep
easy-chair to comfort him, and the food was quickly prepared. They ate when they were ready, on a cushion by the
fire, which burned clear, without smoke, all light and
bright. There were two courses, meat and fish, wine of
Auxerre and Soissons, white linen, good food. The lady was

eager to serve; she gave her lord all the best, and wine with
each bite to please him the more.]

Pleasure in wine and food reaches a sort of climax in Watriquet de Couvin's *Les Trois Dames de Paris*. The disastrous
ending to the binge therein described owes much to antifeminism and perhaps to an antipathy for excessive gluttony, but
the author lets pass some descriptions of wine and food that
are notably sympathetic. The expedition begins with Dame
Tifaigne, the milliner:

> . . . "Je sai vin de riviere
> Si bon qu'ainz tieus ne fu plantez.
> Qui en boit, c'est droit santez,
> Car c'est uns vins clers, fremians,
> Fors, fins, frès, sus langue frians,
> Douz et plaisanz à l'avaler."   [III, 146]

["I know a Rivière wine so good that there was never planted
any like it before. Drinking it is instant comfort; it's a clear
wine, brilliant, robust, cool and fine, sparkling on the
tongue, smooth and pleasant to swallow."]

The ensuing feast includes fat goose, a platter of garlic, and
hot cakes, followed by waffles and pastries, cheese and almonds,
pears, spices and nuts, and round after round of Grenache wine.
They drink themselves into insensibility and worse, but not
before one of the ladies has delivered a little lecture on the art
of sipping:

> "Hé, que tu as la gorge gloute,"
> Dist Maroclippe, "bele niece;
> Je n'aurai encor en grant piece

But tout le mien, mais tout à trait
Le buverai à petit trait,
Pour plus sur la langue croupir;
Entre .II. boires .I. soupir
I doit on faire seulement:
Si en dure plus longuement
La douceur en bouche et la force." [III, 149]

["Oh, sweet niece, what a greedy gullet you have," said
Maroclippe; "I'm not going to finish drinking mine for a
long time; I'll drink it very slowly in little sips, to let it
lie better on the tongue. Between every two swallows you
should exhale once; that way its sweetness and strength last
longer in your mouth."]

Watriquet de Couvin is no enemy to pleasure. In *Les Trois
Chanoinesses de Couloigne,* he describes in the first person the
charming sight of the three ladies as they sit in their bathtubs:

Lors commenchames à mengier.
Ma table estoit assez près d'eles;
Si les vi vermeilles et beles
Et esprises de grant chaleur,
Que leur fesoit avoir couleur
Li bains chauz et li bons vins frois,
Dont assez burent sanz effrois.
Là fumes aise de touz poins. [III, 141]

[Then we began to eat. My table was right near them, and
I saw how pink and pretty they were and kindled with the
heat; they were rosy from the hot bath and the good cool

wine that they drank plenty of without any trouble. We were comfortable there in every way.]

To top matters off, the minstrel recites them stories.

Sexuality is of course a main component of fabliau hedonism; but discussion of it is so much in need of the fullest possible context that it will have to be reserved for the next chapter. Meanwhile the main lines of sentiment are clear. The fabliaux are full of sensory pleasure, and quite a few of them turn on a general conception of the good life that involves little more. The successful young man in *Le Foteor* goes away having enjoyed some good meals, a warm bath, plenty of sex, and money to boot. The axis of good living (and thus of punishment) for the priest in *L'Evesque qui benei le con* is permission to keep a "wife," to dine on goose and peppered chickens, to drink wine, and sleep on a mattress. The jongleur of Ely's vision of life (scorned, however, by the King as "folie" [II, 248–249]) includes free meals or extravagant ones, lots of drink, sleeping late, fun, games, rising at noon, and knowing pretty women.

Turning from ends to means, one would expect a hedonistic culture to be interested in money, and the fabliaux do not surprise us. They are virtually unanimous on the subject. Money is valued as it gives access to pleasure, and also for its own sake. There is a persistent small rain of coins, a continual traffic of rewards, payments, and bribes, a continual totting up of prices, values, and sums.[7]

One virtuoso passage on sums is the dinner bill already quoted from *Le Prestre et le chevalier*. Another is the dramatic monologue of the jongleur Boivin de Provins disguised as a rich peasant in front of the house of Mabile the whore. He has

only twelve pennies to his name, but pretends to be counting
a much larger fortune:

"Deüsse bien de mon argent
Tout seul par moi savoir la somme:
Ainsi le font tuit li sage homme.
J'oi de Rouget .XXXIX. saus,
.XII. deniers en ot Giraus,
Qui mes .II. bués m'aida a vendre.
A males forches puist il pendre,
Por ce qu'il retint mes deniers!
.XII. en retint li pautoniers,
Et se li ai je fet maint bien.
Or est ainsi, ce ne vaut rien.
Il me vendra mes bués requerre,
Quant il voudra arer sa terre
Et il devra semer son orge!
Mal dehez ait toute ma gorge,
S'il a jamés de moi nul preu!
Je li cuit molt bien metre en leu;
Honiz soit il et toute s'aire!
Or parlerai de mon afaire:
J'oi de Sorin .XIX. saus;
De ceus ne fui je mie faus,
Quar mon compere dans Gautiers
Ne m'en donast pas tant deniers
Com j'ai eü de tout le mendre;
Por ce fet bon au marchié vendre.
Il vousist ja creance avoir,
Et j'ai assemblé mon avoir.
.XIX. saus et .XXXIX.,

Itant furent vendu mi buef.
Dieus! c'or ne sai que tout ce monte!
Si meïsse tout en un conte,
Je ne le savroie sommer;
Qui me devroit tout assommer,
Ne le savroie je des mois,
Se n'avoie feves ou pois,
Que chascuns pois feïst un sout:
Ainsi le savroie je tout.
Et neporquant me dist Sirous
Que j'oi des bués .L. sous,
Qui les conta, si les reçut;
Mes je ne sai s'il m'en deçut
Ne s'il m'en a neant emblé,
Qu'entre .II. sestiere de ble,
Et ma jument et mes porciaus
Et la laine de mes aigniaus
Me rendirent tout autrestant.
.II. foiz .L., ce sont .C.,
Ce dist uns gars qui fist mon conte;
.V. livres dist que tout ce monte."   [*Rych* II,
                                        111A, 112A]

["I really ought to reckon up all by myself how much my money comes to; that's what all wise people do. I have thirty-nine sous from Rouget, but Giraut, who helped me sell my two oxen, got twelve deniers of it. May he hang from the gallows for keeping my deniers! The rascal kept twelve, and I did very well by him. Well, that's the way it is; it doesn't matter. He'll come asking for my oxen when he has to plant his barley and wants to plow his land. Damn my throat if

he ever gets any profit out of me! I know how to put him
in his place; damn him and all his race! But now to talk
about my business. I have nineteen sous from Sorin. I didn't
cheat the least bit for them, for my friend Martin Gautier
wouldn't have given me as many deniers as I got from just
the smaller part (of my goods). So it was good to sell at the
market. He wanted credit, but I have all my money in one
place. Nineteen sous and thirty-nine, that's what my oxen
sold for. God, I don't even know how much that makes! If
I added it all together I wouldn't know how to find the
total. If you counted it all up for me I wouldn't get the
hang of it for a long time if I didn't have beans or peas,
and let each pea stand for one sou; that way I'd understand
it all. Still, Sirou told me I got fifty sous for the oxen; he
got the money and counted it. But I don't know if he fooled
me and took some, because two measures of grain and my
mare and my pigs and the wool from my lambs brought
me just the same amount. Two times fifty makes a hundred,
that's what a boy who counted it said. He said it amounts
to five pounds."]

We can be sure that the fabliau audience followed this account—and especially Sirou's presumed theft of eight sous—
with as much absorbed attention as did Mabile and her crew,
who are completely taken in by the performance.

A fabliau may recommend care in the stewardship of money
(*Fole Larguesce*) or a princely largeness of dispensation (*Lai
d'Aristote* [*Reid,* 70–71]). It may be unsympathetic toward certain of the rich (V, 158), especially toward rich peasants or
rich clerics, or it may admire and respect them (V, 215). It

may warn conventionally against avarice (*Les Sohais* [*Liv*, 142, 146]), or may in various ways cynically accept money as the root of the affections. The old woman in *Le Prestre teint* has her fist full of coins as she avers that one should help out one's friends in need (*Liv*, 259). In *Le Sacristain I* the spendthrift borgois, who has reduced himself to poverty and his wife to tears by his extravagance, murders a monk, then ends up safe and snug with a hundred livres and a side of pork to boot.

In the matter of money the fabliaux are deeply touched by neither the genteel tradition that was later to make the discussion of money seem somehow vulgar, nor by the Christian condemnation of cupidity. The thirteenth-century lai *Le Vair Palefroi*, which some consider a fabliau and others do not, is interesting in this regard, for although it has all of the style and sentiment of the romance mode, it is penetrated throughout with a concern for money. The young hero, Sir Guillaume, has an income of "no more than two hundred pounds," while the heroine's father, a prince, is "worth a thousand a year," and is at pains to inform the young suitor of this fact, as well as that her most recent suitor had five hundred pounds. But she is being held for an offer from someone of the highest rank. The tale might have turned at this point into a contest between evil wealth and virtuous poverty—the young lovers begin to regret that the lady's father is so rich—but it does not. Instead, the lady suggests that the knight go to his rich old uncle (whose income is specified as "more than sixty marks in fine gold") and get a promise of three hundred pounds in land to put up as part of the marriage agreement. Once the marriage has taken place, the land can be returned. The uncle (a friend and contemporary of the lady's father) agrees, but betrays the lovers

by asking for the lady's hand himself! He is gladly accepted
by the father; the heartbroken lady's complaint contains a dia-
tribe against wealth:

> ". . . cil viellars par sa richece
> A ja de moi reçut le don.
> . . . .
> Nus ne me puet vers lui tensser,
> Quar mes pere aime couvoitise
> Qui trop le semont et atise.
> Fi de viellece, fi d'avoir!
> Ja mes ne porra nus avoir
> Fame qui soit haute ne riche,
> Se granz avoirs en lui ne nice.
> Haïr doi l'avoir qui me part
> De celui. . . ."[8]

["That old man has been given my hand just because of his
riches. . . . No one can oppose him because my father loves
greed: it urges him and stirs him up. Fie on old age! Fie
on riches! Nobody will ever be able to take a wife who is
noble or rich unless he has great wealth. I hate the wealth
that keeps me from him."]

But the tale has a happy ending. The lady escapes and marries
Sir Guillaume, and the young pair are forgiven by their elders.
In three years, we are assured at the end, the old prince dies,
leaving everything to Guillaume: "all his land . . . which was
very rich and well stocked; he held a thousand pounds in land."
Then the very rich uncle dies, leaving all of *his* assets to Guillaume as well.

Whether the poem is a true fabliau or not, the double value

system of *Le Vair Palefroi* holds for many fabliaux; and it accords
well enough with what we have observed (see above, chap. 2)
of the materialist coloring of the whole culture. In the undoubted fabliau *Le Chevalier qui fist parler les cons* the courtly
covering over the materialist ethic is even more transparent.
The contrast in the characters of knight and squire would seem
at first to be a contrast between careless aristocratic open-
handedness (the knight has pawned and spent most of what
he had) and a more conservative "lower-class" concern for
worldly goods. It is the squire who contrives to sell a remaining
palfrey to redeem the knight's gear for a tournament. On the
way—they are down to their last twelve pennies—it is the
squire who steals from off a tree the very rich clothes of a bevy
of bathing nymphs. At the nymphs' complaint, the knight
forces the squire to return the booty:

> "Ce seroit trop grant vilenie
> De fere a ces puceles honte."
> "Or tenez d'autre chose conte,"
> Fet Huet, "et ne soiez ivres:
> Les robes valent bien .C. livres,
> Car onques plus riches ne vi.
> Devant .XIIII. anz et demi
> Ne gaagnerez vos autretant,
> Tant sachiez aler tornoiant."
> [*Rych* II, 44C, 46C]

["It would be a very base thing to put these girls to shame."
"But consider something else," replied Huet, "and don't be
silly; the clothes are worth at least a hundred pounds. I
never saw richer ones. You won't make as much in fourteen

and a half years, no matter how much you know about going
to tournaments."]

But the knight returns the clothes, and the nymphs, who are
fairies, decide to reward such courtesy by making him rich
through a number of magical gifts. Huet continues skeptical,
calling "anyone a fool who carelessly throws underfoot what
he holds in his hand"(50C). But in the next episode, having
used one of the gifts to terrify a priest into abandoning his
mare, his fur cape, and half his money in the road, the knight
is vindicated:

> Or est tot liez li chevaliers;
> A Huet baille les deniers
> Dont ill i avoit bien .X. livres.
> "Huet," dist il, "molt fuse ore ivres,
> Se j'eüse ore retenues
> Les robes et lessiees nues
> As franches puceles senees.
> Bien sai de voir, ce furent fees:
> Riche guerredon m'ont rendu.
> Ainz que noz aion despendu
> Tout cest avoir ne tout gasté,
> Aron nos de l'autre a plenté."
>
> [*Rych* II, 52C, 54C]

[Then the knight was overjoyed. He gave Huet the ten
pounds worth of deniers. "Huet," he said, "it would have
been crazy if I had kept the clothes and left those wise and
generous girls all naked. I know for certain that they were
fairies. They have repaid me richly. Before we have spent
all this or lost it, we will have plenty more."]

And so it happens, in a hilarious parody of the romance motif of the magical gift; along with honor the knight enjoys money to the end of his life.

In *Les Trois Boçus* the materialist ethic implied by the action easily overrides the conventional moralization of the conclusion in a way typical of many fabliaux. The conclusion goes as follows:

> . . . onques Diex ne fist meschine
> C'on ne puist por denier avoir;
> Ne Diex ne fist si chier avoir,
> Tant soit bons ne de grant chierté,
> Qui voudroit dire verité,
> Que por deniers ne soit éus.
> Por ses deniers ot li boçus
> La dame qui tant bel estoit.
> Honiz soit li hons, quels qu'il soit,
> Qui trop prise mauvès deniers,
> Et qui les fist fère premiers.   [I, 22–23]

[. . . God never created a girl that you couldn't have for money. To tell the truth, God never made anything so precious, no matter how good nor how dear, that it couldn't be had for money. It was for his money that the hunchback got the lady who was so beautiful. Shame on the man, whoever he may be, who cares too much for filthy money, and shame on him who invented it.]

But the action supports mainly the first part of this conclusion. The rich hunchback in question is not notably avaricious, though he is the richest man in town and has spent his life making money. Except for his jealousy over his young wife,

he is actually open-handed, generous (I, 15). The wife, meanwhile, successfully uses the good sum of thirty pounds to get
a young man to do the dirty work of removing from her prem-
ises the corpses of three hunchback minstrels she has accidentally smothered to death while hiding them from her husband.
In the course of the business her husband is accidentally done
away with as well. She pays the young man gladly, we are
told, as she considers it a good bargain. Now free of her husband, she looks forward to a painless life. Beneath the medieval
cruelty towards the deformed, and beyond the mildly antifeminist sentiments, the moral of the story holds: money can buy
anything.

Money is of course materialist symbolism of the plainest
kind, but it also symbolizes certain kinds of power. In the
fabliaux it is linked with a high valuation of ingenuity or cleverness. The fabliaux do not honor vice for its own sake, but
they do celebrate the getting of money, goods, or pleasure
through wit—whether legally or illegally. Wit is one of the
few great resources of the powerless and the dispossessed. As
Marie de France puts it:

> . . . mult valt mielz sens e quointise
> e plus aide a meinte gent
> que sis aveirs ne se parent.   [Warnke, 147]

[Brains and ingenuity are worth more and are a bigger help
to a lot of people than money or family.]

It is the weapon of the servant, of the woman, and par excellence of the poor scholar. In celebrating this virtue, then,
the fabliaux are to an extent subversive of Christian teaching,
of the class basis of feudal society, of the conventional notion

of sex roles, and of conventional ideas of stability, economy, security, and justice.[9]

Fabliau wit operates, in fact, in an ethical system of its own, surrounded by the other fabliau values that we have been discussing, but usually ignoring conventional morality. Poetic justice, it is true, often accompanies the triumph of wit, but justice is not necessarily on the side of virtue.[10] Fabliau victims may be completely innocent, as the fat priest in *Le Prestre qui ot mere a force,* and Tibout, the sharecropper in *Le Sacristain II,* who simply has the bad luck to be living in the path of the tale's events. At best, fabliau justice favors some virtues and punishes some vices more than others. In the tale of *Brifaut,* a thief steals from an unintelligent but otherwise blameless peasant a huge piece of cloth by jostling him in the market crowd. The thief makes off with the cloth and "disposes of it as he pleases; for anyone deserves to lose something if he foolishly lets it be grabbed" (*JO,* 11). The devastating ingenuity of the knight of *Le Prestre et le chevalier* is exhibited mostly for its own sake, but also to punish the rich priest's lack of hospitality. The same may be said about *Le Bouchier d'Abeville,* in which a rich priest's whole household is grossly exploited.[11] In both of these, and in many another piece, anticlericalism would itself have been sufficient to provide tacit justification for the hero's plain violations of ordinary Christian morality in his treatment of the priest. But anticlericalism, it might be imagined, is itself the other side of a defense of honest religion. The clerics who are punished in the fabliaux are gluttons, whoremasters, perverters of their sacred calling. However, while the fabliaux massively imply that these rascals get what they deserve, they do not typically offer us a vision of the good priest by contrast and in praise.[12] Venal persons are often the

"bad guys" of the fabliaux, but there are few "good guys" who
are such merely by being good in the Christian sense. The
humble, the simple, the charitable have a hard time of it in
this cosmos. Even the good peasant whose exemplary life finally
justifies his entry to heaven has to secure entry through a truly
impressive power of argument:

> "Vilein," dist Diex, "et ge l'otroi;
> . . . .
> Bien sez avant metre ton verbe."   [*Reid*, 22]

["Peasant," said Our Lord, "I grant it. . . . You really know
how to put across your argument."]

The "wicked" victims of fabliau ingenuity are not victimized
so much because they are wicked or hypocritical as because
they are competitors; they are already self-proclaimed entrants
into the contest of beating the system. As such they fit perfectly
into the fabliau taste for wit or ingenuity as competition;
sometimes, indeed, they win.

The contest of wits is an important structural element in
many a fabliau. The center of *Boivin de Provins* is a battle—
virtually hand-to-hand—between the hero and the whores
Mabile and Ysane. Trick is similarly traded for trick in *Le
Prestre et les deux ribaus*. The protagonists of *Les Deus Changeors*
exchange embarrassing sallies almost formally, as do those of
Le Sentier battu. *Les Trois Dames qui troverent l'anel I*, actually
three separate fabliaux, is organized at once as a contest:

> Oiez, seignor, un bon fablel.
> Uns clers le fist por un anel
> Que .III. dames .I. main troverent.
> Entre eles .III. Jhesu jurerent

> Que icele l'anel auroit
> Qui son mari mieux guileroit
> Por fère à son ami son buen.   [I, 168]

[Listen, lords, to a good story. A clerk made it about a ring that three ladies found one morning. Among the three of them they swore by Jesus that whichever fooled her husband best to give her favors to her lover would get the ring.]

La Borgois d'Orliens is seen as a contest between wife and husband, and it is perhaps to put something in balance against the wife's formidable powers that the husband is characterized as he is at the beginning:

> Riches mananz a desmesure.
> De marcheandise et d'usure
> Savoit toz les tors et les poins,
> Et ce que il tenoit aus poins
> Estoit bien fermement tenu.   [*JO*, 21]

[. . . rich beyond measure. He knew all the tricks and turns of trade and moneylending, and what he got his hands on was really held onto.]

The wife's ingenuity is devoted to making her husband "cuckolded, beaten, and happy"—a classic fabliau theme. The values of the poem epitomize the close fabliau interconnections, then, between money, cleverness, and pleasure, especially sexual pleasure.

The exercise of wit that leads either to money, to sensory pleasure, or both is so common in the fabliau as to need no elaborate demonstration here. But the phenomenon of the contest of wits points to yet a third source of the valuing of wit,

namely, wit itself. The gratuitous love of it plays all through
the fabliaux, and it arises often in pure form. In *Les Trois Aveugles* a well-to-do clerk pretends to give to one of a group of
three traveling blind men a valuable coin. Each of the victims
thinks one of the others has it. They head for a wonderful,
costly celebration at an inn in Compiègne. The clerk, who is
from Paris, and is characterized (in perhaps a reference to scho-
lastic intellectualism) as knowing a lot about good and evil
("Qui bien e mal assez savoit" [*Goug,* 1]), follows them just
to see what will happen. The editor of the poem regards the
actions of the clerk as "crudely immoral," his treatment of the
blind men offensive to the modern reader, if less so to the
medieval (p. xi). The point, however, is that we are expected
to share from the hero's point of view the pleasure of the work-
ing out of the trick for its own sake. In this pursuit, as we
have seen with other examples of fabliau morality, the conventional rules do not hold. In the end, in a second display
of ingenuity, the clerk relieves the embarrassed blind men from
an impending beating by the tavern keeper by agreeing to pay
their bill, then tricks him out of getting the payment. Though
the fabliau ends with a one-line remark that one shouldn't
shame other people, the force of the poem is in the relishing
of the tricks and of the wit that devises them.

It is only in this sense that we can understand the tale of
Barat et Haimet, the very champion rascals and thieves. The
brothers come by their talent naturally: their father has been
hanged as a thief. Haimet is so light-fingered that he steals
eggs from the nest of the magpie (which is the thief among
birds). Barat challenges him—the contest again—to return
the eggs to the nest without the bird's knowing it. While

Haimet is doing just this, high in the branches of an oak tree,
Barat climbs up and steals the pants off his brother's backside
("li anble du cul ses braies," *Nar*, 122). Their companion
Travers, a lesser practitioner, at this display of virtuosity decides
to give up the profession:

> "N'a tel larron jusqu'à Nevers
> Con est Baraz, si con moi sanble.
> Bien est lerres qui larron enble.
> Mais ge n'ai avuec vous mestier,
> Quar ge n'ai de vostre mestier
> Vaillant quatre deniers apris.
> Teus cent foiz seroie ge pris,
> Que vous eschaperiez par guile.
> Ge me retrairai a ma vile,
> Ou ge ai ma femme espousee.
> Folie avoie golousee,
> Qui voloie devenir lerres.
> Ge ne suis fou ne tremelerres;
> Ge me sent tant fort et delivre
> Qu'assez gaaignerai mon vivre
> Se Dieus plaist, des or en avant.
> Ge m'en vais, a Dieu vous coment."
>
> [*Nar*, 124]

["It seems to me that there isn't a thief from here to Nevers
like Barat. He is a good thief who can steal from a thief.
But I have no business with you; I haven't learned four cents
worth of your trade. I'd be caught a hundred times while
you would cunningly escape. I'll return to my village where
I have my wedded wife. I must have been crazy to want to

become a thief. I'm neither a fool nor a gambler; I'm strong
and active enough to earn my living from now on, if God
wills. So I'm going; and God keep you."]

In thus returning to respectability Travers sets up a contest
between moral systems. The remainder of the tale tells of the
elaborate efforts of Travers to defend himself, his wife, and
his home from the depredations of his erstwhile colleagues—
especially as regards a side of bacon that is repeatedly stolen
and then retrieved by the harassed villager. Travers comes out
well enough considering the one-sidedness of the array of talents. He finally proposes a truce: that they divide his meat.
The tale ends with the observation that Travers, who raised
the pig, never got the better part of it:

> Por ce fu dit, segnor baron,
> Mal conpeignon a en larron.   [*Nar,* 148]

[This is why it's said, my lords, that a thief makes a bad
companion.]

The tale illustrates, but with imperturbable acceptance, not
only the moral it perfunctorily offers at the end, but also that
which we find at the end of *Le Vilain qui conquist paradis par
plait:* "Mielz valt engiens que ne fait force" (III, 214)—"Cleverness counts for more than strength."

In this context, the various fabliaux that celebrate champions
of stupidity can be recognized at the same time as celebrating
cleverness. Many a cuckolded husband in the fabliaux is persuaded that he should not believe his eyes, but the wife of *Le
Vilain de Bailluel* persuades him that he is dead! Massive ig-
norance about sexuality is the major vice of the various fools

in *Jouglet, La Sorisete des estopes, Le Fol vilain,* and *Le Sot chevalier.*
The hero of the last, however, does so much damage and comes
out so well that he must be counted rather as one of the symbols
of disorder—encompassed by no system of values at all—which
grin at us from more than one niche in this literature.

It is also an appreciation of instability, a familiarity with
the possibility of social disorder, that lies behind some of the
extraordinary fabliau taste for verbal comedy, for the comedy
of misunderstanding and double meaning.[13] The first half of
Le Roy d'Angleterre et le jongleur d'Ely is a dialogue of that sort
between the king and the jongleur:

> "Où est vostre vile, daunz Jogler?"
> "Sire, entour le moster."
> "Où est le moster, bel amy?"
> "Sire, en la vile de Ely."
> "Où est Ely qy siet?"
> "Sire, sur l'ewe estiet."
> "Quei est le eve apelé, par amours?"
> "L'em ne l'apele pas, eynz vint tous jours
> Volonters. . . ."
> "Tot ce savoi je bien avaunt."
> "Don qe demandez com enfant?
> A quei fere me demaundez
> Chose que vus meismes bien savez?"
>
> [II, 243–244]

["Where is your town, Mr. Jongleur?" "Around the church,
sire." "Where is the church, fair friend?" "In the town of
Ely, sire." "Where is it that Ely is?" "Next to the river."
"If you please, by what name do you call the river?" "You

don't call it; it always comes by itself. . . ." "I knew all
that before." "Then why act like a child? Why ask me
something you already know yourself?"]

The element of lèse majesté reappears in *La Male Honte,* which
turns on a bequest made by a *preudom* named Honte, who directs
that his goods be put in a bag *(male)* and given to the King.
A friend of his tries to deliver to the King "la male Honte"
(which also means "foul shame") with predictable results. But
comic safe-conduct for abuse of the establishment[14] is not the
only motive for fabliau verbal wit; other pieces turn for their
humor on nothing more specific than simple misunderstanding.
At the climax of *Les Perdris* the priest sees a preudom running
after him with a sharp knife. The preudom is shouting at the
top of his lungs:

> "Ainsi nes en porterez mie . . .
> Bien les en portez eschaufées;
> Ça les lerrez, se vous ataing."   [I, 192]

["You'll never get away with them . . . You're carrying
them nice and hot, but you'll leave them if I catch you!"]

The pursuer thinks that the priest has run off with two roast
partridges. The priest, however, is running to escape what he
takes as an attempt at castration. *Le Prestre qui ot mere a force*
turns on a misunderstanding by an old woman who, hearing
that the bishop is going to suspend *(souspendre)* her son the
priest, thinks that he is going to hang *(pendre)* him. And so
on.[15] A goodly number of fabliaux finally turn on conscious
verbal manipulation by the protagonists, including a group in
which the action turns on several double entendres.[16] Verbal
wit of these kinds is of course not unique to the fabliau, but

the values it is based on—ironic celebration of the human propensity for error, of the power of words to deceive, to protect
assault, to shift shapes, to manipulate fortune—accord well
with what we have already observed of the fabliau ethos.

Thus far we have dealt—on the theory that no literary text
is free of values—with the values illustrated, embodied, or
implied by the plots and texture of the fabliaux. It remains to
deal with what the poems say about values directly. That self-
conscious didacticism is not an essential element in the genre
is made clear by the fact that a third of the fabliaux do not
contain moralistic or sententious expressions of any kind. The
minstrel Jean de Condé is willing to accept the fact that some
people like a *truffe* better than *une bien grande auctorité* (IV, 47),
jokes and sly mockeries better than sermons (VI, 260). Watriquet de Couvin agrees (III, 137). Indeed, some dozen fabliaux
announce their purpose to be simply to provide amusement or
refreshment.[17] But as we have already remarked in chapter one,
a hundred or so fabliaux do contain moralistic advice of one
sort or another, often in the form of proverbial expressions;
more than four hundred such expressions occur in our texts.[18]
A few texts such as *Fole Larguesce, La Housse partie,* and *La
Bourse pleine de sens* are so exclusively edifying that they barely
qualify as fabliaux.[19]

As we have already observed, the overtly sententious or didactic passages in the fabliaux are often only loosely related to
their plots.[20] Many of the proverbs or wise sayings with which
fabliaux begin and end either have no necessary connection
with the ethical import of the main action or relate to the
action so generally that the structure of the tale could never
have been predicted from its overt moral. Sometimes different
manuscript versions of the same tale offer different morals.[21]

If fabliaux often carry a moral, they only infrequently embody it.

This is, however, a common enough trait in medieval literature. That the medieval criteria of relatedness between a tale and its overt moral should be looser than ours derives no doubt in part from the high medieval valuing of didacticism itself. The period regarded as a commonplace the notion that there is moral profit in every text, as St. Paul had said to the Romans (15:4): *Quaecumque enim scripta sunt, ad nostram doctrinam scripta sunt.* One can imagine many a forced or remote moralization to have been generated in this spirit. Several more specific motives have been suggested for the gratuitous moralizations in the fabliaux. Some "morals" may have been added to protect the story in certain circles from the imputation of immorality. Some no doubt derive from the well-known teaching of the rhetoric books: it is proper to begin or end a composition with a sententious expression. Others may represent play of one sort or another with the medieval taste for moralization itself.[22] Most, perhaps, were put in by authors careless of formal rhetoric, who sensed the effectiveness of proverbial expressions as a method of closure, bu were not much concerned about which proverb would best fit. But such disparity between fabliaux and their expressed morals creates no difficulty in our present investigation of fabliau ethos. In one way, indeed, it is an advantage. For its gratuitousness, its naked commonplaceness, makes this fabliau moralizing all the more reliable as an index of what its audience takes for granted. Acceptable independently of the literary context, it is part of their habitual thinking.

In this overt moralizing, specifically Christian exhortations to virtue are notably absent. Indeed, it would require a considerable effort to find in fabliau moralizing anything about love or charity or, for that matter, about orthodox virtue of any kind. The ending of *Le Chapelain* is almost unique for its pious conclusion condemning vice (for you'll always get caught) and applauding good works (VI, 253–254). A few fabliaux recommend moderation, and a few courtesy.[23] Some virtues are perhaps implicitly recommended by the opposing of their corresponding vices, as in the several instances of the criticism of greed and of clerical venality. But for each such criticism there is a passage that, cheerfully or cynically, accepts the same vices.[24] Recommendation of virtue is more often than not undercut by practical considerations. The moral of *Le Povre Clerc* is that one should give bread to a person one never expects to see again—because you can never tell what will happen if you don't. The clerk would never have revealed the wife's secret if she had granted him the lodging he requested (V, 200). *Brunain, la vache au prestre* concludes with the recommendation that one should give oneself up to providence—for you can't multiply your goods without risk (*Nar,* 97). In this case a poor cow given as alms returns home with the better cow of the priest in tow.

The stated wisdom of the fabliaux is thus overwhelmingly practical, and worse. "Don't fly before you have wings." "Beware of little eyes and proven thieves." "Repentance comes too late when all is lost—you can lose out by waiting too long— who wants everything loses everything." "Importunity softens all." "Don't behave against your nature." "A fool never gives up." "The more forbidden, the more incentive." "Who goes, feasts; who sits, dries up." "The habit doesn't make the hermit." "The bad herder feeds the wolf." "Troubles you can cook and eat are better than ones that give no pleasure." "There's many a slip twixt the cup and the lip." "Often the innocent pays the penalty." "If you have a pretty wife, don't harbor clerks." "It's not wise to put your wife out at night."[25] Such warnings against women are most common. "He's a fool who believes his wife more than himself." "Women are very smart; they know a lot about trickery." "Don't try to trick a woman; for each of your tricks she will do ten or fifteen or twenty."[26] It is entirely characteristic that most of the antifeminist conclusions are appended to tales that actually celebrate female ingenuity.

If there is a single dominant tone in the overt moralism of the fabliaux, it is that of irony, the irony of surprise, of reversal, of a justice that is fashioned by chance or by oneself. "He who seeks deceit will find it." "You intend to deceive someone who deceives you first." "She brewed what she drank." "He wiped my nose with my own sleeve."[27] This taste for irony harmonizes with the taste for wit and for wordplay in the fabliaux to suggest in the audience a developed awareness of the instability of life. Their materialism and hedonism are not naive, but are played out against the practical, proverbial wisdom that is revalidated by experience from generation to generation. This audience may be a Christian one, but within it the Christian ethos shares important space with another ethos, sub-Christian and no doubt pre-Christian, which is neither fugitive nor trivial. In this culture it is marshalled in the face of a felt reality by people who, as Faral once put it, "never had as good reasons to be never sure of what the next day would bring."[28]

CHAPTER V

Sexuality and Obscenity

LL OF THE EXTENDED DISCUSSIONS OF SEXUALITY and obscenity in the fabliaux are relatively recent, liberated, no doubt, by recent shifts in our attitudes toward both of those subjects. Bédier allowed himself only a page on "fabliaux obscènes"; Nykrog devotes to "l'obscenité des fabliaux" a whole chapter.[1] Nykrog's treatment, however, is weakened by an incomplete account of the extent of fabliau "obscenity," and by his seeing in it a simple contrast between what is acceptable and what is self-consciously and exaggeratedly smutty, with a strong line of demarcation between them:

> He [the storyteller] can then do one of two things: either he respects the frontier and keeps on the good side, yet not without signaling to the reader that he is going to brush close by; or he transgresses, most often with vividness [éclat], so that no one can help noticing that he is committing an infraction. For despite all, the boundary of decency fills him with enough respect that he is quite incapable of going and coming across it without attracting any attention at all. Like a naughty child, he insists that you see that he has been disobedient.
>
> That is the character of obscenity in the fabliau: it wishes to shock by openly offending decency. It is direct and naive pornography. [Nyk, 216]

Nykrog does not venture any historical analysis. Though he naturally (and wisely) refuses to assign the two sides of the frontier to different social or intellectual groups (which would

weaken his thesis that the fabliau is a courtly genre), he concludes that in the Middle Ages, as in later ages, some courtly
people were amused by coarseness and others not.

Jürgen Beyer's chapter "Formen schwankhafter Tabudurch-
brechung im Fabliau," in his rather difficult *Schwank und Moral*
(pp. 94–106), is mainly concerned with the mechanics of obscene humor in the fabliaux, the Freudian "technique of ov-
ercoming repulsion" (p. 98). His analysis, like Nykrog's, assumes the existence of a basically unchanged Western-Christian
sense of the obscene. In the fabliaux, he says, this sense is
either confronted aggressively and directly for the purpose of
comic shock (pp. 100–104), or played with by means of a
variety of euphemistic metaphors (pp. 104–111). Beyer departs
from Nykrog, to my mind correctly, when he recognizes that
the shock effect of so-called obscene words in the fabliaux is
hard to measure (p. 103), and that many technically "euphemistic" words are not used as euphemisms, but rather for the
comedy of the difference between what is being said and what
is actually meant.[2]

Like Beyer's treatment, that of Wolf-Dieter Stempel, published almost at the same time, puts great emphasis on medieval
obscenity as an artistic problem, and spends a good deal of
energy on finding aesthetic justification for it in the fabliaux.
The assumption here again that there is a perennially clear line
of demarcation between genteel and obscene, which allows for
an almost automatic conclusion that unvarnished terms in the
fabliaux always create a shock, get a laugh, and thereby justify
themselves aesthetically as a direct source of humor. Other
presumed sanctions for the use of obscenity are satire, and burlesque of courtliness. One result of this theory is an exaggeration
of the satiric and burlesque elements in the fabliaux.[3]

Two essays in the Cooke-Honeycutt collection are also relevant to the present subject. Thomas D. Cooke's "Pornography, the Comic Spirit, and the Fabliaux" (*CH*, 137–162) is to date the most extensive study of the fabliaux as pornography. Based on a comparison of the fabliaux with traits derived by Steven Marcus principally from Victorian pornography, Cooke's finding is that "some in part and some almost in their entirety, exhibit definite pornographic elements" (p. 146). While this is true in terms of certain traits taken individually—male orientation; the attention to sex organs, especially the penis; sexual aggressiveness; the absence of "strong personal relationship"; the use of taboo words; and so on—the fabliaux rarely if ever support a tone and feeling similar to that of Victorian pornography, and Cooke comes to this conclusion by paying particular attention to fabliau humor.

Roy J. Pearcy's "Modes of Signification and the Humor of Obscene Diction in the Fabliaux" (*CH*, 163–196) is an analysis of obscenity and euphemism largely in epistemological terms, correlating euphemisms with the illusory and obscenities with the real. He concludes that obscene diction in the fabliaux signifies espousal of a particular attitude of mind, "materialistic, analytical, existential," in conflict with another one, "speculative, synoptic, idealistic"; in short, that this diction is evidence that the fabliau "establishes its own ethos" (pp. 194–195).

Most recently, in his book on the fabliaux, Philippe Ménard offers a chapter on "grivoiserie et grossièreté." It provides an accurate and sensible overview of the subject, giving due attention to the great variety of tones with which "vulgar" subjects and language are treated in the genre. But he nevertheless leans throughout, as do Nykrog and Beyer, on the notion of

a fixed hierarchy of sensibilities, preestablished for the Middle
Ages. "Indecent" references, then, are seen against a permanent
backdrop of good taste, which they almost always self-consciously offend:

> The authors of fabliaux are no more ignorant of good
> manners than are the courtly romancers. If they violate
> the proprieties openly, it is always with some ulterior
> motive. . . . One of the most important motivations is
> perhaps the desire to make the audience laugh by pro-
> nouncing coarse words, improper remarks. . . . One can
> guess that in more than one author of fabliaux there is
> the desire to shock [*faire scandale*] in the manner of an
> outrageously painted clown, the intention to make people
> laugh by launching challenges to modesty and defiance
> to polite usage.[4]

Of the views mentioned above, Pearcy's seems to be the
most congenial to those to be presented here. But the present
account differs from all of them in emphasizing the full extent
and variety of usage in the fabliaux, and it deals with the
problem of fabliau obscenity in terms more historical.

I shall be assuming that sexual humor largely exploits, and
is a way of coping with, the frustrations that inhibit the free
play of sexuality in a given culture—including both the manifold difficulties of sexuality itself and the specific taboos placed
on sexual expression by the culture. Obscenity, then, is relative
to the culture—to the time and place.[5] The use of so-called
"obscene" terms, I assume, is primarily a way of evoking sexuality with directness; it can be used to manipulate or violate
taboos against such direct evocation—but only in the measure
that the culture does in fact exercise such taboos.

In this light the sexual humor of the fabliaux has some special historical interest. It suggests that the fabliau audience did not take very seriously the medieval Christian-ascetic injunctions against sexual pleasure, for it rarely seems to be playing with taboos that come principally from that direction. Its basic sexual humor seems to come, rather, from an older and perhaps deeper source—the inherent frustrations of sexuality itself: the perennial problems (and thus the comedy) of sexual opportunity, privacy, potency, compatibility, rivalry—and any other obstacles in the way of sexual satisfaction. Fabliau humor easily turns to the mild pleasure of using "obscene" terms, along with a whole array of synonyms, to evoke sexuality with directness. So used, the terms do not often seem to be carrying a heavy charge of feeling, nor, by the same token, a heavy burden of taboo. The direct contemplation of sexuality clearly transgresses *some* cultural injunctions, but in this culture they are easily transgressed, especially in the protective environment of a jointly shared funny story. Contrary to Nykrog's thesis, then, in many fabliaux the words that can be called obscene do not seem to be designed to shock the audience; the effect or the humor of the tale is often elsewhere.

On the other hand, there is another group of fabliaux which seem to be responding to verbal taboos that are felt more strongly than in the first group: they avoid certain words in referring to sexual activity, and sometimes make negative comment upon them. In speculating on the source of these stronger taboos, we cannot rest fully content with the truism that some folks have a lower tolerance for smut than others. For there is another palpable source of verbal taboo in the rapid spread, in the thirteenth century, of the courtly ethic. In showing sharply divergent responses to so-called obscene terms the fabliaux seem to be recording the impact of relatively new taboos, the mixed reception of these taboos in the fabliau period, and indeed, some opposition to them.

By and large the fabliaux are uninhibited and direct regarding sex. In referring to intercourse, the most commonly used verb is *foutre,* "fuck." It is used once or more in at least twenty-five of the fabliaux.[6] In a dozen of these the author uses the term in his own voice, as part of the narrative; in twenty it is used by characters in the dialogue. If this number in any way still suggests restraint, it is only because of the co-presence of a rich array of variations. Some of these are undoubted euphemisms—and we shall presently take up that problem in detail—but the gamut extends continuously from self-conscious delicacy to naked specification. It testifies to an inveterate interest in the subject and to a pleasure in the analogies, and thus in the linguistic variations, that sexual activity suggests.

Male domination and aggression take an expected place in the metaphors for copulation; it is to give justice, to dub, to take the maidenhood, to give the King's blows, to prick, and to beat or whip in a variety of terms: on the rump, with the thong *(corgie)* of the cistern, or with the hammers or mallets to which testicles are inveterately compared. Expressions of attack and assault carry us well into the military domain. Ample experience in the field, in one case, has "torn her banner to shreds." Figures of equitation are inevitable; one may "ride indoors" *(en loge)* or "mount without reins or saddle." Too much sex in *La Veuve* is to "squeeze the mare."[7]

In the area of animal imagery, intercourse is described at some length as a ferret's hunting for a rabbit in its lair, a squirrel's searching for nuts, as feeding or watering a horse,

and as feeding a piglet. A further set of analogies is based on
eating: to have the final course, to have some bacon or a roast,
to nurse, to be skewered or turned on the spit. There are various
agricultural terms: to seed a garden, to grind (grain), to plow
a field, to reap, to crush grapes, to exercise pasture rights, to
draw in the shafts; and terms taken from a miscellany of other
familiar activities: to open the door, beat the drum, crack nuts,
give the cure, polish the ring, measure the length, broach the
cask, forge, get plugged, get greased, and to sharpen up with
a stone.[8]

Verging toward direct specification are some terms of syn-
ecdochic character: to bend or curve or turn someone over, to
move the loins or the behind; and a number of passages abandon
figurative speech completely.[9] Finally, there is a small array
of jargon having a clear general import, while the precise shades
of meaning remain in doubt: *prendre à la torcoise* and *enteser* (V,
209); *faire le ravescot* (I, 263); *bravoillier* and *bocillier* (*Ros,* 101;
129n.); *riber* (VI, 269); *ramener le con de Rome* (VI, 148); and
various contributions of Gautier le Leu: *mateculer, cotener, her-
diier, creponer.*[10]

We shall not need to classify the foregoing substitutes for
foutre to see immediately that they represent a great range of
variations in delicacy and explicitness. Some of them are manifestly more explicit even than *foutre,* and few could be called
purely euphemistic. There are, however, as Nykrog and others
have observed, a number of expressions for intercourse in the
fabliaux that are more or less clearly polite: to play the game
of love, take one's pleasure or delight, do one's will or that of
one's partner, to sleep or lie with or in the arms of, and so
forth; and in a number of instances the author announces that
he is going to decline any comment at all.[11] To these instances

we might add some expressions that are less polite but at least rather neutral: to serve someone, to do it, to do one's business *(besogne,* or *mestier),* to be at the work *(oevre),* to be a man, to do good or foolishness, to be touched, to be restored or eased or satisfied *(aasiez).* In *Auberee* the lovers "do what they were brought together for." Elsewhere it is the twin flesh, the thing that a woman loves above all else, and having one's due *(rente).* [12]

As we might expect in a literature dominated by men, male sexuality is given somewhat more prominence than female; references to the penis are common. The ordinary word, used in at least thirty-five fabliaux, is *vit,* usually translated into Modern English as "prick" or "cock." Though *vit* is obviously taboo in some contexts, it is clearly less taboo in Old French than the Modern English terms are at present, so that translation tends to make *vit* sound somewhat more shocking than it was. It is unselfconsciously used by female characters in at least six fabliaux. [13] In *L'Esquiriel* (V, 102–103) two females discuss the taboo. As with *foutre,* the simple term is generously supplemented with synonyms covering a whole range of analogy and euphemism. It must be said that (with the possible exception of Gautier le Leu) the fabliau authors do not expend much imagination in this area. The most notable property of *vit,* of course, is its size. Conventionally it is big and well-made *(bien carré);* [14] in this it is compared to a lance, a champion's baton, a stake, a spit, a ram, a coulter, and that of a packhorse. [15]

The most common euphemisms are "thing," "member," or "tool." [16] The additional expressions that approach analogy are for the most part commonplace: pipe, staff, lance, root, club, horn, horse. The motifs involving small animals have been mentioned above. [17] Otherwise, it is variously a relic, a sharp-

ening-stone, a parsnip, various kinds of innards or sausages,
a fish, and a waterbird. Twice in *Le Moigne* it is personified:
"this lecher," "his fun-loving young noble." Twice in versions
of *Les Trois Dames qui troverent un vit* it is identified by the
Abbess as "the bar of our gate."[18] A disproportionate share of
what variety we find among these terms belongs to Gautier le
Leu and to fabliaux that make an issue of the subject: *L'Esquiriel*
and *Le Pescheor de Pont seur Saine.*[19]

As we know from Jean de Meun's *Roman de la rose* (discussed
below), the common Old French word for testicles, *coilles* or
coillons (Modern English "balls"), was taboo in certain circles
by the end of the thirteenth century (see below, pp. 146–150).
In the fabliaux it is used as freely as is *vit,* although less frequently, along with an even more homely range of synonyms.
Coilles are neutrally referred to as pendants, couplings, gear,
or as a "thing" *(afère).* They are sometimes described as large,
swollen, and hairy, and are compared to a variety of sacks and
purses. Other analogical references are to bellows, seeds, hammers or mallets, bells, balls of yarn, eggs, pork-rind, kidneys,
and twins. In two stories the twins are two "grooms" *(mareschal)*
who guard the "horses."[20] Less often mentioned, but apparently
as freely, are other details of male sexuality. There are seven
or eight ways used to describe erection, and in at least five
fabliaux the ejaculation of semen is mentioned with some con-
creteness.[21]

The female genitals are referred to with equal freedom. The
common term, *con,* is less taboo than *vit* in some contexts,
especially for women, and it carries a good deal less sexuality
than the associated Modern English "cunt."[22] The word itself
appears in at least twenty-six fabliaux; its synonyms and euphemisms are for the most part quite banal: tool, hole, belly,

entrance, gate, beaten path, ring, valley, wound, fountain. Some expressions turn on conventional medieval notions of female appetite: glutton, pig, Goliath, "the place where the sickness is harbored in women."²³ The animal motif includes "Connebert," a name derived from the commonplace pun on *con/connin* (rabbit), and "Morel," a name for a black horse. Two fabliaux offer catalogues of *cons* of all kinds.²⁴

So many fabliaux turn on verbal play of one sort or another that sexual puns would seem inevitable. Nykrog notes two puns on *vit* and its homophones (*Nyk*, 212). The first occurs in a fabliau about a man who has a marvelous ring—

> Tant com il avoit en son doit,
> Adès son membre li croissoit.   [III, 51]

[As soon as he had it on his finger, his member would get big.]

The euphemism *membre* is used consistently in the story; but when the man comes to a fountain and dismounts,

> Si lava ses meins et son *vis*.   [III, 51]

[He washed his hands and his face.]

In the second case, a young man uses the euphemism "squirrel" to explain a certain commotion under his clothes. In response to his companion's further interest, he explains:

> "Douce amie, se Dieus me saut,
> Il se leva or de son cruet . . .
> En non Dé, quar il est toz *vis*."   [V, 105]

["Sweetheart, as God save me, it is coming up out of its hole . . . in God's name, for it is very much alive."]

To this small store of puns anyone with the requisite imagination can contribute. Surely there is a pun in a maxim uttered by two whorehouse pimps *(houliers)* in *Boivin de Provins:*

"Lessons les mors, prenons les *vis.*"   [V, 59]

["Give up the dead; take hold of the living."]

The elegant courtliness of *Guillaume au faucon* is nearly destroyed near the end by a pun on *faucon* (falcon/false cunt); the author pointedly insists on it as "two words in one" *(deus moz a un).*[25] The author of one version of *Les Quatre Sohais Saint Martin* is so pleased with the pun on *connue (known/"cunt-ed")* that within a few dozen verses he elaborately repeats it.[26] Gautier le Leu is fond of punning on words that have the prefix *con-: conmandet, consentit, conbatés, conquis.*[27] A clear pun on *foutre* occurs in a satiric treatment of the French spoken by an Englishman. "Are you Auvergnat or Netherlandish?" he is asked. "No, no," he replies, "mi *fout* Anglois" ("I'm English," II, 180). There is probably no end to the number of additional places in the fabliaux where puns may be suspected.[28]

I have led the reader through this account in some detail in order to show that we cannot accept Nykrog's estimate of fabliau sexual usage: "When a teller of fabliaux has an occasion to be coarse *(grossier)* he abstains in at least one case in two. In a number of cases which is certainly not less than half, he passes rapidly over the delicate situation, using a euphemism compatible with courtly language" *(Nyk, 213).* It is true that of the fifty or sixty fabliaux in which explicit reference to intercourse might be made, in some thirty the word *foutre* is not used. However, synonyms are not necessarily euphemisms; we have seen that many of the available substitutes are neither

courtly nor euphemistic. Nor do euphemisms invariably indicate an exercise of taste. Some fabliaux use euphemistic
expressions in some places and more direct ones in others. The
author of *Aloul* uses *afère* (I, 279) and *couple* (I, 267) apparently
for the rhyme; elsewhere he uses *coilles*. The husband in *Le
Fevre de Creil* uses *foutre* (I, 234) in ordinary conversation and
the euphemism *marteler* in an attempt at wit (I, 236). The
author of *Celui qui bota la pierre* gives the use of *foutre* to his
characters, but reserves for himself some elaborate metaphors
(VI, 148–150) that call even more attention to themselves than
simple directness would have. Pearcy has shown brilliantly how
in some fabliaux the euphemism is artistically correlated with
the hypocritical or with illusion (*CH*, 177–188). The author
of *Gombert et les deus clers,* for instance, uses euphemisms—five
or six of them—until the moment of truth, when one clerk
inadvertently reveals to the miller what has happened to his
daughter; then he uses "an agglomeration of obscenities," including *foutre*. Again, in *Le Pescheor do Pont seur Saine,* the wife
uses euphemisms—*afère, riens, ostil*—while trying to maintain
the fiction that her marital happiness does not depend on sex.
At the end, however, when she verifies that her husband has
recovered his supposedly lost penis, her "spontaneous outburst
of honesty" is signaled by the dropping of euphemism:

> "Mesire a son vit recouvré,
> Nostre Sires i a ouvré."   [III, 74]

["Master's got his prick back—it's the work of Our Lord!"]

Taking into account the verbal taste of the tellers rather
than the number of isolated instances of usage, we can say that
only about a quarter of fabliaux tellers presented with the opportunity to be "coarse" clearly avoid coarseness.[29]

While fabliau sexual terminology, as we have seen, is not
simple, nor either heavily inhibited or heavily self-conscious,
it does not compare in range of reference to what we could
find in Roman satire and epigram or in Attic comedy.[30] Medieval French sexuality was by no means as unfettered as that
of classical antiquity. In the fabliaux we are usually quite far
from the highly elaborated sensuality (or the pornography) of
other cultures. Scenes of lovemaking, however explicit, involve
remarkably little prolonged description. Of course there is appreciation, in passing, of sexual attractiveness. In their idea
of beauty the fabliaux are mostly high medieval, and they thus
share some traits with romance. But they generally eschew the
detailed inventory and any but the most conventional similes.
When they are described at all, beautiful females in the fabliaux
are usually white-skinned and have adolescent figures,[31] though
here and there a certain admiration for plumpness creeps in,
as in the bedtime imagination of a lovelorn monk who has
ridden past some pretty girls that morning:

> "Se je tenoie le plus crasse
> Et la plus mole entre mes bras. . . ."
>
> [*Rom* 44: 561][32]

["If I might hold the plumpest and softest in my
arms. . . ."]

The fabliaux share with romance the idea that lovemaking is
best in the nude; often, bathing together comes first. There
is easy reference to sexual initiative and sexual foreplay. Extreme
sexual ineptitude is made fun of, and extremes of pleasure are
occasionally mentioned.[33] But these topics are rarely dwelt
upon. There is no elaboration, no lingering over the details
for their own sake. *Le Moigne* does venture (part of a monk's

dream) an inventory of vaginas for sale in a market. The first two are superlatively ugly, but the third is ideal:

> L'entree ert douce comme miex,
> Et s'estoit primes de ce point
> Que li paus volages li point,
> S'ot gros bauchet et sist sor boche.
>
>   [*Rom* 44: 562]

[The entrance was as sweet as honey, and it was so fresh (?) that its down was just growing out, and it had a large barrier (? = hymen?) and was placed on a mound.]

Other references to the more intimate complexities of female anatomy are rare. There is one passing mention (apparently axiomatic) of the difficulty of feminine hygiene.[34] The shape of the vagina prompts some crude jokes on the theme of its creation by means of a spade or axe *(Du Con qui fu fait a la besche);* and its position near the anus provides evidently comic material on the fool's initiation in *Le Sot chevalier.* A variation is the conceit, in *Berengier au lonc cul,* of a woman disguised as a knight who is remarkably "long-assed."[35]

There is of course an abundance of comic sexual fantasy in the fabliaux, and a certain amount of sexual magic. The titles of fabliaux variously herald a woman who serves a hundred knights, a knight who can make vaginas talk, and a ring that causes erections.[36] Sexual energy is estimated generously: three to five climaxes per encounter is common, and in *Le Prestre et Alison* it is nine times a night.[37] As with endurance, so with physique. Phallic championship—a matter of unimaginable size—belongs to the apprentice in *Le Fevre de Creil:*

Devers le retenant avoit
Plain poing de gros et .II. de lonc. . . .
Tozjors en aguisant se tient
Por retrère delivrement,
Et fu rebraciez ensement
Come moines qui jete aus poires . . .
Rouges come oingnon de Corbueil;
Et si avoit si ouvert l'ueil
Por rendre grant plenté de sève,
Que l'en li péust une fève
Lombarde très parmi lancier
Que jà n'en lessast son pissier . . .
Ne que une oue à gorgueter
S'ele éust mengié un grain d'orge. [I, 231-232]

[Around the base it was a full fist thick, and two hands long. It kept itself always perked up to be drawn readily, and it got uncovered just like a monk reaching for pears. It was red as a Corbueil onion, and it had an eye so open to give plenty of juice that if you threw a Lombard bean right into it you wouldn't keep it from pissing any more than a goose would be kept from swallowing if she had eaten a grain of barley.]

The only other comparable description is that of the prize merchandise in the "obscene market" of *Le Sohait desvé (Nar,* 103). But wonders of this sort are almost never less than comic in their conscious exaggeration, and when they are not used simply to exploit the inherent funniness of sex, they are celebrating other motives—such as the appreciation of sexual pleasure, the respect for (or anxiety over) potency, the desirability of a competent mate—that we can safely call normal.

Indeed, sexual activity in the fabliau is normal to the point of narrowness. Intercourse only rarely strays beyond the missionary position. Some expressions suggest variety without much specification:

> Cilz s'aparoille et monte sus
> Qu'amont, qu'aval, que sus que jus;[38]
> Ainsis fist à pou de sejour
> Dès le couchier jusques au jour.   [I, 324]

[He got ready and climbed on—up, down, high and low; he worked like that without much rest from bedtime till dawn.]

One of the students in *Gombert et les deus clers* brags of having taken the miller's daughter "from behind and from beside" (*derriere et encoste*, [*Nar*, 92]). Another ingenious clerk works again and again *"par darriere"* to affix a tail on a silly girl who wants to fly in the air (IV, 209–210). Something of the same posture must be imputed to the young couple in *La Gageure*. The agreement is that she will grant him her love if he first kisses her behind, but in the course of the operation his objective changes.[39] There are a number of expressions, so rare as to elude accurate modern comprehension, that might enlarge the picture;[40] and a number of scenes leave one in doubt as to precisely what is going on.[41] The female on top occurs so seldom as to occupy the denouement of *La Damoiselle qui sonjoit:*

> "Or fetes tost, si alez jus,
> Je revoeil ore aler desus;
> Ce n'est pas, ce m'est avis, honte
> Quant homme faut, se fame monte." [V, 210]

["Now hurry up and get down; I want to get on top now.
I don't think there's anything wrong if the woman climbs
on when the man falls off."]

All in all, the fabliaux do not refer to the range of sexual
positions recited, for example, even in *Richeut*.[42]

If sexuality does not become much of a technique in the
fabliaux, it does not become much of a mystique either. What
commentary we get on the subject is usually brief and com-
mendatory. In *La Dame qui se venja du chevalier,* lovemaking
is called "praiseworthy because it makes you completely forget
poverty, boredom, and pain" (VI, 24). In *Boivin de Provins* the
prostitute Mabile tells her pretended widowed uncle that it is
as foolish to go too long without a woman as to go too long
without food (V, 60). Perhaps more disinterested is the warning
at the beginning of *Le Pescheor de Pont seur Saine* that a husband
who doesn't make love with his young wife as well as he can
will lose her love and have no happiness:

> Quar jone fame bien peüe
> Sovent voudroit estre foutue.   [III, 69]

[For a well brought up young woman would like to be laid
often.]

The emphasis on female appetite in this passage is typical.
It is one of the persistent topics in the fabliaux, and there are
doubtless those who see behind the lustful fabliau woman only
some red-eyed clerics sublimating, in their fierce antifeminism,
a deep fear of castration and of female domination. While it
is likely that some forms of medieval antifeminism *are* based
on fear of female sexuality (medieval thought attributed superior

sexual appetite to the female)—the so-called "antifeminism" in the fabliaux is so various in its quality and tone as more often to support the claim of admiration for women than fear and hatred.[43] It is the same for female sexual initiative as for the many examples of female cleverness and enterprise of other sorts.

There are admittedly some baldly crude and unsympathetic treatments of female appetite, though even here we are more likely to be repelled by the quality of the narrative tone and authorial comment than by the actions of the female characters themselves.[44] The treatment of the wife in *Le Fevre de Creil* is largely unsympathetic, though both her hypocrisy and her lustfulness are mitigated by the fact that temptation is deliberately put in her way by her husband. The emphasis and texture of the story are such, indeed, as to suggest that the satire on lascivious women serves another theme: celebration of the phallus. The same can be said of *Le Pescheor de Pont seur Saine,* which, in the course of showing that the wife will desert the husband if he loses his penis, actually celebrates the husband's sexuality. Male prowess is likewise a strong motif in the otherwise antifeminist *Cele qui se fist foutre sur la fosse de son mari* and *La Pucele qui voloit voler. Le Vallet aus douze fames,* under the appearance of antifeminism, actually celebrates monogamy, as the young wife undertakes to disabuse her husband of the notion that he can handle twelve women by proving that he can hardly handle one. The extreme of fabliau ambivalence on this score is in *La Dame qui aveine demandoit;* its crude, scatological ending is preceded by some of the most engaging passages on mutual sexual satisfaction and regard in the entire corpus (I, 318–320).

Elsewhere female appetite is given dramatic motivation, or

made acceptable as part of the workings of nature. Some fabliau women respond to desire uninhibitedly because of their innocence. Others give in to force, or to logic, or, in proper courtly fashion, to suitably prolonged importunity. Yet others react naturally against being deprived of their rights by old and incompetent mates, or by young and stupid ones, or by malicious ones. A line or two in *Un Chivalier et sa dame et un clerk* (II, 232) presents female initiative as a charming generosity; the tale as a whole is almost profeminist in tone.

The disparity between female needs and desires on the one hand, and female speech on the other, is several times the theme of fabliau scenes, but female hypocrisy is not always the issue. Jean Bodel's *Le Sohait desvé* allows a good measure of sympathy to the sexually frustrated wife. She receives her husband, returned from an absence of some months, with a warm embrace, a comfortable chair, and an excellent meal by the fire. But once abed, he falls asleep, and she, left with her desire, dares not wake him for fear of being thought lascivious (*Nar*, 102). Instead, she falls asleep, has an erotic dream, and wakes him accidentally. After suitable explanations, marital concord is restored. Another suggestion of fabliau sympathy with the sexual plight of women in a male-dominated society is found in *Le Chevalier qui fist sa fame confesse,* wherein a wife confesses:

> "A paine porroit-l'en choisir
> Fame qui se puisse tenir
> A son seignor tant seulement,
> Jà tant ne l'aura bel ne gent;
> Quar la nature tele en ont,
> Qu'els requierent, ce sachiez-vous,

> Et li mari si sont vilain
> Et de grant felonie plain,
> Si ne nous oson descouvrir
> Vers aus, ne noz besoins gehir;
> Quar por putains il nous tendroient,
> Se noz besoins par nous savoient;
> Si ne puet estre en nule guise
> Que n'aions d'autrui le servise."   [I, 183]

["You can hardly find a woman who could depend entirely on her husband, no matter how fine and handsome a one she has. For women have a nature that makes them have certain desires, if you know what I mean; and husbands are so crude and full of hostility that we don't dare be open with them or tell them our needs. Why, if they heard us ask for what we needed they'd think of us as whores. So it's impossible for us to get along without help from outside."]

This speech is made, ironically, to the speaker's husband, who is disguised as a monk-confessor; but it is meant as a deathbed confession, and it has a certain ring of conviction to it.[45] By and large in the fabliaux, for women as for men, sex is naturally desirable because pleasurable. It is something to get and enjoy, like food, wine, or money. The fabliau audience manifestly has among its accepted values a lot of room for a relatively unselfconscious, axiomatic, direct pleasure in sex. It is another aspect of the hedonistic materialism that we have been tracing as the dominant ethos in this literature.

The fabliaux do not show an extraordinary or morbid interest in any aspects of sexual experience other than very conventional heterosexual lovemaking. Autoeroticism is not taken up,[46] nor is oral intercourse. Mention of sodomy is rare. The one reference to intercourse with an animal—a she-ass—is in a dream: *"Si sonjoit . . . qu'i voloit une asnesse foutre"* (V, 139). Barely half a dozen fabliaux mention male homosexuality, and then mainly as an insult or as a comic result of misunderstanding.[47] The motif of the priest hiding naked in the medieval darkness while the cuckold and his servants feel for him with their hands— in the sheepfold, or in the attic among the hanging *charcuterie*— produces some homosexual contact, but there is more emphasis on the comically mistaken resemblance to sheep or to char- cuterie than to homosexuality.[48] In *Le Prestre et le chevalier,* where intercourse between males is for once proposed, it is proposed as a comically outrageous threat rather than as an invitation, and it never takes place (II, 81ff.). *Le Prestre comporté* brushes by, but does not really touch, necrophilia: the wife does not realize at once that the lover-priest she is hugging has just been strangled by her husband (IV, 7).

If sexual reference verges at all toward extremes, it is in the area of sadism. Three fabliaux contain scenes of castration, of a priest in each case. In *Le Prestre et le leu,* a peasant digs a ditch to catch his wife's lover. Into it falls a prowling wolf, then the priest-lover, then the servant-girl sent by the wife to look for him. The peasant kills the wolf, castrates the priest, and chases the girl away (VI, 51–52). The piece is only twenty- eight verses long; there are no further details. More room is given for sadistic emphasis in *Le Prestre crucefié.* The cuckold- husband is a master carver who comes back home early from market. On his approach the wife persuades her lover to hide naked in the workshop as if he were one of the crucifixes. But the preudom senses at once what has happened, and indulges in the luxury of a leisurely meal before he begins sharpening his knife. He commands his wife to carry a candle before him into the shop, and instantly identifies the immobile impostor. Remarking that he has to correct this botched piece of carving, he cuts off the priest's genitals. The priest flees; before the story ends he is knocked down into a slough and held for fifteen pounds ransom (I, 194–197).

Gautier le Leu, as we might expect of the fableor with the oddest mind, takes this motif to even farther extremes in *Connebert*. Here the cuckold is a blacksmith who not only witnesses the offense but overhears the ensuing conversation:

> "Amie doce,
> Don estes vos trestote voie?"
> Ele respont: "Se Dex me voie,
> Vostre est mes cuers, vostre est mes cors
> Et par dedanz et par defors,
> Mais li cus si est mon mari."   [*Liv*, 228]

["Sweet love, to whom do you completely belong?" She replied: "As God may see me, my heart is yours, and my body, inside and out; but my ass is my husband's."]

The lover then replies with a conceit on the action of intercourse that Gautier is fond of:

> ". . . li cus soit siens. . . .,
> Mais je lo li batrai sovant;
> Ce li met je bien en covant."   [*Liv*, 228]

["Let your ass be his; I guarantee you I'll beat on it for him often."]

The couple are seized by the smith and his servant. The smith refuses two hundred pounds ransom, preferring, he says with simple sarcasm:

"Mais vo coille qui maintes foiz
Me bat mon cul sor mon defoiz."   [*Liv,* 229]

["Just your balls, that spite me so much by beating on my
ass."]

Don li va la coille enhaper,
Que il avoit au cul pandue.
Sor l'estoc li a estandue,
Si a feru cinq clos parmi,
Les quatre entor et l'un parmi.   [*Liv,* 229]

[Then he grabbed the balls (the priest) had hanging by his
ass, laid them on the anvil-block, and drove five nails
through, four around them and one in between.]

The smith then lays a razor on the block and sets fire to the
bundles of fuel around the forge. Faced with death by burning,
the victim castrates himself and flees. What he leaves behind—
"balls as big as two kidneys; the skin so big and ruddy you
could make a purse out of it" (*Liv,* 230–231)—is found well
roasted in the coals and is eaten by dogs.

Connebert is perhaps the most brutal of the fabliaux. Its violence is approached only by that of the antifeminist *La Dame
escoillee,* which culminates in the pretended extraction of testicles from the wounded buttocks of a contrary mother-in-law.
Sadism is present, finally, in the spurred beating of the women
in *Les Tresces (Reid,* 27), and in *Constant du Hamel,* where the
hero, at his wife's suggestion, rapes the wives of his three ene-
mies as the latter watch helplessly through a hole in a barrel.

This cumulative recitation may make the fabliaux sound
worse than they are. We are dealing here with only five out
of some hundred and fifty texts. In none is there any hint of

reciprocating masochism. Furthermore, the sexual sadism in each of the elaborated texts is made indirect, oblique to an extent, by other and more powerful motives that it seems to be serving. In *Connebert* it is hatred (and envy?) of the clergy. The issue of *La Dame escoillee*—the most fiercely sexist of the fabliaux—is domination: "Damn the woman who defies a man" (Dahet feme qui despit home!" [VI, 116]). And *Constant du Hamel* is suffused with social antagonism toward the peasant's oppressors. What sexual cruelty there is in the fabliaux, then, is not always very sexual.

Sexual themes are occasionally associated with excretory jokes. Urination, referred to quite naturally in the fabliaux,[49] is only rarely the subject of humor. In *Les Trois Meschines* it is connected with the reliable comedy of flatulence. The plot is a mad one concerning three girls who buy some powder that has to be wetted with urine before they can use it for makeup. Brunatin agrees to hold the pot of powder while Agace wets it. But Agace has some difficulty:

> N'i pissast el sanz esforcier,
> Mès ele i a mise sa force . . .
> Et .I. trés grant pet li eschape, . . .
> Pet fist du cul et poudre vole.   [III, 78]

[She couldn't piss without making an effort; so she pushed hard and a great big fart escaped, . . . Out of her ass came the fart and away flew the powder.]

The tale ends with a debate over who should pay for the powder and a demand for a judgment by the audience. The brief *Gauteron et Marion* is based on farting during intercourse:

> "N'oïtes vos le pucelage
> Qui s'enfoï quant vos boutastes?"   [III, 49]

["Didn't you hear (explains Marion) my virginity flying out
when you shoved in?"][50]

Other instances of the theme, some not even marginally comic,
are designed to support insults of one sort or another,[51] or
verge toward the fully scatological.

Scatology, like sadism not one of the areas of fabliau humor
most amusing to us, must nevertheless be recognized as an
accepted theme. A number of sexual encounters have a scatological climax on the ground that when the male's *grain* (that
is, semen) for feeding the "animal" is all used up, all he can
produce is *bran*.[52] *Jouglet* turns on the uncontrollable diarrhea
of a fool-figure (IV, 112–127). In *Charlot le Juif,* a minstrel
makes a gift of a rabbit-skin full of excrement as a revenge
(III, 226). The wife in *La Crote* tricks her husband into tasting
a turd (III, 46–48). *La Couille noir* concerns a peasant and his
over-proud wife. When she accidentally discovers (after five
years of marriage) that his genitals are not white but black,
she hales him before the Bishop of Paris and demands a judgment against him. The husband replies to the Bishop:

> "A vous, sire, me clain
> De ma fame, qui tot mon fain
> A torchier son cul et son con
> Et la roie de son poistron,
> M'a gasté à faire torchons."   [VI, 93]

["I'm making a complaint to you, sire, against my wife,
who has ruined all my hay by making wipes to wipe her
ass and her cunt and the parting of her rump."]

The wife falls into the trap:

> "Vos i mentés par les grenons,"
> Fait ele, "dans vilains despers:
> Il a cinc ans que ne fu ters
> Mes cus de fain ne d'autre rien."
> "Non," fait il, "jel savoie bien:
> Por c'est ma coille si noircie."   [VI, 93–94]

["You're lying in your whiskers, you crude peasant: in five years my ass hasn't been wiped with hay or with anything else." "No," he said, "I knew it; that's why my balls are so black."]

After we take note additionally of the use of a couple of popular or proverbial expressions (I, 116; V, 62–63), we have accounted for virtually all the instances of scatology in the fabliau. The theme, though accepted, is a minor one.

Since all medieval attitudes towards sexuality necessarily exist in a context of Christian puritanism, it is surprising how little implicit response there seems to be in the fabliaux to the alleged sinfulness of sexual concupiscence, either through symptoms of guilt or in calculated postures of defiance of Christian teaching. Medieval church doctrine, we remember, held that the only licit intercourse was between spouses, and that its only justification was the good of offspring. Intercourse for any other purpose, and any sexual pleasure, even between spouses, was considered sin. It was only late in the period we are studying, late in the thirteenth century, that Thomas Aquinas was willing to concede that the sexual pleasure that proceeds from lawful intercourse might be good; but it remained a sin to seek such pleasure. As John Noonan points out, St. Thomas might have

raised the question "whether pleasure itself was not sometimes
a need. . .," for the sake of health. But the Church failed to
sanction sexual pleasure even as an intermediate value.[53]

In the fabliaux sex for procreation is rarely taken up; pregnancy occurs rarely, mainly by mistake, or is used (or pretended)
as an alibi.[54] The orthodox religious taboo on sexual pleasure
has very little force. Of course some humor comes from the
manipulation of taboos that have overtly Christian backing,
particularly the perennial sexual activity of priests, nuns,
monks, and friars. Occasionally the superior sinfulness of sexuality among the clergy is rubbed in by reference to religious
office. Alison the whore is told that the priest with whom she
is about to be bedded will teach her the *Credo in Deum* (II,
18). Another priest, after intercourse, kneels to his mistress
"as if before an altar" (VI, 149). A monk, bargaining for a
beautiful *con* in the market, offers a reduced price along with
his prayers and psalms (*Rom* 44: 563). A bishop is tricked into
blessing the *con* of his mistress, and a priest hidden behind
the curtain responds with "amen" (III, 185). A prioress recognizes her abbess's lover as their abbot and visitor:

> "Par le langhe dont Dieus parla,
> Compaingnes, c'est nos viseteres;
> Chi poons bien prendre materes
> Orendroit à nos souverains.
> Que feus d'infier arde les rains
> Qui au riber espargneront;
> Et tout cil qui em parleront
> En mal soient de Dieu maudit!"   [VI, 269]

["By the tongue that God spoke with, sisters, it's our visitor!
From now on we can take a good lesson from our superiors:

may hell-fire burn the loins of all who don't play around,
and God damn those who speak ill of it!"]

These and other manifestations of anticlerical comedy, however,
seem almost always to come down on the manifold worldliness
of the clergy—so well attested in our records that it would be
difficult to tell where history leaves off and satiric exaggeration
begins—rather than on sexuality itself as sin.[55]

If the fabliaux show a remarkably unruffled enthusiasm for
sex, they are nevertheless of two minds as regards "obscene"
language. Some exist in a cultural milieu in which terms which
at other times and places might be called obscene seem to be
part of the ordinary vernacular. The authors of some fabliaux
use these words freely—and give them to their characters, including women—in contexts in which the humor does not
seem to depend on the shock of usage felt to be forbidden.
We must thus visualize a mixed audience, which, in the mood
to hear fabliaux, expected to hear plain language, along with
a rich array of metaphorical variations, without embarrassment.
One of the fabliaux puts it in just these terms:

> . . . quant ce vint après souper,
> Si commencierent à border
> Et contoient de lor aviaus
> Lor aventures, lor fabliaus,
> Tant que li uns foutre nomma.   [III, 81–82]

[. . . when it came time, after supper, they began to crack
jokes and told about their amusements, their escapades, their
stories, until someone mentioned fucking.]

On the other hand there are fabliaux that consistently use
euphemisms, either courtly or neutral, or that contain direct

attacks on bad language.[56] That we are presented with an historical issue here, rather than with some perennial and simple division between nice people and vulgar ones, is suggested by the tone—that of a contemporary issue—that surrounds the instances of debated usage. When they debate usage, the fabliaux do not seem to be contemplating obscenities newly flung into the face of long-established standards so much as the reverse: they seem to be responding to an outbreak of decency. We can readily identify this historically as the radical strengthening of certain linguistic taboos in the thirteenth century by the spread of the ethic of courtliness or gentility.

From what we know of the habitual sexual attitudes of the knightly class of feudal society—Marc Bloch calls it "frankly realistic"[57]—we should expect that if courtly erotic doctrine was something substantially new, its norms of usage were new too. That the doctrine of clean language had to be learned and was at first only imperfectly adopted and assimilated is suggested by such well-known early evidence as the erotic directness, along with *con, foutre,* and scarcely less explicit metaphor in some of the poems of the first known troubadour, William IX of Aquitaine.[58] Searching early Old French romance for the same symptoms, we find in *Eneas (ca.* 1160), alongside elaborate indoctrination on the symptoms of courtly love, outbursts by the Queen and by the heroine Lavinia on the sexuality of Eneas that contain language that the code surely would have proscribed.[59] But early courtly literature is not generous to us with such slips. As Philippe Ménard reports (*Rire et sourire,* pp. 691–694) the language of twelfth- and thirteenth-century French romance is remarkably pure. Of the (mostly three-letter) words in Old French that might later be classified by genteel standards as taboo, Ménard finds the verb *pissier* used only

three times in a century. The scatological term *merde,* and the
word *cul,* equivalent to medieval English *arse,* are just as rare.
Taboo sexual terms are even rarer in these romances. The word
vit is not found at all in the romances examined by Ménard,
and only the twelfth-century Anglo-Norman trouvère Hue de
Rotelande uses the female equivalent, *con* (in the diminutive,
cunet, Ipomedon 2269).[60] It is Hue, too, who is the only author
of a predominantly serious, non-burlesque romance to use *foutre*
(ibid. 8648, 10517). Hue, of course, is possessed of a comic
temperament rare for trouvères, and he may be looking for a
certain shock effect in the context of courtly taboos. But after
examining his use of these terms in context—he uses them
only in a mood of high enthusiasm—it seems to me just as
likely that, as with the passages in *Eneas,* the taboos here have
not yet taken firm root.

That the *chanson de geste* in the same period is equally pure
in diction[61] is not surprising. The epic tradition has little to
do with the subject matter that concerns us here. Considering
the preoccupation of courtly literature with erotic matters,
however, the purity of courtly language is clearly a programmatic matter.

Programmatic, and didactic, as is made certain by one of
the commandments of the God of Love in perhaps the purest
example of French courtly didacticism, Guillaume de Lorris's
Roman de la rose (ca. 1237):

> "Après garde que tu ne dies
> Ces orz moz ne ces ribaudies:
> Ja por nomer vilaine chose
> Ne doit ta bouche estre desclose:
> Je ne tieng pas a cortois ome
> Qui orde chose e laide nome."[62]

["Next guard yourself against using any dirty words or expressions. Your mouth should never open to name a vulgar thing. I don't consider a man refined *(cortois)* who mentions dirty and ugly things."]

This is the doctrine pure and simple.

Within the same generation Jean Renart, author of romances, had already taken the same position at the beginning of his charming *Lai de l'ombre* (ca. 1221):

> Vilains est qui ses gas en fet,
> Qant ma cortoisie s'aoevre
> A dire aucune plesant oeuvre
> Ou il n'a rampone ne lait.
> Fox est qui por parole lait
> Bien a dire.

[He is vulgar who makes fun of me when I show my courtliness by telling a pleasing tale that has in it nothing offensive or ugly. He's a fool who gives up speaking well for the sake of a quip.][63]

In his romance *Galeran de Bretagne*, while describing its heroine, he protests somewhat too self-consciously, regarding that part of her beauty hidden under her clothes,

> . . . que cortoisie me deffent
> Que je ne nomme appertement.[64]

[that courtesy forbids me to call it openly by its name.]

The same courtly social bias—*vilanie* on the one hand, *cortoisie* on the other—is evident at the beginning of Henri d'Andeli's *Lai d'Aristote* (ca. 1242). Henri will say nothing that smacks of vulgarity:

> Quar oevre ou vilanie cort
> Ne doit estre escoutee a cort,
> Ne ja jor que ge vive en m'uevre
> N'orroiz vilanie remuevre,
> Ne vilain mot n'i reprendrai
> En oevre n'en dit que ge face,
> Ne ne quier estre troveur
> De nule riens en mon vivant
> Ou vilain mot voist arrivant.   [*Reid*, 71]

[For a work that runs to vulgarity shouldn't be heard at court. Never in my life will you hear any vulgarity repeated in my work, nor will I use a vulgar word in any work or tale that I write. While I live I'll not author anything where you'll see a vulgar word introduced.]

The emphasis here is particularly meaningful when we consider that the *Lai d'Aristote,* while charmingly and impeccably courtly in tone, has a comic plot. It is—except for its style and tone—a fabliau.

The idea of the need for a purified diction in courtly or genteel circles was expressed by Provençal lyricists themselves, and was later propagated in guides to courtesy and polite conduct. It was early taken up in a comically ironic manner, and appears in a variety of bawdy texts, usually with the apology, as Chaucer put it, that "The wordes moote be cosyn to the dede."[65]

That other fabliaux contain a reply to this courtly promotion of clean language is evident, though the precise timing and extent of it is hard to judge. Since few fabliaux can be dated, we cannot trace the movement with any chronological fineness. It is important to remember, too, that all the while there is a good amount of unruffled and unreflective persistence of the common idiom, used not so much in response to specifically verbal taboos (whether courtly or Christian) as for the less complicated pleasures of direct reference to or shared invoking of uninhibited sexuality. Even when a linguistic issue is raised, we cannot distinguish with certainty in each case which responses derive from specifically courtly influence and which from others. It will help to keep in mind, however, that even though the courtly tradition may be expected to have taken some cues from Christian moral tradition in its fashioning of a system of conduct, the two traditions are rather far apart on the subject of obscene language. The courtly system proscribes it; medieval Christianity has no formal doctrine on it at all.

In the courtly system this proscription is very much a matter of taste or style; it focuses on words, not on morals. Except as it later is merged with and submitted to Christian morality— as in Dante and in prose romance—the system in no way denigrates sexuality or sexual pleasure in themselves. The sources of medieval courtly verbal taboos are necessarily obscure. There was of course a well-developed, if fluctuating, set of terms considered obscene in polite circles in the ancient world.[66] But we have no evidence of the nature of colloquial usage as the vernacular developed in the centuries before the fabliau period. Just as the school comedies and other forms of clerical humor make clear that the learned or literary Latin tradition of obscenity was in vigorous condition by the twelfth century, courtly notions of clean and dirty language may largely represent the survival and then the revival of what Quintilian once called "the good old rules of Roman modesty."[67]

In any case it is a reasonable assumption that the rules of diction codified with the courtly rules of conduct in the twelfth

century, and then self-consciously promulgated by indoctrination for some centuries thereafter, were intended for a population that had an insufficiently developed notion of the obscenity of language. Whatever the state of verbal taboos may
have been in the pre-courtly period, it would seem inevitable
that in proscribing certain words and expressions, in banishing
them from its newly exclusive social sphere, the courtly tradition made those words and expressions more obscene, and
newly vulgar.

Perhaps surprisingly, the topic of obscene—as distinct from
profane—language does not come up in canon law, and it is
only rarely mentioned in the writings of the Church fathers.
In the Christian tradition, language is mentioned as obscene
mainly because it refers to acts or images considered obscene.
Obscene words, according to Augustine, would not even have
existed had it not been for Adam and Eve's sin, which turned
sexuality itself into a shame-laden thing. The words are forced
on us when we attempt to discuss sexuality; modesty is invoked
to avoid not the words, but the thoughts of shameful things.
Augustine (following the example of Paul in Romans 1:26)
consciously avoids obscenity of language in discussing human
generation, but it is clear that for him the linguistic taboo
comes mainly by transference from the subject.[68]

These distinctions, along with the context of images, references, and action in a piece will often give some indication
as to which taboos are the source of the fabliau conflict or
debate on obscenity. What creates a persuasive impression that
this debate is mainly a response to the courtly ethic is that it
most often does focus emphatically on words. It is a matter of
style or taste, not of morals.

Some fabliau punning and some uses of sexual euphemism,

metaphor, and direct statement obviously have behind them
courtly contexts already felt strongly enough to be worth playing with. The pun in the elegant *Guillaume au faucon* (discussed
above) is a likely example. We can expect Nykrog, in his exhaustive study of the whole genre as a courtly burlesque, to
have turned up a good many more: for instance, the use of the
"creation by Nature" topos to introduce the phallic description
in *Le Fevre de Creil;* the wife's formal dedication of her *cul* to
her husband in *Connebert;* the reference to semen as a soothing
ointment in *La Saineresse;* the references to "fountains" and
their "guardians" in a number of fabliaux.[69] There is assuredly
some verbal play with the courtly context when a handsome
and elegantly groomed young man, who will otherwise maintain a consistent gentility with a lady and her maid in regard
to his *servise,* coolly identifies himself as a "fucker" *(fouterres;*
I, 308).

Condemnation of misguided play with courtly verbal taboo
is very clearly evident in *La Dame qui se venja du chevalier.* The
mistake occurs while the lady and her lover are in the midst
of lovemaking:

> Le chevalier, qui est deseure,
> En mi le vis l'a esgardée;
> Si la vit de douchor pasmée,
> Dont ne pot celer sa folie,
> Einz dist une grant vilanie:
> Demanda li à cele foiz:
> "Ma dame, croitriez vos noiz?"   [VI, 24–25]

[The knight, who was on top, looked right at her face and
saw her swooning with pleasure. Whereupon he couldn't
suppress his foolishness, but said something very vulgar.

Right then he asked her, "My lady, would you crack some nuts?"]

The question is more than ill-timed, for *croistre noiz* is a vernacular synonym for *foutre*. The lady's love is instantly withdrawn, and she takes apt revenge.

Some of the other instances of overt response to the rules of polite diction are defenses based on (often pretended) female delicacy. In *La Dame qui aveine demandoit pour Morel* it has evidently been fortified by courtly teaching:

> "Toutes fois qu'avec moi seras,
> Soit en lit ou en autre place,
> Et tu vourras que je te face
> Se jolif mestier amouroux:
> Se me diras: 'Biax freres doux,
> Faites Moriax ait de l'avainne.' "
> Cele li respont com cortoise:
> "Biax freres douz, de ce t'aquoise . . .
> Miex aim c'on me couppast la gorge
> Que je tel outrage féisse."   [I, 320–321]

["Whenever you're with me, whether it's in bed or another place, and you want me to do some of that pleasant, lovely business with you, say to me 'Fair sweet brother, feed Blackie some oats'." She replied like a well-bred person: "Fair sweet brother, drop the subject; I'd rather have my throat cut than do such an indecent thing."][70]

Yet other responses to the issue are rather against the rules than for them. We have enough of the fragmentary *Jugement* (VI, 154–155) to see that it turns on a contest in a nunnery over who can say *le plus bel mot,* by which is meant, apparently,

the most explicit anecdote. In the part that we have, Sister
Ysabel overcomes her modesty, at the Abbess's urging, to make
a creditable performance. The audience is asked to judge the
winner. A similar contest takes place in *Les Trois Chanoinesses
de Couloigne*. But first the three ladies, "well versed in the
theory and practice of love" (III, 138), having invited the minstrel to dinner, hear some of his own *bons mos*. To begin he
recites a piece having obviously courtly interest. Then they
command him to recite another,

> Qui parlast plus parfondement
> De paroles crasses et doilles,
> "Si que de risées nous moilles."   [III, 141]

[. . . which would make deeper use of vulgar, suggestive
words, "so that you get us wet with laughter."]

He recites a fabliau, now lost, which gave some prominence
to a character called *li Cons* (III, 142). Nykrog (*Nyk,* 219)
gives this passage some emphasis as providing general evidence
of "the comic power of obscene words" in the fabliaux. But
surely the significance of the passage is more restricted. The
adjectives *crasses* and *doilles* (literally "fat" and "soft, ductile"),
with their voluptuous overtones, suggest here a special instance
of linguistic hedonism. This is one of the last of the fabliaux
(Watriquet wrote in the 1320's), produced in an upper-class
milieu in which the courtly rules have become strong enough
to make conscious defiance of them a special source of humor
and of pleasure.

The new gentility generated even more overt defense of the
vernacular in other fabliaux. There is, in fact, a describable
group of four anti-prudery poems: the two versions of *La Da-*

moisele qui ne pooit oïr parler de foutre, La Pucele qui abevra le polain, and *L'Esquiriel.* The principal character in the first three is a young woman with normal sexual desires but with serious verbal inhibitions. In two versions she is called stuck-up—*desdaigneuse* (III, 81; V, 24). She can't stand to hear words having to do with sex. In one they give her heart pains; in another she always faints; in the third she feels as if she had taken a vomitory. She has few suitors, and her father finds it hard to keep a male servant. The hero is a clever young *vallet* or clerk who comes visiting or asking for a job. In one version the young man, whose name is David, replies thus to the father's warning about his daughter's heart attacks when she hears the word *foutre:*

> Daviez prist sa boche à terdre,
> Et puis crache autresi et moche,
> Con s'il aüst mangiée moche;
> Au vilain dist: "Ostez, biaus sire;
> Si vilain mot ne devez dire!
> Taisiez por Deu l'esperitable,
> Que ce est li moz au deiable:
> N'en parlez mais là o je soie!
> Por .c. livres je ne veldroie
> Veoir home qui en parlast
> Ne qui lecherie nomast,
> Que grant dolor au cuer me prant!"   [V, 27]

[David began to wipe his mouth, then to clear his throat and spit as if he had eaten a horsefly. He said to the peasant "Stop, good sir; you shouldn't use such a vulgar word: Quit, for holy God's sake; that's the word of the Devil! Don't talk like that where I am! For a hundred pounds I wouldn't want

to hear anyone who said it or mentioned lechery—it gives
me pains in my heart!"]

David—like his brethren in the other versions—is apparently so
innocent that he can be safely entrusted to the daughter's bed.
The story always ends with a prolonged mutual seduction, by
means of a rich array of circumlocutions and animal metaphors—
of ponies, squirrels, fountains, meadows, and the like.

The author of *La Pucele qui abevra le polain* offers a few ed-
itorial remarks, opening his tale by announcing that it is not
a vulgar one, but just to make people laugh (moz por la gent
faire rire, IV, 199). He comments on the father's inability to
keep a servant by explaining—as to speaking of *foutre*—

> Il n'est nus qui ne prengne some
> As joenes genz, ce est la some,
> Et c'est à toz .I. molt doz mot.
> El monde n'a sote ne sot,
> Ne vielle de .IIII^{xx}. anz,
> Qui ne soit durement joianz,
> Quant el en oit .I. sol mot dire,
> Au meins l'en estuet il à rire.   [IV, 200]

[Anyone who took account of young people, all in all, would
find that to all of them it's a very fine word. There isn't a
fool of either sex in the whole world, nor an old woman of
eighty, who wouldn't be quite delighted to hear even one
word about it—at least you should get a laugh out of it.]

Nykrog (*Nyk,* 218) draws from the last line the conclusion
that the word *foutre* was in itself automatically funny. However,
in the context the line more likely means: It delights most
people to hear even a single word on the subject; rather than

feeling the anxiety of a prude, *at least you should get a laugh out of it*. There is an interesting slip or confusion on the use of the term *coilles* later in the poem. In the dialogue in which the lovers are presumably using euphemistic metaphors for the parts of the body, the girl describes her breasts as two "sheep's balls"(!), *coilles de mouton* (IV, 204); moments later, when she finds the clerk's *coillons* and asks what they are, he uses the conventional euphemism "two marshals," *dui mareschal* (IV, 205). The authorial slip would seem to suggest that except for the peculiar demands of this plot the word *coilles* did not carry much taboo in this author's milieu.[71] Near the end of the fabliau the author remarks:

> Par cest essanple monstrer vueil
> Que femes n'aient point d'orgueil
> De foutre paller hautement,
> Quant il foutent tot igalment.   [IV, 206]

[I want to show by this example that women should not be too proud to say *foutre* out loud when all the same they're doing it.]

L'Esquiriel opens quite differently from the other three poems, not with a prudish girl, but with a prudish mother. The unique dialogue between mother and daughter is in fact poorly related to the concluding episode of seduction-by-circumlocution, except that both deal with linguistic taboos. The mother—a wealthy matron of Rouen—warns her daughter not to talk too much, not to talk foolishly, and "emphatically above all"—

> "Que ja ne nommez cele rien
> Que cil homme portent pendant."   [V, 102]

[". . .not to mention that 'thing' that these men carry hanging."]

Pressed for its name, the mother refuses—"we women aren't supposed to mention it in any way"—but after a couple of wildly ingenious guesses by the daughter, she gives in.

> "Ja soit ce qu'il soit deveez,
> Et que droit et reson le dit,
> Je te di bien que ce est vit."   [V, 103]

["Well, forbidden as it may be, since it's right and reasonable, I tell you truly that it's called *vit*."]

Here the author capitalizes on the fact that the word *vit* in Old French (like "prick" and "cock" in Modern English) has a number of common and harmless homonyms. He has the girl give an unusually rhetorical discourse on the harmless familiarity of the forbidden word:

> Quant la pucele ce oï,
> Si s'en rist et si s'esjoï:
> "Vit," dist ele, "Dieu merci, vit!
> Vit dirai je, cui qu'il anuit,
> Vit, chetive! vit dist mon pere,
> Vit dist ma suer, vit dist mon frere,
> Et vit dist nostre chamberiere,
> Et vit avant et vit arriere
> Nomme chascuns à son voloir.
> Vous meïsme, mere, por voir,
> Dites vit, et je toute lasse
> Qu'ai forfet que vit ne nommaisse?
> Vit me doinst Dieus que je n'i faille!"
>   [V, 103]

[When the maiden heard this she was pleased and laughed. "*Vit,*" she said, "God be thanked, *vit!* I'm going to say *vit* no matter who cares. *Vit!* wretched me! my father says *vit,* my sister says *vit,* my brother says *vit,* and our maid says *vit. Vit* here and *vit* there—everybody says it as they please. Truly, even you say *vit,* mother; and I, poor me, what have I done wrong not to say *vit?* God give me one that I fail not!"]

That these texts are taking up an issue that extends beyond the fabliaux is attested by a well-known passage in Jean de Meun's continuation of the *Roman de la rose* (ca. 1277). Jean puts into the mouth of Reason an extended and noble defense of plain language, precisely directed against the courtly prohibitions we have already quoted from the first part of the poem. Dame Reason is speaking to the lover, and in one of the learned discourses that Jean de Meun is so fond of, Reason, making passing mention of Jupiter's castration of Saturn, uses the word *coilles* (v. 5537). The Lover (to whom the Rules of the God of Love have been addressed in the first place) is horrified:

> "Mais oï vous ai nomer ci,
> Si com mei semble, une parole
> Si esbaulevree e si fole
> Que, qui voudrait, ce crei, muser
> A vous emprendre a escuser,
> L'en n'i pourrait trouver defenses."[72]

["But I just heard you say, it seems to me, a word so shameless and improper that anyone who wanted to pass the time trying to excuse you would not be able to find a defense."]

Reason is too occupied with another argument at that moment,
but later on the Lover returns to the attack:

> "Si ne vous tieng pas a courtoise
> Quant ci m'avez coilles nomees,
> Qui ne sont pas bien renomees
> En bouche a courteise pucele;
> Vous, qui tant estes sage e bele,
> Ne sai con nomer les osastes,
> Au meins quant le mot ne glosastes
> Par quelque courteise parole,
> Si com preudefame en parole.
> Souvent vei neïs ces nourrices,
> Don maintes sont baudes e nices,
> Quant leur enfanz tienent e baignent,
> Qu'eus les debaillent e aplaignent,
> Si les noment eus autrement."   [6928–6941]

["I don't consider you polite when you just said coilles to
me—they aren't very praiseworthy in the mouth of a polite
maiden; I don't know how you, so wise and fair, dared to
mention them, at least without glossing over the word with
some polite expression, the way a respectable woman speaks
of them. Often I see that even these nurses, many of whom
are frivolous and stupid, when they hold and bathe their
children, and undress and fondle them, they refer to them
in other ways."]

Reason smiles, and patiently explains that God created these
things (she mentions *coilles* and *viz,* v. 6966) and put into
them marvelous powers of generation, for perpetuating the
species. The Lover responds even more prissily to this further

display of grossness, pointing out that God may have made the things, but at least he didn't make the words, which are completely vulgar (tuit plein de vilenie, v. 6986). Reason's reply, at some length, is that she speaks plainly, as God teaches, and has no need of glossing:

> "Se je, quant mis les nons aus choses
> Que si reprendre e blasmer oses,
> Coilles reliques apelasse
> E reliques coilles clamasse,
>
> . . . .
>
> Me redeïsses de reliques
> Que ce fust laiz moz e vilains.
> Coilles est beaus nons e si l'ains;
> Si sont, par fei, coillon e vit;
> Onc nus plus beaus guieres ne vit.
> Je fis les moz e sui certaine
> Qu'onques ne fis chose vilaine."   [7109–7120]

["When I gave the names to the things that you dare thus blame and criticize, if I named *coilles* relics and called relics *coilles*, . . .you would have said that "relics" was an ugly, vulgar word. *Coilles* is a beautiful name and I like it; in faith, so are *coillon* and *vit*. I know of none more beautiful. I made the words and I'm certain I never made anything vulgar."]

Reason goes on to comment on the disuse of plain terms by some women:

> "Se fames nes noment en France,
> Ce n'est fors desacoustumance,
> Car li propres nons leur pleüst,

> Qui acoustumé leur eüst;
> E se proprement les nomassent,
> Ja certes de riens n'i pechassent."
>
> [7131-7136]

["If women don't name them in France, it's nothing but getting out of the habit, for the right names would please those who were used to them; and if they called them by their right names, surely there would be nothing sinful about it."]

Nykrog leans rather heavily on these six verses to argue that medievals, according to Jean de Meun, were not "accustomed" to these words, that Jean envisages free use of them "only in theory," and that the historical attitude of the epoch was to condemn them.[73] In declining to accept this judgment we might marshal Jean's satirical characterization of the Lover as a very special, rather than typical, representative of the epoch, with his prim adherence to the Rules of his lord Amor. Nykrog uses the Lover's reference to the euphemisms of relatively ignorant nurses to suggest that lower-class people shared the Lover's sensibility. But the rather diaphanous sexuality of the picture that Jean evokes, of female nurses fondling naked male infants, suggests a stronger reason for linguistic taboo in this situation than universal disapproval of certain words. Jean has the Lover, in fact, come around finally to the admission at least that anyone who knows French should understand these words, so easy are they to grasp:

> ". . .Bien les i puis entendre,
> Qu'il i sont si legier a prendre
> Qu'il n'est nus qui franceis seüst
> Qui prendre ne les i deüst."   [7185-7188]

In another part of the discussion Reason's speech implies that besides the customary occasions for more-or-less genteel euphemisms, other more intimate situations called forth a customary directness:

> "Chascune qui les va nomant
> Les apele ne sai coment:
> Bourses, harneis, riens, piches, pines,
> Ausinc con ce fussent espines;
> Mais quant les sentent bien joignanz,
> Eus nes tienent pas a poignanz;
> Or les noment si come eus seulent."
>
> [7141–7147]

["Every woman who goes around mentioning them calls them I don't know what: purses, gear, things, cruets, even pine cones, as if they were prickles; but when they feel them right up close they don't find them prickly. Then they call them the way they do usually."]

Jean here imputes to the epoch what we have found in the fabliaux generally: an element of tutored gentility, a range of synonyms of varying degrees of decency (or obsceneness), and occasions when taboo terms are used in direct evocation of sexual experience. Jean's own practice in the rest of the poem further suggests that the self-consciously aggressive linguistic position is the Lover's, not Reason's. Here and there, Jean uses *coilles,* and *con,* and graphic metaphors such as we have found in the fabliaux, without particular emphasis, as if normally.[74] Indeed, even the purist Guillaume de Lorris, in a moment of inattention, uses the word *cul* (anus), which is avoided in courtly literature.[75]

The historical issue we are raising here is more serious than the material illustrating it. Are we dealing, in the fabliaux, with sexual attitudes that have at best a vagrant, peripheral relationship to the values of the culture, or with something central? Did courtly usage set itself up at an already well-defined frontier between established decency and obscenity, or is a new definition of decency—and thus of vulgarity—pushing itself in over an older, simpler, and perhaps more persistent set of values? The conservatism and the relative unselfconsciousness—the normalcy—of fabliau sexual attitudes suggests a quite real stratum in medieval sensibility, one that coexists with, underlies, and probably antedates both courtly purity and Christian puritanism. Fabliau directness of diction almost certainly antedates courtly delicacy. While it is unimaginable that there were no taboos surrounding the language of sexuality before the courtly period, fabliau diction seems to show that the re-invention of courtesy, and thus the complementary re-invention of vulgarity, must have deepened those taboos decisively. They made the fabliaux for later periods newly obscene.

CHAPTER VI

The Fabliaux in Medieval French Culture

PART FROM PROVIDING A GENERAL INTRODUC-
tion to the genre, this study has aimed to show
that the fabliaux should be taken seriously as evidence in medieval French cultural history. Much of the foregoing discussion
does provide evidence that the genre is not a fugitive or peripheral one, but represents a definable area of sensibility central
to the culture of the period.

The emergence of the genre suggests, as does the emergence
of every literary genre, that a newly prominent or newly dominant set of values and feelings was finding a newly adequate
mode for its expression and celebration. Furthermore, the genre
does not emerge in isolation, as if it represented a cultural
novelty or idiosyncrasy. Rather, it is a version, an artistic elaboration, of a long-standing genre of the oral tradition, and
most of the other medieval written genres—romance, lai, Latin
"comedy" and *ridiculum*, beast epic, fable, exemplum—share
key traits of style, structure, or sentiment with it.

Fabliaux were produced for amusement, enjoyment, and that
in no segregated fashion. They were recited aloud in mixed
company, often in convivial circumstances, and they everywhere
suggest the pleasure characteristic of comedy, of the surrender
to confidence, of the sharing of the story with others. Further,
the fabliaux in their own time were not a class literature. They
were shared by and within all classes, and they sensitively reflect
the strains and ambiguities that the feudal class system was
feeling in the period. Fabliau imagery overwhelmingly records
ordinary experience. The genre has long been recognized by
social historians as a rich source of factual data on the details

of daily living, but its circumstantial realism is far from incidental: it is central to its style and to its ethos, as well as to its surface historicity. Paradoxically, it is even in one of the persistent literary defects of the fabliau, its frequent weakness of plotting, that its insight into contemporary life and values most clearly appears. For the audience of many a fabliau gives up some of the pleasure of plot-interest for the equal pleasure of sharing and savoring the wit, the irony, and the texture of ordinary experience.[1]

If the fabliau's material cosmos is precisely that in which its audience was currently living, so is its ethos. This ethos, rooted in a deeply human taste for material goods and sensory pleasure, for food, drink, and uncomplicated sexuality, cannot be appreciated merely in negative terms, as "anti-courtly" or "anti-Christian." It has its own rather formidable integrity. The recurrence in text after text of the same attitudes and values makes clear that we are not dealing here with a random miscellany of jokes having a random miscellany of tendencies, but with a body of literature expressing a consistent value system.

Let us give this system a name—I have already called it "hedonistic materialism," but "materialistic hedonism" would have done just as well—and let us assume that the name includes that taste for irony that I have mentioned as one of its traits. Thus equipped with a respectable philosophical label, the system will be readily seen to have three attributes important for our inquiry. One is coherence, namely the quality of being a system; the next is an historical life of its own; and the third is a locus, a place in medieval French culture.

The force and integrity of the fabliau ethos comes in part from the fact that its traits seem mutually to reinforce each other and to create a plausible and stable system. I need not linger long on the affinities of various forms of appetite to the general espousal of physical pleasure, nor of this philosophy in turn to a view that values money very highly and sees the universe mainly in terms of material goods. This congeries of traits is particularly receptive to the high valuation of cleverness or wit, since cleverness in the fabliaux is, as we have seen, a powerful instrument in the procurement of goods and pleasure. Cleverness turns a face the other way, linking the materialism of the fabliaux with what we might call its "political" philosophy, a kind of individualism, if not egalitarianism, in which wit levels distinctions of station and gender, and opens the prospect of pleasure to whoever can manage it. This philosophy is not so entirely naive as to create for its adherents a *Schlaraffenland*. It is penetrated by, and sits comfortably with, an irony and a cynicism that along with cleverness recognize error and miscalculation, and hedge themselves against instability and defeat with traditional formulations of practical wisdom and with laughter.

This ethos has enough resemblance to one widely to be found in modern American society (to take an example) that I do not need to argue very strenuously for either its stability as a system or its historical existence. Even if modern America and fabliau France were not historically related, and there were no conceivable filiation between the values of the one and the values of the other, we would have to remark that the traits of the value system I am describing have a perennial affinity for each other. And it would be a safe guess that they did not come together for the first time in thirteenth-century France, but represent an old—a very old—configuration in human civilization, that expressed itself in fabliau-like stories long before the Middle Ages and continues to do so still. This ethos is more dominant and more noticeable in some periods and places than in others. When it is recessive, obscured from historical view, we can still imagine it to persist in subterranean ways, its values shared and transmitted in oral tradition rather than in written form, a deep and ancient stratum in Western culture. It is this kind of stratum, I suggest, that the fabliaux represent in the culture of their time.

By "stratum," by the geological metaphor, I mean to suggest that the fabliau ethos, however old, must not only have a history but also a place, and that it shares that place with other systems of feeling and value, with other cultural strata having their own histories. Turning from geology to anthropology, we might alternatively imagine the rich complexity of a given culture to consist of a number of subcultural systems, each more or less well defined because of the affinity, coherence, and persistence of its traits, and each coexisting with the others in a complex variety of ways. In this formulation, then, the fabliaux could be seen, if not as the production of a social class, then as the expression of a subculture that, like the large and powerful contemporaneous subculture of the Christian religion, runs across class lines and forms its membership on another principle.

Hindsight now enables us to see that even Bédier was giving us a pointer toward this alternative to his theory when he admitted that despite the bourgeois origin of the fabliaux, there was ample evidence that the texts that have survived were recited and enjoyed among *grands seigneurs,* just as the most aristocratic genres were enjoyed in "bourgeois" circles. He concluded, we recall, "that there was in the thirteenth century, up to a certain point, a confusion of genres and promiscuity of audiences (*promiscuité des publics*)."[2]

We have seen (above, pp. 26-27) that the same observation,

in more emphatic terms, was made in 1924 by Edmond Faral, at the time that he was arguing for the fabliau's having ultimately originated in antique Latin comedy and its having proximately issued from the learned Latin comedy of the twelfth century. "The fabliaux," he wrote, "are neither the creation nor the property of a particular social class, but represent rather a propensity which was that of an entire epoch. A taste for coarse joking seems indeed to have cohabited in the same breasts with more subtle and refined tastes. This is why it is an historical error to say that the fabliaux belong to 'bourgeois' literature: it is advisable to say simply that they belong to 'realistic' literature."

For us the key words here are "cohabited in the same breasts." The observation is acute, and psychologically true. So true that even Nykrog, at the very end of his complex and exhaustive argument for the aristocratic character of the fabliaux, allows himself a similar perception. He concedes that despite the advent of courtly ideas, tendencies that he calls "less refined" existed in the very same bosoms (dans le sein même) of refined society during the whole course of the thirteenth century (tout le long du XIIIᵉ siècle). He goes on to repeat that "these two opposing tendencies did not limit themselves to the social level"; he sees a struggle between them as probably extending "into the spirit of each individual, the new ideas of sophisticated circles seeking to snatch it from the domination of archaic grossness." His argument closes with a picture of medieval man's joining in himself "contrasts more violent and deep than have men of later generations," participating "at the same time in yesterday's primitivism and in the delicacy of a refinement to come."[3]

There is much to comment on in these closing concessions.

We shall turn in a moment to the dualism of this view, and the implication that it must always involve conflict. For now, what is most interesting is first that Nykrog finally comes to confirm Faral's view that fabliau values and attitudes share space, as it were, within individuals of different social classes; and second, that by calling them "archaic" and a "primitivism," he acknowledges that they constitute something historically older than the courtly system. We have already, then, from the century's major students of the genre, something of a formulation, however partial or oblique, of the view that we have been developing here. The fabliaux represent a value system that coexists, along with an indeterminate number of other value systems, in a wide range of individuals in the culture. We might say that the individuals who share this system, by virtue of sharing it, constitute a cultural stratum, or subculture, that has, among other things, its own literature and its own history. We can imagine the members of this subculture as having affiliations with it of varying strengths and durations. They may much of the time pay more attention, at least outwardly, to other memberships or allegiances. But at certain times and places they variously acknowledge, appreciate, relish, and live by its tenets, and they meet with others to share and commend its values.

This kind of formulation may well sound like a ponderous (or pretentious) way to describe the place of comic stories in a given society. But it has the advantage of enabling us to make some discriminations about the meaning of the fabliaux that less complex formulations seem to blur. I mean particularly the discrimination of those values, and that humor, that seem to arise inherently out of the fabliau world view, as opposed to those which arise from it contrastively, because of the co-presence of other systems. The contrastive value of the fabliaux is to my mind overemphasized in our usual assessments of their humor. Not that conflicts among subcultural systems are not an important and perennial source of literary effect. Whenever one set of values is found to dwell in close proximity with the sentiments, the doctrine, the behavior and laws prescribed by another system, the materials are at hand for a variety of possible literary exploitations: satire, parody, burlesque, and particularly irony. There is such a rich and easily reachable vein of meaning in these contrasts that we are sometimes tempted to conclude that contrast or juxtaposition is the only source from which the effect is coming; and this is particularly tempting when one of the systems seems more important or dominant or respectable than the other.

When in *Saint Pierre et le jongleur* St. Peter wins in a crap game for souls, especially when his jongleur opponent is led to suspect him of cheating (V, 73), we are acutely and deliciously aware of the co-presence and the contradictions of two systems being used in the creation of humor. Similarly, when a wealthy bourgeois mother warns her daughter that "we women" aren't allowed to use such words as *vit* (V, 102); or when we are told that a baron's daughter habitually faints when she hears the word *foutre* during recital of fabliaux (III, 82), we readily appreciate that two standards of usage (standing for two different value systems) are at issue. Nykrog's thesis that the fabliaux depend on the co-presence of the courtly system thus virtually limits the meaning of the fabliaux to the contrastive sort.[4]

The fact is, however, that the fabliaux generate a great deal of meaning and feeling that does not seem to depend on contrast or juxtaposition with other value systems. All of the tricksters who compel our grudging admiration in the fabliaux are not St. Peters; many are just great tricksters. The thief who steals a peasant's piece of cloth in a dense crowd by sewing the end of it to his clothes and walking off; the brother thieves Barat and Haimet, who completely defeat the apprentice Travers for possession of a side of bacon; the ingenious knight who devastates a rich priest's household in *Le Prestre et le chevalier;* the similarly talented butcher of Abeville; the clerk who tricks the blind men in *Les Trois Aveugles*—are appreciated by the fabliau audience mostly for their own sake. It is perhaps true that no value system is proof against the contrastive effects that someone in its audience might consciously or subconsciously bring forward. Thus in the fabliau of *Barat and Haimet* the decision of Travers the apprentice to go straight because of lack of talent provides a backdrop of contrastive value that produces some of the poem's humor; and perhaps all tales of trickery are susceptible to some such implied or assumed shadowing by "straight" values. Nevertheless, in many fabliaux this sort of effect is clearly neither suggested, planned, exploited, nor productive of an important part of the tale's meaning. In them the audience appreciates and even applauds the success of the "trickster" or "rascal" much as a modern reader might appreciate the skill of a great international jewel theft or of a perfect payroll robbery.

The case is even plainer if we turn to the sexual morality of the fabliaux. When, in *Le Sohait desvé* of Jean Bodel, a loving but sexually frustrated wife dreams, by her husband's side, that she goes to a great fair where nothing is on sale but penises (*Nar,* 102), the humor of the situation seems to owe less to contrasting value systems than to certain inherent values and conditions within the fabliau view of sexuality itself: the insistency of desire, the pleasure of intercourse, the obstacles to satisfaction, the seductions of fantasy, the contest of the sexes. Furthermore, when the author uses the term *vit* throughout, and gives it to the wife to use in her dialogue with her husband (*Nar,* 107), we have no sense here, either, of an issue *between* value systems as regards verbal usage. The term, as in many other fabliaux (and with many other key colloquial terms), seems to be the normal and natural usage of the author and characters, evoking sexuality without either parody, or irony, or impudence either.

Self-consciously proclaimed sensualism knowingly and impudently aimed at Christian teaching *is* found at the borders of the corpus of fabliaux and in peripheral genres. As such it helps us delimit and distinguish the fabliau ethos from others with which it is too often confused.

In the fabliaux of the talented Gautier le Leu there is occasionally a perfervid excessiveness that suggests a temperament most congenial to the mood of confrontation. The sadism of his *Connebert* is remarkably insistent, as if to conjure up by its own violence a vision of the moral system it outrages. The same can be said of the scatology of his *Les Deus Vilains,* and of the comedy of threatened homosexual attack in *Le Sot chevalier.* In *Dieu et le pescour,* a piece not usually accepted as a fabliau, Gautier's irreverence toward Jesus borders on actual sacrilege. He is undoubtedly the author of a piece entitled *Du con,* called by its editor "one of the most obscene of the Middle Ages" (*Liv*, 233), which is not a fabliau but a "sermon joyeux" related to the famous *Lai du lecheor,* and a glorification of female sexual parts that far exceeds any fabliau in its almost hysterical enthusiasm.

Once we define this note of calculation, exaggeration, and impudence just on the edges of the fabliaux, we can identify it with a number of other well-known works which, however much they share some traits with the fabliaux, should not be lumped with them; they are a different genre, have a different ethos, and represent a different cultural situation. It is in this way that we can distinguish from the fabliaux proper the remarkable stanzaic poem *Richeut*. *Richeut* deals, in largely the same style, with the same key value traits: sex, money, and cleverness, material goods and pleasure—and even ends with an episode much like that of the fabliau *Le Prestre et Alison*. Yet its literary structure is more like that of a mock-heroic romance than of a fabliau (the heroine is the super-whore Richeut), and, more important, the structure of its ethos is different; it is outrageously and self-consciously impudent, and its cynicism is soured into an enveloping pessimism and moralism. Where the fabliau occasionally refers to some stray deviation from the missionary position, Richeut's son Samson runs epically through the whole catalogue of possibilities:

> Sanson les fout totes sovines,
> Les genoz lor met as poitrines,
> Il croist en coste
> Et a copresse et a soposte;
>
> . . . .
> A bachet [= brachet?] et a pissechien.
> Plus set Sansons,
> Car il les croist a estupons
>
> . . . .
> Maintes en monta sor les dos
> A cui il fist croistre les os.[5]

[Samson fucks them lying right down with their knees at their chests. He fucks them sideways and down on them (?) and over them (?); . . . dog-fashion (?) and with a leg up.

Samson knows even more, for he screws them bent over
forwards. . . . With many he gets on their backs and makes
their bones crack.]

Where the fabliaux touch comically and even affectionately on
the transgressions of nuns, *Richeut* is almost sadistic. Samson,
ordained a priest, becomes a chaplain, and corrupts a whole
nunnery, then robs it. He makes the abbess pregnant and she
becomes a minstrel *(jugleresse)*. Samson does not simply seduce
a woman, but also "her niece and her aunt and her sisters,"
"her mother, her daughter, and her cousins." "From lechery,"
it says, "Samson never has rest" *(Rich,* 222, 224). What humor
there is in a text such as this has a crazy glitter in its eye that
the fabliaux rarely if ever suggest.

Of a different but related sort are some of the episodes in
the *Renart* cycle. The *Confession de Renart* (branche 14) is locked
into a violent affront to monasticism. In one sequence Renart
confesses himself a heretic and sodomite; then, after an insulting
discussion of various monastic orders, he explains why he cannot
become a monk himself. The explanation falls into the class
of *encomia vulvae* that was to become a minor genre in the thirteenth century:[6]

> "Et je conment dont le feroie?
> que nul mal souffrir ne porroi[e]
> et que conserrer ne me puis
> de Hersant ne de son pertuis?
> Pertuis? El mont n'a si grant chose,
> mout est hardiz qui nomer l'ose,
> que por seulement que m'en menbre
> me fremisent trestuit li menbre
> et herice toute la char.
> Par mon chief ce n'est mie eschar;

ce est or li plus nobles nons

qui soit en cest siecle que cons." [*Ren* 5, 48]

["And how could I do it, unable to tolerate any pain, or to keep myself away from Hersant and her hole? Hole? There isn't so great a thing in the world. He is a brave man who dares name it; why, when I just think of it all my parts quiver and all my flesh prickles. By my head it's no joke: the very noblest name in this world is cunt."]

There follows an enumeration of the marvelous powers of *le con*. Renart ends his confession with a couplet celebrating "the very good and beautiful order consisting of male and female," then his "confessor," Hubert the Kite, counters with a highly unpleasant description of the aforementioned Hersant and her venerable part. Of similar tone and import are the sermon delivered at Renart's funeral by the Archpriest Bernard the Ass (*branche* 17, ed. Martin, vv. 870–912), and the passage recounting the collaboration of Renart in the work of King Connin, the construction of a giant vulva from the parts of animals (*Ren* 5, 24–36).

The borders between genres are scarcely distinct, but these documents in cynical clerkly anti-asceticism do go well beyond the fabliaux in the perversity and impudence with which they confront the Establishment. Their humor, while touching on fabliau subjects, is describably different from fabliau humor. The latter is the humor of normal sexuality; the former, the humor of special forms of repression and of truancy. It is as if monasticism, for instance, had an exaggerated need for comic release, and produced a sexual humor correspondingly more fervid, more febrile, more challenging, and much more clearly based by parody on the forbidding presence of Christian orthodoxy.

By the same token, the style and ethos of the fabliaux are

similarly to be distinguished from those of the "grotesque realism" which Mikhail Bakhtin rather uncritically lumps together from virtually all the manifestations of medieval humor—including the fabliaux—in his celebrated study of the background of Rabelais (1940).[7] In their transcendence of class limits the fabliaux are, in a sense, a sort of "people's laughter," but they mainly eschew the grandiosity, the exaggeration, the grotesquerie of the Rabelais tradition. Their ambivalence is decidedly not that of fleshly decay and degradation on the one hand and overwhelming fecundity on the other. (Pregnancy rarely occurs in the fabliaux.) They have not, largely, a potbellied kind of humor.

Although they give every evidence of having been shared as social entertainments, the fabliaux in no way suggest the kind of universal holiday fare, the immemorial folk celebrations, envisioned by Bakhtin. There is a perhaps difficult but important distinction to be made between the production and enjoyment of the fabliaux and the variety of festive or furtive activities in the Middle Ages that might variously be called "concessionary," or "marginal." I am thinking of the Boy Bishop and the Feast of Fools, of carnival, of obscene imagery in cathedral sculpture, and comic drawings in the margins of sober texts. The possible analogies with fabliau are many, and easy, and they are often made.[8] But they rest on questionable assumptions. I have tried to suggest already some of the ways in which fabliau is *not* dependent on direct juxtaposition, as carnival *is* dependent upon Lent, and the Boy Bishop upon the real Bishop. It is not at all likely that the fabliau ethos is as marginal in medieval culture, and as merely mischievous, as are the apes and rabbits and compound little monsters that cavort and copulate in the margins of manuscripts.

Let me terminate my argument with three reasons why we should be on guard against undervaluing the fabliaux as evidence for cultural history, and why we should look at them with a new seriousness. The first is that, since the fabliau ethos is not the official, accepted ethos of the Establishment, which in the Middle Ages meant that it had severely limited chances of being recorded in writing at all, what we have in writing must be recognized as very likely only a partial expression of the subculture that it represents. In some circles we should expect this literature to have been suppressed rather than preserved. One hundred fifty texts is a remarkable number for us to have in any case, but we ought to remember that these composed, rhymed, and written-down tales are only the top layer of what must have been a mass of stories shared orally, and on an unimaginable scale. The fabliaux ought to be regarded not as a minor literature, but rather as archaeological evidence: fragmentary remains, preserved in written form, of an important stratum of the culture that has otherwise left few traces. We need increasingly to face up to the fact that what we deal with in the Middle Ages is mainly the official culture of the period, and that without taking due account of the period's unofficial, private, unbuttoned, confidential feelings—to which humor is a very dependable index—we falsify our histories.

Another reason to take the fabliaux seriously is that their ethos is too important in human experience to ignore. Whatever one may think of it, one cannot remove it from the picture of the human condition, nor from history. It simply cannot be swept over to the margins as an example of childish truancy. Indeed, it celebrates values that are perhaps too central to the human condition, too essentially comic to allow us to hold it steadily in mind as a particular historical phenomenon at all.

I have not found it particularly helpful to follow Bakhtin's lead and to sum up the authority of the fabliau by whatever connection it may have with the folk, and the fecundity of earth, and a tradition of folk wisdom that goes back to the dawn of culture.[9] But I *am* struck, reading Langer's *Feeling and Form*, by how much a theory of the form of comic drama in general produces ideas applicable to the fabliau. The fabliaux, like comedy, do celebrate the sense of life, of self-preservation, as Langer puts it, of "instinctual life modified in almost every way by thought, a brainy opportunism in face of an essentially dreadful universe." They too express "the elementary strains and resolutions of animate nature, the animal drives. . . , the delight man takes in his special mental gifts." Their protagonists too act out "a contest with the world," and they too "triumph by wit, luck, personal power, or even humorous, or ironical, or philosophical acceptance of mischance."[10] A literature, no matter what its scale, that explores and recommends this area of experience cannot be so marginal as we often make it.

There are powerful pressures in our own culture to push fabliaux out of proper perspective. My third reason for taking the fabliau more seriously is that the Judaeo-Christian tradition—or rather the Anglo-American Protestant version of it—makes the fabliau seem much more contrastive, much more impudent, much more conceivable only as temporary truancy, or in terms of short-term temporary license, than it was in its own time. This tradition confronts the fabliau with a rival ethos that is purer, sharper, more intense, and more uncompromising than anything encountered in medieval Catholicism except at *its* outermost fringes.

Coupled with the religious tradition in our own culture is

the genteel tradition of taste, style, and behavior which has since made the fabliau tradition "vulgar." We ought to keep in mind that gentility has had seven centuries to develop, elaborate, and domesticate itself in us since the thirteenth century; then it was a newly formed ethos, belonging to a subculture which, in comparison to that of the fabliaux, was a very small one indeed.

A third pressure on us, related to the other two, is our inveterate sense of cultural coherence, our sensitivity to and uneasiness with contradictory ideas, contradictory feelings, contradictory codes. The notion of the fabliau ethos as representing a valid system of feelings and attitudes, a system existing at the same time and in the same persons with Christianity and with courtly gentility—a coexistence, furthermore, that is surrounded with neither anxiety nor guilt—is almost more than we can comprehend. Yet the phenomenon is not so exotic in our own experience. We may not admire it, but we should perhaps recognize it as a phenomenon: the madam who goes to church, and the Sunday vestryman who goes to the brothel on Friday night; the Sicilian Communist atheist who has his children baptized; the easy coexistence of ideals and expedience in some politicians, of the morals of Christian love and of "business is business" in so many businessmen. The cult of moral consistency and the beauty of moral integrity have in modern times been hard on moral compartmentalization; something like moral compartmentalization is the target of much of our classic satire of hypocrisy. It has not commanded enough study in modern psychology or sociology. Perhaps we shall yet find it more widespread than we imagine, and, like it or not, a perennial if not absolutely necessary device for survival in complex, contradictory cultures.[11]

In any case, the fabliau period apparently accepted the compartmentalization of values in the individual as a normal part of socialization. The point is easily seen in the table of contents of MS. B.N. 19152: a collection of moral tales; then one of fables; then a poem on the signs of the Last Judgment; then a saint's life; then two moral poems; then two fabliaux; then two courtly poems; then a monologue of a mercer; then twenty-one more fabliaux; and so on.[12] It is seen everywhere in the thirteenth-century village of Montaillou as described by Le Roy Ladurie. The village, though intimately documented by the Inquisition for its heresy, which argues a powerful religiosity, is yet a living fabliau. One need only follow the career of the curate Pierre Clergue, who during his affair with Beatrice de Planisolles lay with her once on Christmas Eve and on another occasion in the village church.[13] Of his affair with Grazide Lizier—whom Ladurie calls "a Joan of Arc of loving"—Grazide testified to the Inquisition: "In those days it gave me pleasure, and it pleased the curate too to know me carnally and to be known by me; so I didn't think it was a sin, and neither did he. But now with him it wouldn't be a pleasure. So if he knew me carnally from now on, it would be a sin" (p. 218).

Thinking of the various components of thirteenth-century French culture in terms of subcultural systems has the advantage of clarifying for ourselves the manifold ways in which they do or do not interact in the society, and it tends to respect their historicity more than might other approaches. If we have rejected social class as explaining the fabliau, we should also be wary of psychoanalytic theory, which would tend to reduce fabliaux to symptoms of permanent tensions in the psyche, just as religious exegesis would see them simply as signs of the permanent and vicious propensity of the soul toward concupiscence. These formulations may have their uses, but they do not work well when we propose the historical question: what to make of the writing up, in literary form, of so many fabliaux in the thirteenth century? We ought to be able to look on it as documenting a cultural development, an episode in the history of sensibility, of a swelling of the interest, and of the power, in a lot of people, of a particular complex of ideas and feelings.

We have seen that we have other evidences of the same cultural development. The hedonism and materialism and the ethic of cleverness of the fabliaux find a rough correspondence in the economic, commercial, and social development of the period. They are clearly symptomatic of some of the ideas and feelings that contributed to the creation of towns and the commercialization of the countryside, the increase of social mobility and the creation of social illusions. But if we were content to see the fabliaux as simply corroborating the historical picture provided by the socioeconomic facts, we would be badly missing the point. The fabliaux are in themselves a more precise, more accurate, more subtle, and more complex evidence of how people felt in that culture than the socioeconomic data could ever provide, and they would provide an insight into the culture had no socioeconomic facts survived at all. The genre emerged just as did the romance a half-century before, because a certain complex of ideas and feelings had gained enough power and currency in that time and that place to need a newly efficacious form through which it could be acknowledged and shared.

Notes

CHAPTER I

1 Joseph Bédier, *Les Fabliaux: Etudes de littérature populaire et d'histoire littéraire du moyen âge,* 5th ed. (Paris: Champion, 1925; 1st ed. 1893); Per Nykrog, *Les Fabliaux: Etude d'histoire littéraire et de stylistique médiévale* (Copenhagen: Ejnar Munksgaard, 1957).

2 See Bédier, *Fabliaux,* pp. 28–37; Nykrog, *Fabliaux,* esp. pp. 3–18; Hermann Tiemann, "Bemerkungen zur Entstehungsgeschichte der Fabliaux," *Romanische Forschungen,* 72 (1960), 406–422; Jean Rychner, "Les Fabliaux: Genre, styles, publics" in *La Littérature narrative d'imagination,* Université de Strasbourg, Centre de Philologie Romane (Paris: Presses Universitaires de France, 1961), pp. 42–54; Omer Jodogne, "Considérations sur le fabliau," in *Mélanges . . . René Crozet,* ed. Pierre Gallais and Yves-Jean Riou, 2 vols. (Poitiers, 1966), 2: 1043–1055; Omer Jodogne, *Le Fabliau* (printed with J. C. Payen, *Le Lai narratif*), Typologie des Sources du Moyen Age Occidental, fasc. 13 (Brepols: Turnhout, 1975); Reinhard Kiesow, *Die Fabliaux: Zur Genese und Typologie einer Gattung der altfranzösischen Kurzerzählungen,* Romanistik, 10 (Rheinfelden: Schäuble, 1976), chap. 2; Willem Noomen, "Qu'est-ce qu'un fabliau?" in International Congress of Romance Linguistics and Philology (14th, 1974, Naples), *Acts* (Napoli: Gaetano Macchiaroli, 1981), 5: 421–432; and Nico van den Boogaard, *"Le Nouveau Recueil Complet des Fabliaux (NRCF),"* Neophilologus, 61 (1977): 335.

3 Bédier (pp. 436–441) admitted 147 poems to the canon; Nykrog (pp. 311–324) lists 160. The *NRCF,* edited by W. Noomen and N. van den Boogaard and still in progress, will contain 127 titles, omitting some 23 poems from Nykrog's list, adding four others, and treating as alternate versions within accepted titles 14 poems that Nykrog lists as separate fabliaux. Of these titles there are 276 manuscript copies extant; see N. van den Boogaard, "Les Fabliaux: Versions et variations," *Marche Romane,* 28: 3–4 (1978): 149–161.

4 Cf. Knud Togeby, "Les Fabliaux," *Orbis Litterarum,* 12 (1957), 88–89, 96–97. The term *fablius* appears in a list of familiar genres, along with romance and chanson de geste, in some MSS of the *Roman de Renart;* see E. Martin, ed., *Le Roman de Renart,* 3 vols. (Strasbourg and Paris,

1882–1887), branche 2, v. 7. This branche of the *Renart* is possibly dated about 1176, leading to the supposition that the fabliaux were flourishing by that time; see H. R. Jauss, *Untersuchungen zur mittelalterlichen Tierdichtung*, Beihefte zur Zeitschrift für romanische Philologie, 100 (Tübingen, 1959), pp. 178–180 and n. 1. But the passage in other MSS reads *fables*, not *fablius*; see, e.g., Martin's variants (III, 87), and the more recent edition by Mario Roques, *Le Roman de Renart*, *CFMA*, 6 vols. (Paris: Champion, 1948–63), branche iii, v. 3739 (=*Ren* II, 16).

5 Nykrog, *Fabliaux*, 324–325. Nykrog's figures will no doubt be revised upward by publication of the *NRCF;* see van den Boogaard, "Le Nouveau Recueil," 336.

6 Jean Rychner, *Contribution à l'étude des fabliaux*, Université de Neuchâtel, Recueil . . . de la faculté des lettres, fasc. 28, 2 vols. (Neuchatel: Faculté des Lettres, and Geneva: Droz, 1960), esp. 1:131–136.

7 Edmond Faral, *Les Jongleurs en France au moyen âge* (Paris: Champion, 1910), chap. 1.

8 Wendelin Foerster and Hermann Breuer, eds., *Les Merveilles de Rigomer, von Jehan*, 2 vols., Gesellschaft für Romanische Literatur, 19, 39 (Dresden, 1908–1915), vv. 3059–3061. Cited in Nykrog, *Fabliaux*, p. 23.

9 Bédier, *Fabliaux*, pp. 389–398; Faral, *Jongleurs*, pp. 32–43; Stephen L. Wailes, "*Vagantes* and the Fabliaux," in Thomas D. Cooke and Benjamin L. Honeycutt, eds., *The Humor of the Fabliaux* (Columbia, Mo.: University of Missouri Press, 1974), pp. 43–58.

10 Raymond Eichmann, "The Question of Variants and the Fabliaux," *Fabula*, 17 (1976), 41–42; and Bédier, *Fabliaux*, pp. 127–128, correctly observe that most of those may well be formulaic references to sources real or imagined.

11 Edmond Faral, ed., *Le Manuscrit 19152 du fonds français de la bibliothèque nationale* (Paris: Droz, 1934), p. 10; Rychner, *Contribution*, 1:135–140; Rychner, "Les Fabliaux," pp. 50–51.

12 Nykrog, *Fabliaux*, pp. 44–50; see also the comment by L.-F. Flutre, "Le Fabliau, genre courtois?" in *Frankfurter Universitätsreden*, 22 (1960), 78–82, to the effect that the Lyons MS, which Nykrog regards as the unique surviving specimen of an unbound copybook, must have been part of a bound collection.

13 See for example Robert Hellman and Richard O'Gorman, trans., *Fabliaux: Ribald Tales from the Old French* (New York: Crowell, 1965), 79; cf. Thomas D. Cooke, "Two Ozark Analogues to Two Old French Fa-

bliaux," *Southern Folklore Quarterly*, 44 (1980), 85–91, for analogues to *Le Prestre et la dame* and *Les Trois Meschines*.

14 Bédier, *Fabliaux*, esp. pp. 118–148, 250.

15 For further references to passages indicating oral sources, see Bédier, *Fabliaux*, pp. 127–130. Jean de Condé, author of *Le Pliçon*, remarks that he has often been asked to put "laughs" up in rhyme ("risées à rime mettre," VI, 260).

16 Cf. Anthime Fourrier, *Le Courant réaliste dans le roman courtois en France au moyen-âge*, 1 (Paris, 1960); C. Muscatine, *Chaucer and the French Tradition* (Berkeley, 1957), pp. 41–58; Erich Auerbach, *Mimesis*, trans. W. R. Trask (Princeton, 1953), pp. 131–134; Carla Cremonesi, "Spunti di realismo sociale nella poesia di Chrétien de Troyes," *Studi in honore di Italo Siciliano*, 2 vols. (Firenze, 1966), 1:279–288; Philippe Ménard, *Le Rire et le sourire dans le roman courtois en France au moyen âge (1150–1250)* (Geneva: Droz, 1969); D. H. Green, *Irony in the Medieval Romance* (Cambridge, 1979), esp. pp. 119–131.

17 For editions see Nykrog, *Fabliaux*, pp. 295–296; on classifications see the useful remarks of Togeby, "Les Fabliaux," p. 87.

18 Fifteen are edited by Gustave Cohen et al., *La "Comédie" latine en France au XIIᵉ siècle*, 2 vols. (Paris, 1931). The genre is discussed by Cohen, pp. v–xiv; Edmond Faral, "Le Fabliau latin au moyen âge," *Romania*, 50 (1924), 321–385; F. J. E. Raby, *A History of Secular Latin Poetry in the Middle Ages*, 2 vols. (Oxford, 1934), 2: 54–69, 126–132; Edmond Faral, ed., *De Babione* (Paris, 1948), pp. xxxiii–lxvii; G. Vinay, "La Commedia latina del secolo XII," *Studi Medievali*, N.S. 18 (1952), 209–271; Nykrog, *Fabliaux*, pp. xlviii–lii; Thomas Jay Garbaty, "Pamphilus, De Amore: An Introduction and Translation," *Chaucer Review*, 2: 2 (1967), 108–134; M. M. Brennan, tr. and ed., *Babio: A Twelfth-Century Profane Comedy*, Citadel Monograph Series, 7 (Charleston, 1968), pp. 1–47; Jürgen Beyer, *Schwank und Moral: Untersuchungen zum altfranzösischen Fabliau und verwandten Formen*, Studia Romanica, 16 (Heidelberg: Carl Winter, 1969), chap. 1; Keith Bate, ed., *Three Latin Comedies*, Toronto Medieval Latin Texts, 6 (Toronto, 1976), pp. 1–10; Ian Thomson, "Latin 'Elegiac Comedy' of the Twelfth Century," *Genre*, 9:4 (1976–1977): 329–344; Joachim Suchomski, *"Delectatio" und "Utilitas": Ein Beitrag zum Verständnis mittelalterlicher komischer Literatur*, Bibliotheca Germanica, 18 (Bern: Francke, 1975), pp. 110–157; Joachim Suchomski, ed., *Lateinische Comediae des 12. Jahrhunderts* (Darmstadt: Wissenschaftliche Buchgesellschaft, 1979), pp. 1–26. Full bibliographical

references will be found in *Commedie Latine del XII e XIII Secolo,* Pubblicazioni dell'Istituto di Filologia Classica dell'Università di Genova, nos. 48, 61, 2 vols. (Genoa, 1976–1980).

19 Thus the "snow baby" theme of the fabliau *L'Enfant qui fu remis au soleil* is the same as that of the comedy *Mercator* and of the tenth-century Latin song "Modus Liebinc." On medieval Latin clerical humor see Raby, *Secular Latin Poetry* 2, esp. chaps. 13 and 14; Helen Waddell, *The Wandering Scholars,* 7th ed. (London, 1934); George F. Whicher, trans., *The Goliard Poets,* 2d ed. (New York, 1950); Edwin H. Zeydel, trans., *Vagabond Verse* (Detroit, 1966), pp. 14–43; Beyer, *Schwank und Moral,* chap. 4; Wailes, *"Vagantes,"* pp. 43–58; Peter Dronke, "The Rise of the Medieval Fabliau: Latin and Vernacular Evidence," *Romanische Forschungen,* 85 (1973), 275–297, esp. 279–296; Suchomski, *"Delectatio" und "Utilitas,"* pp. 100–110; and, in a wider context, Peter Dronke, "Profane Elements in Literature," in Robert L. Benson and Giles Constable, eds., *Renaissance and Renewal in the Twelfth Century* (Oxford: Clarendon, 1982), pp. 569–592.

20 On legends see Enrico de' Negri, "The Legendary Style of the Decameron," *Romanic Review,* 43 (1952), 166–189. On sermon realism see G. R. Owst, *Literature and Pulpit in Medieval England,* 2d ed. (Oxford, 1961), and Siegfried Wenzel, "The Joyous Art of Preaching; Or, the Preacher and the Fabliau," *Anglia,* 97 (1979), 304–325.

21 Ensuing references will be to the editions of Roques and of Martin (see n. 4, above) in that order. Commentary: Lucien Foulet, *Le Roman de Renard* (Paris, 1914); John Flinn, *Le Roman de Renart dans la littérature française et dans les littératures étrangères au moyen âge* (Paris, 1963); Jauss, *Untersuchungen,* pp. 178–239.

22 For further comparison see below, chap. 6.

23 Editions: Jakob Ulrich, *Trubert, altfranzösischer Schelmenroman des Douin de Lavesne,* Gesellschaft für romanische Literatur, Band 4 (Dresden, 1904); G. Raynaud de Lage, *Trubert, fabliau du XIIIᵉ siècle* (Geneva: Droz, 1974). See also Luciano Rossi, *"Trubert:* Il trionfo della scortesia e dell'ignoranza. Considerazioni sui *fabliaux* e sulla parodia medievale," *Studi Francesi e Portoghesi 79,* Romanica Vulgaria Quaderni, 1 (L'Aquila: Japadre, 1979), pp. 5–49, esp. 27ff.; Pierre-Yves Badel, *Le Sauvage et le sot: le fabliau de Trubert et la tradition orale* (Paris: Champion, 1979).

24 Ed. I. C. Lecompte, "Richeut, Old French Poem of the Twelfth Century," *Romanic Review,* 4 (1913), 261–305; repr. and trans. by Donald Eugene Ker, "The Twelfth-Century French Poem of Richeut: A Study in History, Form, and Content," Ph.D. diss., Ohio State University,

1976 (Ann Arbor: University Microfilms International), pp. 182–265. On genre, date, and allusions see Ker, "Richeut," pp. 1–92, 175–180; Bédier, *Fabliaux*, pp. 305–309; Lucien Foulet, "Le Poème de *Richeut* et le roman de *Renard*," *Romania*, 42 (1913), 321–330; P. A. Becker, "Von den Erzählern neben und nach Chrétien de Troyes," *Zeitschrift für Romanische Philologie*, 56 (1936) 246–247; Edmond Faral, "Le Conte de Richeut," Bibliothèque de l'Ecole des Hautes Etudes, fasc. 230 (Paris, 1921), pp. 253–270; Alberto Vàrvaro, "Due note su *Richeut*," *Studi Mediolatini e Volgari*, 9 (1961), 227–233.

Because of the likely preexistence of a Richeut cycle, the twelve references to Richeut in other texts cannot be used to date the poem. The one contemporary reference in the poem, to King Henry's great desire for Toulouse (vv. 991–992), depending on which King Henry, might refer to ca. 1159 or to as late as 1242. Ker, "Richeut," pp. 77–93, lists the arguments for the traditional attribution of an early date. In view of the verse-form, and of the elaborateness with which the materials are developed, I favor a late date. Cf. Philippe Ménard, *Les Fabliaux, Contes à rire au moyen âge* (Paris: Presses Universitaires de France, 1983), 226 and n. 3.

25 Ed. Karl Warnke, *Die Fabeln der Marie de France*, Bibliotheca Normannica, 6 (Halle, 1898).

26 Ed. Pierre Nardin, *Jean Bodel: Fabliaux*, 2d ed. (Paris: Nizet, 1965); for the list see *Les Deus Chevaus*, p. 149.

27 Noted at the same time by Nykrog, *Fabliaux*, pp. 100–103, 251–255; by R. C. Johnston and D. D. R. Owen, eds., *Fabliaux* (Oxford: Blackwell, 1957), pp. xiii–xviii; and by T. B. W. Reid, ed., *Twelve Fabliaux* (Manchester: University Press, 1957), pp. x–xii. See also Rychner, "Les Fabliaux," pp. 42–44; Jodogne, "Considérations," 105; Jodogne, *Le Fabliau*, pp. 15–16; Beyer, *Schwank und Moral*, 117–143; Elisabeth Schulze-Busacker, "Proverbes et expressions proverbiales dans les fabliaux," *Marche Romane*, 28: 3–4 (1978), 163–174. Two recent (and I think doubtful) arguments for the derivation of the fabliau from the fable are James L. Taylor, "Animal Tales as Fabliaux," *Reading Medieval Studies*, 3 (1977), 63–77; and Wolfgang Bergerfurth, " 'Des fables fait on les fabliaus': Zum Verhältnis von Fabel und Fablel," in Wolfgang Bergerfurth et al., eds., *Festschrift für Rupprecht Rohr* (Heidelberg: Groos, 1979), 61–73.

28 *Petri Alfonsi Disciplina Clericalis, III: Französische Versbearbeitungen*, ed. Alfons Hilka and Werner Söderhjelm (= Acta Societatis Scientarum Fennicae, Tom. 49, No. 4 [Helsingfors, 1922]), version A, vv. 1141–

1174. For the uses of the term "fabliau" see vv. 1248, 1333, 1449, 1470 (variant).

29 The shortest of the fabliaux is *Le Prestre et le mouton* (VI, 50), which goes as follows: "A priest made love with a lady who was married to a knight. The priest had in his house a sheep that used to butt people. One day the pair was together and the sheep noticed that the priest's head was moving. The animal thought that this was his cue to attack. Unseen, he launched himself from a distance and butted the priest right in his shaved crown. He gave him such a painful blow that his head was dizzy. The lady had no more pleasure, for he could serve her no longer. They had to leave off their business. By this, Haiseau wishes to show us that it's a good idea to stay on the alert." And the author of *Le Prestre comporté* (IV, 40; 1164 verses) repeatedly refers to its unusual length.

30 See Oskar Pilz, *Beiträge zur Kenntnis der altfranzösischen Fabliaux*, 1. *Die Bedeutung des Wortes Fablel*, diss. Marburg (Stettin, 1889); Bédier, *Fabliaux*, pp. 30–31; Nykrog, *Fabliaux*, pp. 9–13; Rychner, "Les Fabliaux," p. 42; Kiesow, *Fabliaux*, chap. 3.

31 Nykrog, *Fabliaux*, pp. 14–15; cf. Ménard, *Fabliaux*, pp. 33–34.

32 In Rychner, "Les Fabliaux," discussion, p. 54: "M. Le Gentil: 'Le lai baigne dans l'optimisme et le merveilleux, tandis que le fabliau prend ses racines dans le réel. A cet égard, le fabliau est l'envers du lai.' " Cf. Jodogne, "Considérations," p. 1054: "Ce qui distingue notre genre, c'est le ton: il est trivial, terre-à-terre, sans portée poétique"; Robert Guiette, "Fabliaux," in his *Questions de littérature*, Romanica Gandensia 8 (Ghent, 1969), p. 70: "Il s'agit d'une oeuvre narrative courte, en vers, . . . mais surtout conçue dans le style réaliste"; Alberto Vàrvaro, "Il Segretain Moine ed il Realismo dei Fabliaux," *Studi Mediolatini e Volgari*, 14 (1966), 213: "Il particolare realismo del *fabliau* . . . non vada tanto cercato nell'attenzione agli individui o alle cose o ai paesaggi . . ., non nello svolgimento di una determinata tematica per se stessa realistica, . . . ma soprattutto nel gusto di situazioni esistenziali, etiche, sociali che non solo . . . hanno precisi riferimenti alla realtà contemporanea ma . . . la subiscono e la celebrano nella dimensione originale e specifica."

CHAPTER II

1 Robert Bossuat, *Manuel bibliographique de la littérature française du moyen âge* (Melun, 1951), with supplements in 1955 and 1961; cf. "The

Bourgeois Tradition," a title now regretted, for chap. 3 of my *Chaucer and the French Tradition* (Berkeley, 1957).

2 Edmond Faral, "Fabliaux," in *Histoire de la littérature française illustrée*, ed. Joseph Bédier and Paul Hazard, 2 vols. (Paris, 1924), I, 61; in rev. ed. by Pierre Martino, 2 vols. (Paris, 1948), I, 80. The importance of this view will be taken up in chap. 6.

3 Leonardo Olschki, *Die romanischen Literaturen des Mittelalters* (Potsdam, 1928), pp. 130–131. L.-F. Flutre, reviewing Nykrog in (*Studia Neophilologica*, 29 (1957), 269, quotes Albert Pauphilet as also critical of the Bédier thesis: " 'On oppose généralement à la littérature aristocratique, représentée par les genres narratifs et lyriques, une prétendue littérature bourgeoise et populaire, en violente réaction contre l'autre et représentée surtout par les fabliaux. C'est une vue beaucoup trop sommaire, et dominée par une opposition de goûts et d'esprit entre peuple et noblesse, qui n'a à peu près existé que dans l'imagination des historiens romantiques' " (from *Histoire de la littérature française*, ed. F. Strowski and G. Moulinier, fasc. 1, *Le Moyen Âge* [Paris, 1937], p. 67).

4 Nykrog, *Fabliaux*, pp. 20–28; Alberto Vàrvaro, "I Fabliaux e la società," *Studi Mediolatini e Volgari*, 8 (1960), 276–282, cites additional evidence for a variety of fabliau audiences.

5 See, for instance, *Rych* 2: 101; *Ren* 5, vi; *Ros*, 80; *Reid*, 51; I, 305; II, 49, 52, 77, 249; III, 42; IV, 137; VI, 91; cf. *Rom Rev* 4: 273.

6 Additional examples will be found in the treatment of picturesque similes in Ménard, *Fabliaux*, pp. 170–171. On similar touches of agricultural imagery in the traditional comparisons used in chanson de geste and romance, see the lists in Ménard, *Rire et Sourire*, pp. 112–113, 587–588. For this imagery in Chaucer, see C. Muscatine, "The Canterbury Tales: Style of the Man and Style of the Work," in *Chaucer and Chaucerians*, ed. D. S. Brewer (London, 1966), pp. 91–92.

7 Cf. also II, 16, 85; III, 83; IV, 161; VI, 92, 154; *Liv*, 188; *Rom* 44: 562.

8 Vàrvaro, "Società," pp. 292–293, makes this point to explain in part the relative paucity of city satire of country bumpkins in the fabliaux.

9 J. Lestocquoy, "L'Origine des habitants d'Arras au XIIᵉ siècle d'après les noms de famille," *Annales de la Fédération Archéologique et Historique de Belgique*, 35ᵉ Congrès (Gembloux, 1953), fasc. 3, p. 160; Jean Schneider, *La Ville de Metz aux XIIIᵉ et XIVᵉ siècles* (Nancy, 1950), p. 336; A. Joris, *La Ville de Huy au moyen âge*, Bibliothèque de la Faculté

de Philosophie et Lettres de l'Université de Liège, fasc. 152 (Paris, 1959), p. 338, and references therein.

10 Typical is Raymond Monier, ed., *Le Livre Roisin, coutumier lillois de la fin du XIIIᵉ siècle*, Documents et Travaux Publiés par la Société d'Histoire du Droit des Pays Flamands, Picards, et Wallons, 2 (Paris and Lille, 1932), p. 18, sec. 15; cf. Schneider, *Metz*, p. 340.

11 Schneider, *Metz*, pp. 339-342; cf. Léopold Genicot, *Le XIIIᵉ Siècle européen*, coll. "Nouvelle Clio," no. 18 (Paris: Presses Universitaires de France, 1968), p. 81.

12 Robert Fossier, *La Terre et les hommes en Picardie jusqu'à la fin du XIIIᵉ siècle*, 2 vols. (Paris and Louvain, Béatrice-Nauwelaerts, 1968), II, 653-654; Guy Fourquin, *Les Campagnes de la région parisienne à la fin du moyen âge*, Publications de la Faculté des Lettres et Sciences Humaines de Paris, Série "Recherches," 10 (Paris: Presses Universitaires de France, 1964), pp. 151-153; Genicot, *XIIIᵉ Siècle*, p. 82.

13 Jean Schneider, *Du Commerce à l'aristocratie terriene, Thiebaut de Heu, citain de Metz (vers 1265-1330)*, Mémoires de l'Académie Nationale de Metz, Vᵉ série, tome 3 (1954-55), pp. 13-90; Marie Ungureanu, *La Bourgeoisie naissante, société et littérature bourgeoises d'Arras aux XIIᵉ et XIIIᵉ siècles*, Mémoires de la Commission des Monuments Historiques du Pas-de-Calais, tome 8 (Arras, 1955), pp. 26, 59-61, 113; cf. Genicot, *XIIIᵉ Siècle*, pp. 69, 106, 127.

14 Ungureanu, *Bourgeoisie*, p. 121; A. Sapori, "Rapport," *IXᵉ Congrès International des Sciences Historiques, Paris, 28 août-3 septembre 1950*, I, *Rapports* (Paris, 1950), pp. 284-285; but cf. the reservations of Genicot, *XIIIᵉ Siècle*, pp. 330-331.

15 Genicot, *XIIIᵉ Siècle*, pp. 73-81. For this and the ensuing discussion of socio-economic conditions I am indebted particularly to Genicot, *XIIIᵉ siècle*, pp. 71-138, 195-212, 323-350; Fossier, *Picardie*, 2: 534-735; and Theodore Evergates, *Feudal Society in the Bailliage of Troyes under the Counts of Champagne, 1152-1284* (Baltimore, 1975).

16 Vàrvaro, "Società," pp. 293-297; cf. Nykrog, *Fabliaux*, pp. 94, 97, 104, 106-139 (esp. 109, 117, 119). Vàrvaro cites the prevalence of type-characterization in the fabliaux as further evidence of the acceptability of crystallized social attitudes among all classes.

17 See Genicot, *XIIIᵉ siècle*, p. 87; Fossier, *Picardie*, 1: 388-389; 2: 639, 647, 653-654, 723.

18 See Georges Duby, "Une Enquête à poursuivre: La Noblesse dans la France médiévale," *Revue Historique*, 226 (1961), 18.

19 Ménard, *Fabliaux,* p. 46, gives a summary and bibliography of this activity, to which his chap. 2 is a contribution; see also Marie-Thérèse Lorcin, *Façons de sentir et de penser: Les Fabliaux français* (Paris, 1979), which contains a substantial inventory of fabliau attitudes as well.

20 Of the period generally, Jacques Le Goff remarks: "La *superbia,* l'orgueil, péché féodal par excellence, jusque-là considéré comme la mère de tous les vices, commence à céder cette primauté à l'*avaritia,* le désir de l'argent." *(La Civilisation de l'occident médiéval* [Paris: Arthaud, 1967], p. 313); cf. Genicot, *XIIIe siècle,* pp. 110–111; Jacques Toussaert, *Le Sentiment religieux en Flandre à la fin du moyen âge* (Paris: Plon, 1963), pp. 412–413; Lester K. Little, "Pride Goes before Avarice: Social Change and the Vices in Latin Christendom," *American Historical Review,* 76 (1971), 16–49. Of Picardy, in the middle of fabliau territory, Fossier writes: "La réorganisation des fortunes marque le milieu du XIIIe siècle comme elle l'avait déjà fait du XIe. Il s'était agi alors de substituer aux notions dépassées de la richesse en hommes, mal répartis sur les sols gaspillés, celle d'une efficacité technique et d'une meilleure répartition de revenus. On va plus loin au XIIIe siècle, lorsque le souci du profit financier devient prépondérant dans la société rurale, du chevalier qui veut tenir son rang, au pauvre hère qui espère sortir de sa misère et ne se résigne plus au rôle passif de ses ancêtres" *(Picardie,* 2: 598); "Le monde paysan s'ouvre désormais tout grand sur les nouveautés techniques, le commerce, les échanges mentaux. On ne peut donc plus classer les hommes selon les critères anciens. . . ; en 1200 et surtout après 1250, les hommes sont estimés davantage selon leur revenus que selon leur familles, selon leur poids économique que leur rôle politique" (2: 727; cf. 613, 706, 728).

CHAPTER III

1 Thomas D. Cooke, *The Old French and Chaucerian Fabliaux: A Study of Their Comic Climax* (Columbia, Mo., and London: University of Missouri Press, 1978), p. 13. The climax, says Professor Cooke, "consists of two elements: it comes as a surprise, and yet it has been carefully prepared for in such a way that when it comes, it is seen as artistically fitting and appropriate." However, he limits his attention to the artistically best fabliaux: "I mean only to suggest the ideal, which not all fabliaux fully achieve and which some fall quite short of" (p. 16). A "structuralist" analysis of fabliau action is offered by Roy J. Pearcy, "Investigations

into the Principles of Fabliau Structure," *Genre*, 9 (1976), 345–378; and Mary Jane Schenck, "The Morphology of the Fabliau," *Fabula*, 17 (1976), 26–39, presents a "functional analysis," along the lines of Vladimir Propp's *Morphology of the Folk Tale*. Nykrog, *Fabliaux*, 52–66, does not take up plot structure, but rather classifies fabliau plots by theme: erotic and non-erotic, the former divided into groups and subgroups according to the cast of characters and the outcome of the action. A sustained treatment of fabliau narrative technique that pays due attention to its defects is that of Roger Dubuis, *Les Cent Nouvelles Nouvelles et la tradition de la nouvelle en France au moyen âge* (Grenoble: Presses Universitaires, 1973), pp. 247–264. Ménard, *Fabliaux*, pp. 37–45, offers comments on narrative art with emphasis on plot preparation, surprise, and successful denouement.

2 On transmission from memory, see Rychner, *Contribution*, 1: 141–142.

3 See, e.g., *Le Prestre qui manja mores II* (V, 39); *Le Prestre comporté* (IV, 15–16, 32–33, 39–40); and *Le Vilain au buffet* (III, 205–206).

4 I, 107; the second and third lines, which contribute to the slackness of the narrative, are omitted in the other copy of the poem.

5 See Jodogne, "Considérations," p. 1052; Cooke, *Old French and Chaucerian Fabliaux*, pp. 134–135. The authors of *Les Putains et les lecheors* and *Le Vallet qui d'aise a malaise se met* call their works fabliaux (III, 177; II, 169); both are accepted by all authorities. The *NRCF* banishes from the canon *La Veuve* and *Le Roy d'Angleterre et le jongleur d'Ely*; see van den Boogaard, *"NRCF,"* p. 345, n. 17.

6 See above, chap. 1, n. 32; and Bédier, *Fabliaux*, chap. 11.

7 Nykrog, *Fabliaux*, pp. 231–234, raises the question.

8 *Rhetorica ad Herennium*, IV.10, ed. and trans. Harry Caplan (Cambridge: Harvard University Press, 1954), pp. 252–253.

9 *Ad Herennium*, IV.14: "id quod ad infimum et cotidianum sermonem demissum est." It is clear that not only the choice of words is meant, but also arrangement and figures. Cf. the repetition of the idea of arrangement in IV.15: "Erant enim et adtenuata verborum constructio quaedam et item alia in gravitate, alia posita in mediocritate," and IV.16: "Omne genus orationis, et grave et mediocre, et adtenuatum, dignitate adficiunt exornationes. . . ."

10 Ed. Edmond Faral, *Les Arts poétiques du XIIe et du XIIIe siècle* (Paris: Champion, 1924), p. 312. The expansion of the definition of style to include "persons and things" is apparently due in part to the influence of Horace's *Art of Poetry*. Cf. *Documentum*, 2: 138: "Notandum quod quando materiam prosequimur, observandae sunt proprietates person-

arum et rerum quae describuntur, et immorandum est in assignatione illarum proprietatum quae convenienter attribuuntur personis et rebus de quibus incidit sermo," with examples from Horace (Faral, *Arts poétiques*, pp. 310–311). Faral (p. 86) traces this expansion back to as early as a commentary on Horace dating from before the eleventh century.

11 *The Parisiana Poetria of John of Garland*, ed. and trans. Traugott Lawler (New Haven and London: Yale University Press, 1974) 5: 46–48, 78–79, 84–85 (pp. 86–89). Lawler rightly remarks (p. 252) that it is hard to tell just why John prefers one example to the other, suggesting that presumably *testiculos* was too direct. Faral, however (*Arts poétiques*, pp. 88–89), italicizes the word in this passage as one characteristic of the style.

12 Geoffrey of Vinsauf, *Poetria Nova* (ca. 1210), ed. Faral, *Arts poétiques*, vv. 1883–1187 (p. 255). Cf. *Documentum*, 2: 164 (Faral, *Arts poétiques*, p. 317). Nykrog (*Fabliaux*, pp. 142–143) makes the same point.

13 Cf. also the density of physical detail in *Le Vilain de Farbu (Nar*, 69ff.); *Estormi* (I, 208–209); *Le Prestre teint (Liv*, 258); *Les Perdris* (I, 190); *Gombert et les deus clers (Nar*, 90). For tests largely devoted to extensive listing of the things of the fabliau world, see *Le Dit des marcheans* and *L'Oustillement au villain*, not fabliaux, but printed by Montaiglon and Raynaud, II, 123–129, 143–156. Paul Theiner, "Fabliau Settings," in Cooke and Honeycutt, *Humor*, pp. 119–136, emphasizes the elements of generality, economy, and strict functionalism in fabliau settings, in my judgment much too severely.

14 *Liv*, 174; cf. the trousseau in *Dame Jouenne, Rom* 45: 102–103, and the list of the youth's clothes in *Le Vallet qui d'aise a malaise se met* (II, 164–165).

15 On the formal portrait (*effictio*) in medieval literature, see Faral, *Arts poétiques*, pp. 75–81; Alice M. Colby, *The Portrait in Twelfth-Century French Literature* (Geneva: Droz, 1965); Claes Schaar, *The Golden Mirror* (Lund: Gleerup, 1967), pp. 167–367.

16 Nykrog, *Fabliaux*, pp. 72–85.

17 See, for instance, the descriptions of the hunchback in *Les Trois Boçus* (I, 14); the squint-eyed, club-footed peasant Berengier in *Aloul* (I, 278); the tousled peasant Raoul in *Le Vilain au buffet* (III, 202); the wrinkled old mistress in *Le Prestre pelé (Rom* 55: 546); cf. the exhausted young husband in *Le Vallet aus douze fames* (III, 188).

18 See, respectively, *sa mere voit / Qui li cligne c'outre passast (Reid*, 17; cf. V, 60); *Par la treillie le porlingne, / Felonessement le rechingne* (I, 205); *l'esgarde a estal / Li clers, si c'autre part ne cille (Nar*, 85); *la chiere morte*

(*JO,* 53); *Si enbroncha un poi la chire* (*JO,* 60); *Lors a l'un l'autre regardé* (*JO,* 64); *Bien voit qu'il estoit corouciez;* / *Ses bras li a au col ploiez (Ros,* 79); *Le prestres l'acole, si rist (Ros,* 88); *Ele lo prant entre ses braz:* / *"Sire," fait ele, "ne vos chaille"* (IV, 164); *Si s'entreprendent par les dois (Liv,* 143); *Si l'avoit saisi par la main,* / *A conseil le tret d'une part* (V, 111); *A pris son oste par le doit,* / *Si l'a fet delez lui assir (Goug.* 7–8); *Se degratoit delez son feu* (III, 46); *Gratant son cul* (II, 64); *Grate sa teste de paour* (II, 65).

19 See, e.g., dialogue-in-monologue, a courtly method of expressing mental conflict, in the predominantly courtly *Guillaume au faucon (Reid,* 86); cf. *Le Lai d'Aristote (Reid,* 74–75).

20 The language of sex and of the body is taken up in detail in chap. 5, below. For the rest, some examples are I, 75, 98–105, 186–187; II, 169, 185–186, 196; III, 59–64, 238–243; IV, 50; V, 49, 62–63, 202; *Ros,* 106; *Rom* 34: 283; *Rom* 45: 106; *Béd,* 345. *Les Trois Dames de Paris* is a compendium of tavern-talk; *Saint Pierre et le jongleur* is one of dicing terms.

21 See Bédier, *Fabliaux,* pp. 347–357; Nykrog, *Fabliaux,* pp. 144–165; cf. Dubuis, *Cent Nouvelles,* pp. 266–268; Ménard, *Fabliaux,* pp. 217–219.

22 Bédier, *Fabliaux,* p. 351; Vàrvaro, "Segretain Moine," esp. pp. 207–210.

CHAPTER IV

1 Cf. Ménard, *Fabliaux,* p. 140: "Une libération de l'instinct et une évidente morale du plaisir se rencontrèrent partout ici." Ménard's is one of the most detailed and accurate modern treatments of fabliau morality; see esp. pp. 121–142. Cf. Beyer, *Schwank und Moral,* pp. 130–157.

2 On descriptions of eating in medieval literature, and on the comparatively greater emphasis on eating in the fabliau than in the romance, see Grégoire Lozinski, ed., *La Bataille de Caresme et de Charnage,* Bibliothèque de l'École des Hautes Etudes, sciences historiques et philologiques, fasc. 262 (Paris, 1933), esp. p. 78. Ménard, *Fabliaux,* pp. 65–72, 215–216, makes valuable observations on fabliau food and wine.

3 Cf. also *Dame Jouenne,* ed. A. Långfors, *Rom* 45: 103, 105.

4 Cf. also II, 10, 16, 44; III, 112, 139–140; IV, 138; VI, 179; *Reid* 63, 93; *Liv,* 265–267; *Nar,* 86; and the tavern scenes in IV, 21, 28; *Goug,* 3, 4; *Nar,* 71.

5 Cf. also *Baillet, JO,* 28.

6 For references to mead and beer, see *Liv,* 149–196; *Nar,* 69, 71; cf.
   P. Pfeffer, *Beiträge zur Kenntnis des altfranzösischen Volkslebens, meist auf
   Grund der Fabliaux,* 3 (Karlsruhe, 1901), 31–33.

7 For coins, see II, 14, 17; *WG,* 31–32; V, 220; cf. also Urban T. Holmes,
   Jr., "Notes on the French Fabliaux," in *Festschrift for John Kunstmann,*
   University of North Carolina Studies in Language and Literature, 26
   (Chapel Hill, 1959), pp. 39–44. For rewards and payments: *Rych,* 2:
   107; *JO,* 26; I, 118, 197, 100; V, 117, 210; *Liv,* 180. Other sums:
   I, 310–316; II, 10, 14, 58–59, 164–165; V, 112; VI, 2; *JO,* 32;
   Reid, 32.

8 Ed. A. Långfors, *CFMA,* 2d ed. (Paris, 1957), pp. 19–21. Bédier includes this work in the fabliau canon; Nykrog (*Fabliaux,* p. 15) does
   not, nor does *NCRF.*

9 Wit, *engin,* is very much at home in the fabliau, but of course it is not
   exclusive fabliau property. It appears intermittently in romance, where
   it sometimes underlines romantic values by acting as a device to improve
   or educate its victim. But mostly it is an ethical embarrassment. See
   particularly Robert W. Hanning's complex dealing with the problems
   raised by *engin* in romance in *The Individual in Twelfth-Century Romance*
   (New Haven and London: Yale University Press, 1977), pp. 105–138.
   Though Hanning denies that the weight of *engin* in such a romance as
   Ipomedon has a burlesque or satirical result, his argument makes clear
   that the elements of "rational awareness and analysis" behind *engin* (p.
   123), its exposure of "intractable realities" (p. 135), submit chivalry
   and idealistic love to ironic exposure.

10 This is one conclusion of the analysis of plots made by Schenck, "Morphology": "Resolution does not occur in many fabliaux and when it
   does, it provides an end to the conflict, but not necessarily a just so-
   lution"; "these tales reflect a world where immediate retributory justice
   is administered by the injured party, and where the most clever person, not the good one wins" (pp. 37–38). Cf. also Pearcy, "Investigations," p. 373: "Conformity to the dictates of a traditional Christian
   morality is a variable in the fabliaux. Its services may be enlisted to
   sharpen the comic denouement by certain authors, but it may as
   readily be left in abeyance, or its contravention may be deliberately
   flaunted."

11 There exists, however, a reading of the poem as a comic-religious allegory
   of the scourging of a corrupt priest: Howard Helsinger, "Pearls in the
   Swill: Comic Allegory in the French Fabliaux," Cooke and Honeycutt,
   Humor, pp. 98–103.

12 A rare exception is the priest in *Le Vescie a prestre*. There is a brief characterization of an ideal vicar in *Un Chivalier et sa dame et un clerk* (II, 216–217).

13 Cf. Jodogne, *Le Fabliau*, pp. 19–20, where forty-seven whole fabliaux or major episodes are classified by central motif under Words ("Paroles") rather than under Action ("Actes").

14 Modestly anti-establishment is also *La Vieille qui oint la palme au chevalier*.

15 Other fabliaux turning importantly on misunderstood reference: *Le Clerc qui fu repus derriere l'escrin; Estula; Le Sot chevalier*.

16 For pieces turning on deliberate double meanings of various sorts, see *Le Sentier battu; La Dame qui se venja du chevalier; La Saineresse; Le Vilain au buffet*. For sexual puns, conscious euphemisms, and other forms of wordplay, see *La Grue, Le Heron, La Saineresse*, and the many examples given in Chapters 2 and 5.

17 The case for an actual tradition of this sort is made by Glending Olson, "The Medieval Theory of Literature for Refreshment and Its Use in the Fabliau Tradition," *Studies in Philology*, 62 (1974), 291–313. Most of the following passages from the fabliaux are noted by Bédier, *Fabliaux*, pp. 304–316, and by Olson: I, 70; II, 24, 114; III, 137, 144; IV, 199; V, 157; VI, 24, 68, 198, 260. As Bédier observes, *L'Espervier* (V, 43) and *Le Vilain au buffet* (III, 199) announce a didactic purpose; *La Dame qui se venja du chevalier* (VI, 24) gives fabliaux both purposes: "Les plusors por essample prendre, / Et les plusours por les risées."

18 See Schulze-Busacker, "Proverbes," p. 164. The overt morality of the fabliaux is discussed exhaustively by Beyer, *Schwank und Moral*, chap. 6. Suchomski, *"Delectatio" und "Utilitas"* is focused mainly on theory of comedy and on examples of the moral function of comedy from medieval Latin and German literature.

19 Nykrog (*Fabliaux*, p. 15) excludes *La Housse partie* and *La Bourse pleine de sens*; Jodogne, *Le Fabliau*, p. 18, restores the latter; NRCF restores both.

20 See the discussion of *Cele qui se fist foutre* in Chapter 1, and those of *Les Trois Boçus, Les Trois Aveugles*, and *Barat et Haimet* above in the present chapter.

21 Schulze-Busacker, "Proverbes," p. 173: "Dans la plupart des cas où un proverbe forme le point de départ ou la conclusion d'un récit, il formule une expérience humaine trop générale qui ne contient pas assez d'éléments spécifiques pour que le fabliau puisse être construit à partir de ces éléments." For morals appended to one MS that do not appear in others,

cf. e.g. MS. F of *Auberee* (*NRCF*, 1: 292); MS. B of *La Male Honte* (*Rych*, 2: 27); MS. C of *La Borgoise d'Orliens* (*Rych*, 2: 98); MS. P of *Boivin de Provins* (*Rych*, 2: 119). Carter Revard has made an interesting study ("Fabliaux as Moral Tales: Some Pre-Chaucerian Instances," [unpublished]) of the diverging moralizations of the two MS versions of *Les Trois Dames qui troverent un vit* and of two of the MSS of *Les Quatre Sohais Saint Martin*.

22 Cf. on the moral as defense, Suchomski, *"Delectatio" und "Utilitas,"* p. 168; Beyer, *Schwank und Moral*, p. 121. On the moral used ironically or parodically, idem, pp. 150–153; Nykrog, *Fabliaux*, pp. 101–102. On rhetorical use of sententious material, see the summary by Faral, *Arts poétiques*, pp. 58–59; Nykrog, *Fabliaux*, pp. 102–103. It should be noted, too, that rhetorical teaching urged that the sententious expression rise above the immediate material and be given a form more general and abstract. See Geoffrey of Vinsauf, *Poetria Nova*, vv. 126–133 (Faral, *Arts poétiques*, p. 201).

23 See I, 329: "Faites à mesure et à point, / Quant verrez lieu et tens et point"; II, 256: "Qy par mesure tote ryen fra / Ja prudhome ne l'y blamera"; VI, 31: "cil qui preuz sunt et courtois / I gaaignent sovent ces drois, / Car grant sens gist en cortoisie."

24 See *Liv*, 146: "Que Damerdex celui maudie / Qui assés a et trop golose"; I, 23: "Honiz soit li hons, quels qu'il soit, / Qui trop prise mauvès deniers, / Et qui les fist fère premiers." For anticlerical morals see, for instance, I, 218; *Liv*, 231. On the power of money, see I, 22–23: "Diex ne fist si chier avoir / . . . Que por deniers ne soit éus"; VI, 53: "Tant as, tant vaus, et je tant t'aim."

25 See, respectively, II, 169–170; IV, 149 (cf. VI, 151); V, 36; *Reid*, 97; *JO*, 5; *Warnke*, 306; V, 108 (cf. V, 46); I, 317 (cf. III, 207–208); III, 263; V, 155, 156; VI, 45, 47; *Nar*, 93; *Reid*, 33; cf. above, p. 33.

26 See, respectively, *Nar*, 84; II, 240–241; I, 254 (cf. also III, 198; VI, 33; I, 171, 292).

27 See, respectively, III, 226 (cf. IV, 211); IV, 127 (cf. II, 74); I, 167 (cf. IV, 119; II, 87); III, 245.

28 Edmond Faral, *La Vie quotidienne au temps de Saint Louis* (Paris: Hachette, 1938), p. 266; cf. Vàrvaro, "Segretain moine," p. 212: "qui si tratta non soltanto di una generica intuizione della situazione umana nella sua permanente instabilità, quanto della traduzione di uno specifico modo di essere, legato ad un costume sociale, a tempi ed a luoghi precisi."

CHAPTER V

1 Bédier, *Fabliaux,* pp. 325–326; Nykrog, *Fabliaux,* pp. 208–226. Passing treatment of the subject appears in Bruno Barth, *Liebe und Ehe im altfranzösischen Fablel und in der mittelhochdeutschen Novelle, Palaestra* 97 (1910), esp. pp. 137–148, 190–194.

2 Beyer, *Schwank und Moral,* pp. 105, 109, 110–111. He gives a summary of his views in "The Morality of the Amoral," in Cooke and Honeycutt, *Humor,* pp. 15–42.

3 Wolf-Dieter Stempel, "Mittelalterlicher Obszönität als literarästhetisches Problem," in H. R. Jauss, ed., *Die nicht mehr schönen Künste,* Poetik und Hermeneutik, 3 (Munich, 1968), pp. 187–205. Essentially the same position is taken in the unpublished dissertation of Gérard Marie Burger, "Le Theme de l'obscenité dans la littérature française des douzième et treizième siècles" (Stanford, 1973), pp. 154–249.

4 Ménard, *Fabliaux,* pp. 214–215; see, in general, pp. 143–165.

5 On the cultural relativity of obscenity, see the brief but excellent article by Weston La Barre, "Obscenity: An Anthropological Appraisal," *Law and Contemporary Problems,* 20, no. 4 (Autumn, 1955, entitled *Obscenity and the Arts),* 533–543.

6 See I, 234, 243, 290; II, 20, 21, 81, 82, 84; III, 55, 56, 68, 69, 75, 81–82, 120, 243, 245; IV, 148, 159, 199, 206; V, 24, 61, 92 (noun) 139, 153 (noun), 154 (noun), 156 *(desfoutue),* 156, 177, 178, 181, 182, 208; VI, 148, 150; *Ros,* 99, 100, 103, 104; *Rych,* 2: 69I; *Liv,* 191; .*W.* (see list of fabliaux). Cf. also *foteor* ("fucker" or professional fornicator) used passim in the fabliau of the same name. This number of uses is considerably larger than that reported by Nykrog, *Nyk,* pp. 210–211.

7 *Justicier:* II, 68; *adouber: Ros,* 105n.; *despuceler, tolir le pucelage:* II, 68; *percier: Liv,* 188; *poindre:* V, 88; *boter:* V, 93; *ferir et heurter:* III, 56; VI, 149; *doner, geter les cops le roi:* II, 189; V, 209; *de la crupe:* I, 257; VI, 150; *doner de la corgie: Rom* 62: 5; *ferir des cops:* I, 291; *des maus: Liv,* 182; *(de)marteler:* I, 236, 292; *assaillir:* I, 242; *Nar,* 90; *faire assaut:* II, 16; III, 187; *estour:* II, 190; *conbatre: Liv,* 190; *purfendre sa banere: Rych,* 2: 69M; *chevauchier en loge:* III, 65; *remonter . . . sans frain et sans sele: Rom* 62: 5; *estraindre l'ive: Liv,* 180.

8 *Connins que li fuirons chace:* II, 239–240; *escuiruel:* V, 104–107; *faire Moriax avoir de l'avainne:* I, 320–329; *Le poulain pestre et abevrer:* III, 83–84; *porcelet:* IV, 144–146; *le deerrain mès:* I, 314; *avoir du bacon:* I,

201; V, 92; *faire en rost: Reid,* 41; *aletier:* V, 114; *estre brochie:* I, 235; *courtil semer:* VI, 154; *vous morrés qant jou porrai* (with double meaning?): II, 32; *rebiner sun guaret: Rom* 26: 90; cf. I, 291; *tondre: Ros,* 104n.; *fouler la vendenge:* VI, 150; *prendre le warnehot: Liv,* 221; *se metre es limons, etre boen limonier:* III, 269; *euvre le porte:* VI, 148, 149; *tabourer au tabour:* VI, 147, 149; *croistre (croissir) noiz:* VI, 25, 29, 30; *croistre* (noun), *con crossue: Rom* 26: 89–90; *aprendre la medecine:* I, 258; *garir des maus:* VI, 264; cf. I, 290–292; V, 181–182; *fourbir l'anel: JO,* 28; *mesurer la longhece:* VI, 268; *aforer son tonel: Nar,* 92; *forgier:* IV, 331; *etre vertoillie:* I, 235; *avoir ointes ses valieres:* IV, 137; *retoucher d'un fuisil: Ros,* 103.

9   *Corber:* V, 92, 208; *Ros,* 102–105; *(r)embroncher:* V, 208, 209; *retorner:* I, 313; V, 31; *movoir les rains:* III, 189; *Liv,* 180; *culoner:* III, 240; *culeter:* III, 81; *Liv,* 189; cf. n. 4, above; *apouchier le vit au con:* III, 49; *embatre el con le vit:* III, 121; IV, 209; *entrer entre les cuisses . . . el ventre:* II, 239; cf. also V, 61, 153–156; II, 195; *Reid,* 42.

10   *Liv,* 154, 177; see also Livingston's notes, pp. 295–296, 305–306.

11   *Faire li giu (d'amours):* I, 121; II, 38; III, 282; IV, 48, 137; *faire (avoir) delit (plaisir, deduit,* etc.): I, 200, 242, 246, 297, 298, 314; II, 14, 68; III, 37, 188, 189, 195, 248, 250, 278; VI, 259; *faire talent (volonté,* etc.): I, 182, 294, 298; II, 39, 232; III, 268; *coucher (gesir) o:* I, 162; II, 37, 38, 42; *faire son bel:* II, 41; *ne vous quier fere menssion:* III, 37; cf. IV, 122. See *Nyk,* pp. 73–74, 209; Beyer, *Schwank und Moral,* p. 104; Pearcy, "Obscene Diction," pp. 166–167; Barth, *Liebe und Ehe,* pp. 139–140.

12   See, in order, *servir:* I, 294, 295, 300; II, 232; *le faire:* I, 186; II, 39; V, 120; *faire la besoingne:* I, 235, 320; II, 240; III, 193 (with emphasis on circumlocution); V, 133; VI, 252; *Nar,* 101; cf. *Reid,* 62; *faire mestier:* II, 189; V, 92 *(amouroux,* I, 320); *estre en (faire) oevre:* I, 260; VI, 50, 264; *Liv,* 180; *faire l'ome:* IV, 158; *faire ses boins:* II, 68; III, 237; V, 91; *faire la folie:* I, 240; *Rom,* 34: 282; *adeser de sen rien: Liv,* 155; *rafetier:* I, 260; III, 237; VI, 6; *aasier:* I, 258, 259; IV, 116; *faire ce por quoi assanblé i sont:* V, 14; *la char jumele:* III, 71; *faire icele cose / Que femme aimme sor toute cose:* III, 56; *avoir rente:* I, 322 (cf. I, 295).

13   See III, 74; IV, 130; V, 204–207; VI, 90–92; *Nar,* 107; *Liv,* 189. On the relatively high degree of tabooness of "prick" and "cock" among modern college students, see Timothy B. Jay, "Doing Research with Dirty Words," *Maledicta* 1 (1977), 234–256, esp. table i, p. 247.

14   See, for instance, II, 195; III, 69, 72; IV, 128 *(gros et plener),* 131; V, 32, 181, 208; *Nar,* 103. A small list of shapes and sizes is mentioned

in *Les Quatre Sohais Saint Martin* (V, 204–205). Cf. also III, 52 *(ses braies vont derompant . . . li traïne à terre);* III, 74 *(dur et chaut);* III, 74 *(fier);* III, 83 *(fier);* IV, 205 *(engorgié et roide).* The converse property is mentioned in III, 69 *(mol, vain);* V, 205 *(mol come pelice);* and to three peasants is attributed a *vit . . . noir* (IV, 161; VI, 90–92; *Ros,* 104n.).

15 Respectively, IV, 161; III, 83; I, 236 (also IV, 205); I, 235; V, 30; II, 85; II, 16.

16 *Rien:* IV, 144, 145; III, 73; V, 102; *Liv,* 155; *chose:* I, 119; IV, 130, 131; V, 34; *membre:* I, 233; III, 51–52; *ostil:* I, 232–233, 235; III, 71. Cf. also *genetaires:* I, 282; *chil . . . qui entre les jambes me pent: Rom* 44: 561; *pendeloche:* III, 70; V, 103; *couple:* I, 267, 277; *harnas: Liv,* 195.

17 *Tuiel:* I, 292; *bon bordoun:* II, 195; *espis:* III, 249 (pun); *racine(z):* I, 234, 257; V, 181; *borlivet: Liv,* 154, 296n.; *cornuz:* V, 205; *cheval:* IV, 205; *poulain:* III, 83; V, 30; *Bauçant: Liv,* 180; *baudoin:* VI, 22; *Liv,* 268; see n. 8 above.

18 *Relyke:* IV, 132; *fuisil: Ros,* 103; *pasnaisse: Liv,* 188; *andoille:* I, 282; III, 47; *Liv,* 190, 194; *chaudun:* I, 282; *longaigne de boiel* ("latrine-sausage"?): III, 70; *loche:* V, 103; *plonjon:* V, 103; *cis lechieres, ses damoisiaus reveleus: Rom* 44: 560; *de nostre porte le verrous:* IV, 131; V, 35 *(le toraill).*

19 Their contributions may be identified in the notes above by the pagination: *L'Esquiriel* in V, 101–108; *Le Pescheor* in III, 68–75; Gautier in *Liv.* Livingston's notes, esp. pp. 296, 305–306, 332, and the references therein, are particularly useful on obscene terms in Old French.

20 *Coilles* is evidently a less taboo word than *vit.* However, we find fewer instances of its direct use—I have come across it in only seventeen fabliaux—most likely because it figures somewhat less frequently in fabliau plots. *Pendans:* I, 197; *couple* (?): I, 267, 277; *hernois:* VI, 91; *afère:* I, 264, 279; *granz, enflées, velues:* I, 266; III, 83; VI, 92 *(comme piau d'orce);* VI, 155; *sac, sachet:* III, 83, 84 *(à l'avaine);* V, 30; VI, 93 *(à charbonnier);* *borce:* VI, 92, 155; *Liv,* 231; *fol: Nar,* 103; *grenotes:* VI, 114; *mailliaus, maus:* I, 232; *Liv,* 182; *sone deus cloches* (?): II, 240; *luisiaus:* V, 30; *oes:* V, 105, 107; *cuene:* VI, 155; *roignons: Liv,* 231; *jumaus:* V, 31; *mareschal:* IV, 205; V, 30.

21 Erection is described as follows: *se lever: Rom* 44: 561; *estre à roit, aroidier:* I, 232, 233, 235; V, 104; *croistre:* III, 51, 52; *tendre:* III, 52, 71, 184; *Rom* 44: 560; *Nar,* 106; *arecier:* V, 61; *contremont ercier: Liv,* 195; *drecier:* VI, 22; *Liv,* 268; *estare: Liv,* 156, 188; cf. n. 14 above. The only

reference to ejaculation as a single word that I have found is *parpillier* (IV, 161); otherwise it is described as the production of semen, variously *sève* ("sap, juice"): I, 232; *oignement:* I, 292; V, 182; *provande* ("feed"): I, 326; *la mole des os* ("marrow"): I, 326; *aubun* ("egg-white"): V, 107; and, in a particularly unpleasant analogy in the allegory of the squirrel:

> Si commence à plorer de duel
> Et puis après a escopi,
> Et a vouchié et a vomi.
> Tant a vouchié le fol, le glout,
> Que cele senti le degout
> Aval ses nages degouter.   [V, 107]

[It began to weep from sadness, then afterwards it spit, and threw up and vomited. It threw up so much, the greedy fool, that she felt it running down her buttocks.]

22 On the tabooness of the modern terms, see Jay, "Research," p. 247. On relative tabooness of *vit* and *con* to women, Nykrog *(Nyk,* p. 211) cites *Porcelet:* "metomes non / A vostre rien et à mon con" (IV, 144) and *Le Fevre de Creil:* "à ton ostil / Fai mon con besier" (I, 235). Cf. also *Le Fol vilain:* "men con . . . sen rien" (vv. 255, 266 in *Liv,* 155), and *L'Esquiriel,* where Robin, after using elaborate synonyms for his own parts, refers matter-of-factly to "vostre con" (V, 106). Cf. n. 13, above.

23 *Ostil: Liv,* 158, 195; *pertuis:* II, 239; IV, 146; V, 28 *(desoz lo ventre); ventre:* V, 156; *entrée: Ros,* 104; *porte:* VI, 148, 149; *sentier batu:* III, 249; *anel: Jo,* 28; *Liv,* 177; *vallée, valieres: Rych,* 2: 69; IV, 137; *plaies:* I, 292; cf. V, 180; *fontaine, fontenele:* III, 84; IV, 204; V, 29; *por . . . englotir: Liv,* 194; *gloton: Liv,* 180; cf. V, 114; *porcelez, pors:* IV, 144, 146 *(engoisseus); Golïas* (from *goulu*): *Liv,* 177, 179; *là où le mal aus dames tient:* V, 209; cf. *une goute . . . rains:* IV, 7; *mals ès rains:* I, 293.

24 *Tesniere, tesniere de connin: Ren* V, vi; II, 239–240; *Connebert: Liv,* 157, 189, 205, 227; *Morel:* I, 320–329; cf. *le peleus: Rom* 44: 560. Catalogues: V, 206; *Rom* 44: 562.

25 *Reid,* p. 97. The pun, not remarked upon by Reid or by Nykrog, is discussed by Jodogne, "Considérations," pp. 1044–1045.

26 V, 206; *Rych,* 2: 176–177; the pun is recognized by Robert Harrison in his remarkable translation, *Gallic Salt* (Berkeley: University of California Press, 1974), p. 187. Cf. *descouneüe* in *Rom* 44: 561.

27 *Liv,* 157, 158, 190, 194, 221. In this connection one is permitted to suspect a play on *contesse* in *Le Chevalier qui fit parler les cons,* especially in such a sequence as "Que vos iroie plus *con*tant / Ne longues paroles *con*tant? / La *con*tesse . . ." (*Rych,* 2: 73)

28 For instance, if, as Nykrog's examples suggest, the pun *vis/vit* is licit, it probably also operates in *Tant par avés torblé le vis (Liv,* 179; cf. 307, n. 401; and the same expression used without punning in IV, 79) and in *La bouche li baise et le vis* (III, 282). A. P. Lian, "Aspects of Verbal Humour in the Old French Fabliaux," Australasian Universities Language and Literature Association, Proceedings and Papers of the Twelfth Congress, ed. A. P. Treweek, 1969, pp. 252–253, plausibly suggests a pun on *vit/vie* in *L'Esquiriel* (V, 103): *"Vit me doinst Dieus. . . ."* A certain emphasis makes evident a sexual double entendre on the terms for plowing, seeding, threshing, and winnowing in V, 26.

29 The best examples are *La Borgoise d'Orliens, L'Enfant qui fu remis au soleil, Le Chevalier a la corbeille, Un Chivalier et sa dame et un clerk, Le Chevalier a la robe vermeille, Le Vallet aus douze fames, Les Braies au cordelier, Le Clerc qui fu repus, La Dame qui fist batre son mari, Auberee, Le Sacristain I, Le Vilain qui vit un autre home, La Nonete II,* and *La Dame qui fist trois tors,* in which Rutebeuf almost disqualifies himself from the list by calling so much attention to the need for euphemism (III, 193). The courtly *Guillaume au faucon* is disqualified by its obscene pun, other verbally polite texts by various other infringements of taste, as sadism in *Les Tresces,* and the subject matter in *Une Seule Fame qui a son con servoit cent chevaliers.*

30 See, for instance, Jeffrey Henderson, *The Maculate Muse: Obscene Language in Attic Comedy* (New Haven and London: Yale University Press, 1975), chaps. 4–7; J. N. Adams, *The Latin Sexual Vocabulary* (London: Duckworth, 1982).

31 See, for instance, I, 248: *les hanches et les costéz blans . . . blanc col . . . blanche gorge;* III, 235; II, 11: *la pucelete / Cui primes point la mamelete / Enmi le piz com une pomme;* II, 19, 48; III, 83; V, 28; VI, 72.

32 Cf. II, 41: *grasse, tenre et biele;* III, 37: *crasse, et blanche et tendre;* and the somewhat more satirical instances of the maid-servant in *Aloul,* I, 266: *moult . . . mole et crasse;* and the priest in *Le Prestre et le chevalier* (II, 81–82) who is praised for having four fingers more of fat than his mistress.

33 Nudity and bathing: I, 126, 246, 249, 314; III, 37, 248, 276, 278; IV, 3. Sexual initiative: I, 263, 323; III, 69, 74, 235–236; IV, 7, 26, 164–165; *Nar,* 106; *Rych,* 2: 67, 69. Mutual seduction using anatomical euphemisms: III, 83–84; IV, 205; V, 28–30, 104–105. Sexual in-

eptitude: IV, 116–117, 159; *Liv,* 154, 187ff. Extreme pleasure is indicated occasionally in the dialogue, as in IV, 106–107; and by the image of swooning in III, 121 *(se pasmoit de gieus en aize)* and VI, 24 *(de douchor pasmée).*

34 In *Porcelet,* IV, 144: ". . . *ait non porcelez, / Por ce qu'il ne puet estre nez"* (". . . Let's name it piggy, because it can't keep clean").

35 The same conceit is used in the fabliau-like tale of Isengrin, Brun, and the vilain in the *Roman de Renart,* VI, *Ren,* II, 67–72.

36 *Une Seule Fame qui a son con servoit cent chevaliers de tous poins; Le Chevalier qui fist parler les cons* (2 versions); *L'Anel qui fesoit les vis grans et roids.*

37 I, 290; II, 21 *(".IX. fois");* II, 38, 39; II, 68, 81; II, 232 *("sis fez ou seet");* V, 31, 92 *(".vii. foiz");* V, 182, 208; VI, 154; *Liv,* 155, 253; *Nar,* 90. Nykrog *(Nyk,* pp. 210–211) makes a good deal of this enumeration, remarking that it "insists very strongly on the licentious *(grivois)* character of the expression" *foutre* which it accompanies. On the contrary, it seems to me most often in its exaggeration to heighten the humor of situations without increasing coarseness at all.

38 It is in the same general sense, I think, that one may understand *"en travers et traversée" (Le Heron, Rom* 26: 90).

39   Yl leve sus les dras derer,
                Puis pensout si à bon mester
                Yl sake avaunt un bon bordoun,
                Si l'a donné en my le coun,
                Un gros vit et long et quarré,
                Si l'a en my le coun donné;
                Ensi à ly de ces bras l'afferma
                Ne poeit gwenchir sà ne là.   [II, 195–196]

[He raised up the back of her gown, then thought of a good thing to do. . . . He drew forth a good staff and gave it to her right in the cunt, a big prick, long and well made, right in the cunt he gave it to her, and he held her so close around with his arms that she couldn't squirm this way or that.]

Achieved instances of behind-kissing occur in *Les Deus vilains,* as a grotesque mistake in the dark *(Liv,* 204); and in *Berengier au lonc cul* (III, 260; IV, 64).

40 E.g.: à la torcoise (V, 209); *creponer (Liv,* 177, 305n.); and *culoner* (III, 240) and *culeter* (III, 81; *Liv,* 189), which, though based on the word *cul* ("ass"), in context probably do not refer to anal intercourse, but

either to intercourse from behind, or to the conceit commonly found in the fabliau that during normal intercourse the *cul* of the male moves, and that of the female is beaten upon by the male's testicles.

41 E.g.:   Cil la vait aus jambes saisir,
                       Si l'a couchie toute enverse;
                       Ne la prist pas a la traverse,
                       Ainz l'a acueillie de bout.

                                  [*Constant du Hamel, Ros,* 101]

[He grabbed her legs and laid her down backwards; he didn't take her *a la traverse* (sideways?), but had her *de bout* (endwise?).]

42 *Rich,* pp. 286–287, quoted in part below, pp. 161–162.

43 On female sexual appetite see e.g., St. Thomas Aquinas, *Summa Theologica,* Suppl., Q. 62, Art. 4, Reply Obj. 5 (trans. Fathers of the English Dominican Province [London, 1922]): "in women the humours are more abundant, wherefore they are more inclined to be led by their concupiscences." The idea goes back at least to Aristotle *(Nich. Ethics,* VII, 7). For recent modifications of the traditional view that the fabliaux are antifeminist, see Richard Spencer, "The Treatment of Women in the *Roman de la Rose,* the Fabliaux, and the *Quinze Joies de Mariage,"* *Marche Romane,* 28, 3–4 (1978), 209–213; Ménard, *Fabliaux,* pp. 131–140.

44 See, e.g., the author's footnote on the appetite of the *connin* in *Le Prestre et la dame:* II, 239–240; the description of the woman's desire as a gout in *Le Prestre comporté:* IV, 7; to an extent the male railing in the course of *La Veuve: Liv,* 169, 172, 173, 176, 179; the scatological endings of *Porcelet:* IV 145–146, and of *La Dame qui aveine demandoit:* I, 328. A roundly unfavorable picture of the female emerges from *Une Seule Fame qui a son con servoit cent chevaliers,* but with little or no overt antifeminist comment.

45 It should be noted—times having changed—that Bédier cites this confession, which he calls "répugnante," as one of the instances of severe hatred of women in the fabliaux *(Fabliaux,* p. 324). For another reference to female naturalness and generosity see *Le Roy d'Angleterre et le jongleur d'Ely* (II, 253).

46 Unless one includes the means used by Robin in *L'Esquiriel* (V, 104) to prepare himself to seduce the girl.

47 For instance, as insult, in *La Veuve (Liv,* 179); as misunderstanding, in *Le Sot chevalier (Liv,* 189ff.) and *Celui qui bota la pierre* (IV, 148).

48 See *Aloul* (I, 264, 266–267, 282).

49 See, for instance, I, 232, 241, 262; V, 105; VI, 128; *Nar*, 89.

50 For variations on this situation, see III, 84–85; IV, 145; V, 29–31.

51 In *Du Con qui fu fait a la besche*, the devil, who is entrusted with completing the creation of woman, "made a fart on her tongue, and that's why she has so much chatter" (*Ren*, V, vii); in *Le Pet au vilain*, the devil catches in a sack and carries back to hell the fart of a dying vilain, thinking it is his escaped soul. Since then, explains the author, the souls of vilains have no longer been admitted to hell (III, 103–105). One sequence in *Les Deus Vilains* turns about the flatulence of a sleeping woman; its slapstick ending involves her awakening in the dark, doused with gruel—which she and her husband mistakenly take for a shameful incontinence (*Liv*, 203–205).

52 See *La Dame qui aveine demandoit* (I, 328); *Porcelet* (IV, 145).

53 See John T. Noonan, Jr., *Contraception: A History of Its Treatment by the Catholic Theologians and Canonists* (Cambridge, Mass.: Belknap, 1966), pp. 246–257, 293–295.

54 Pregnancy is mentioned as one of the burdens of marriage in *Le Vallet qui d'aise a malaise se met*, II, 168; and the wife in *La Dame qui fist trois tours* describes herself as pregnant as part of her alibi (III, 197; cf. III, 119); another claims as an alibi to be seeking pregnancy (III, 283). Two fabliaux deal with unsought pregnancy (I, 162; IV, 210–211; cf. *Trubert*, ed. Raynaud de Lage, vv. 2572ff.), and in another it is sarcastically predicted of a priest (II, 86–87).

55 Cf. Ménard, *Fabliaux*, pp. 128–129: "Il faut observer qu'hormis exception les auteurs de fabliaux ne condamnent guère les débordements sexuels au nom de la morale et de la spiritualité chrétiennes"; cf. his excellent general discussion of the clergy in the fabliaux (pp. 121–131).

The records of episcopal courts and visitations are a perennially rich source of information on the misdeeds of the medieval clergy. For the fabliau period see the reports of visitations by the Archbishop of Rouen from 1248 to 1269, ed. T. Bonnin, *Regestrum visitationum archiepiscopi Rothomagensis* (Rouen, 1852), trans. Sydney M. Brown and ed. Jeremiah F. O'Sullivan, *The Register of Eudes of Rouen* (New York: Columbia, 1964), e.g., pp. 20–36; also Faral, *Vie quotidienne*, pp. 41–49; Toussaert, *Sentiment religieux*, pp. 569–572; Gabriel Le Bras, "Le Clergé dans les derniers siècles du moyen âge," in *Prêtres d'hier et d'aujourdhui*, ed. G. Bardy et al. (Paris: Editions du Cerf, 1954), pp. 153–181.

56 Contemporary bowdlerization of copies of fabliaux may also have occurred. If Copy P of *Boivin de Provins* is a rehandling of a version close

to Copy A, then, as Rychner claims, the writer of P suppressed the most obscene passage in the poem; see *Rych*, 1: 80 (but cf. verses A 300 and P 268, *Rych*, 2: 117). The question is made very difficult by the uncertainty in most cases as to which of several copies was made first, and whether one is actually a rehandling of the other.

57 Marc Bloch, *Feudal Society*, trans. L. A. Manyon, 2 vols. (London: Routledge and Kegan Paul, repr. 1967), 2: 308. Italo Siciliano collects instances of sensuality in the medieval romance and in other genres in *François Villon et les thèmes poétiques du moyen âge* (Paris: Nizet, 1934), pp. 148–154.

58 See Guglielmo IX, *Poesie*, ed. Nicolò Pasero (Modena: S.T.F.M., 1973), nos. I–III, V–VI. While directly "obscene" terms are readily found in the non-courtly genres of Provençal poetry (e.g., *sirventes, tensos*), they are much more restricted in use in later *cansós*, except in self-conscious "counter-texts." See William D. Paden, Jr., "Utrum Copularentur: Of *cons*," *Esprit Createur*, 19 (1979), 73; Pierre Bec, *Burlesque et obscénité chez les troubadours: pour une approche du contre-texte médiéval* (Paris: Stock, 1984), esp. pp. 12–13, 16–17.

59 See, for instance, the Queen's rather vulgar comments on Eneas' presumed homosexuality in vv. 8567ff., with pun on *con/connin* in v. 8595; and Lavinia's scarcely more genteel references, vv. 9155–9165 (ed. J. J. Salverda de Grave, 2 vols., *CFMA*, Paris, 1925–1929). For other instances of courtly vulgarity see Siciliano, *Villon*, pp. 150–153.

60 A. J. Holden, ed., *Ipomedon, poème de Hue de Rotelande, fin du XIIe siècle* (Paris: Klincksieck, 1979).

61 Ménard, *Rire et sourire*, pp. 141–142.

62 Guillaume de Lorris and Jean de Meun, *Le Roman de la rose*, ed. Ernest Langlois, 5 vols., SATF (Paris, 1914–1924), vv. 2109–2114.

63 Jean Renart, *Le Lai de l'ombre*, ed. John Orr (Edinburgh: University Press, 1948), vv. 8–13. There may be a direct parody of this kind of courtly prologue on verbal purity in MS A of Gautier le Leu's militantly explicit *Sot chevalier*, when the narrator claims to be telling it *"tout sans meffez et sans mesdiz"* (*Liv*, 187n.).

64 Jean Renart, *Galeran de Bretagne*, ed. L. Foulet, *CFMA* (Paris, 1925), vv. 1307–1308.

65 See, e.g., Guglielmo IX, *Poesie*, ed. Pasero, VII, st. 6:
> e cove li que sapcha far
> faitz avinens
> e que's gart en cort de parlar
> vilamens.

Cercamon, *Poésies*, ed. Alfred Jeanroy, *CFMA* (Paris, 1922), III, st. 6:

> Plas es lo vers, vauc l'afinan
> Ses mot vila, fals, apostitz,
> E es totz enaissi bastitz
> C'ap motz politz lo vau uzan.

Cf. "Edward," in H. Rosamond Parsons, ed., "Anglo-Norman Books of Courtesy and Nurture," *PMLA*, 44 (1929), 420–428, vv. 103–106:

> Unquare te pri ne parlez mie
> De ordure ne de vilanie;
> Les bels contes dois reteinere,
> Et vilainis paroles haier.

Guillaume de Blois, *Alda* (ca. 1170), ed. Cohen, *"Comédie" Latine*, 1, vv. 25–26.

> Inueniet lasciua nimis sibi uerba pudicus
> Lector: materie, non mea culpa fuit.

Cf. Jean de Meun, *Roman de la rose*, ed. Langlois, vv. 15159–15194; *Rich*, vv. 953–956; Giovanni Boccaccio, "Conclusione dell'autore," *Il Decameron*, ed. Charles S. Singleton, 2 vols., Scrittori d'Italia, nos. 97–98 (Bari, 1955), 2: 323–324; Geoffrey Chaucer, *The Canterbury Tales*, "General Prologue," vv. 725–742; "Miller's Prologue," vv. 3171–3186; in *Works*, ed. F. N. Robinson, 2d ed. (Boston, 1957), pp. 24, 48.

66 See Adams, *Latin Sexual Vocabulary*, esp. pp. 214–217, 225–228. The model of genteel Roman doctrine is perhaps Cicero. See, e.g., *De officiis*, I. 29, 35; *De oratore*, III. 41; cf. *Rhetorica ad Herennium*, IV. 34.

67 Quintilian, *Institutio Oratoria*, VIII. 3. 39: "Ego Romani pudoris more contentus." The translation is that of H. E. Butler in the Loeb edition (Cambridge, Mass., 1959), 3: 233.

68 See St. Augustine, *The City of God*, trans. Philip Levine, 7 vols. (London and Cambridge, Mass.: Loeb Classical Library, 1966), XIV, 23, 17.

69 See *Nyk*, pp. 72–82; and Per Nykrog, "Courtliness and the Townspeople: The Fabliau as a Courtly Burlesque," in *CH*, pp. 66–68.

70 See also the wife's response to her husband's reference to Gautier's penis in *Le Fevre de Creil* (I, 233):

> "Quar, par la foi que je vos doi,
> Se plus en parlez devant moi,
> Je ne vous ameroie mie;

Tel honte ne tel vilonie
Ne devroit nus preudom retrère."

Though the speaker is nominally of lower class—her husband is a blacksmith—the author here gives her a rather genteel stance and diction,
in line with many other expressions of mock-courtly sensibility in the
piece. Cf. Jean Subrenat, "Notes sur la tonalité des fabliaux: A propos
du fabliau *Du Fèvre de Creil*," *Marche Romane*, 25, 1–2 (1975), 90. The
source of the verbal taboo expressed by the mother in *L'Esquiriel* is more
difficult to identify. In any case, the forbidden term can hardly be more
obscene in tone than the euphemism she uses:

"ja nule fame,
S'ele n'est se trop male teche,
Ne doit nommer cele peesche
Qui entre les jambes pendeille
A ces hommes."   [V, 102]

71 A similar slip occurs in *L'Esquiriel*, V, 106.
72 Guillaume de Lorris and Jean de Meun, *Le Roman de la rose*, ed. Langlois,
    vv. 5700–5705.
73 Nykrog, *Fabliaux*, p. 222; cf. Daniel Poirion, "Les Mots et les choses
    selon Jean de Meun," *L'Information littéraire*, 26 (1974) 9, where Jean's
    position is related to a new scholastic effort, associated with the "nom-
    inalist crisis," to express things directly.
74 See *Le Roman de la rose*, ed. Langlois, vv. 8796 *(coille)*; 13924 *(con)*;
    15140–15141 *(conin, fuiret*; cf. II, 239–240); 17052, 20040, 20052
    (coillons, coille); 3646 *(cul)*. The whole of Genius's exhortation in favor
    of sex (19543ff.), and Jean's thinly veiled allegorical account of the
    Lover's culminating sexual act (21583ff.) contain dozens of familiar
    metaphors by which the ordinary language described intercourse. Jean
    once does, it must be said, use the topos that what the amorous reader
    might find bawdy should be attributed to the requirements of the subject
    matter (vv. 15159–15194).
75 See *Le Roman de la rose*, ed. Langlois, v. 3646. Ménard *(Rire et sourire,*
    p. 692; *Fabliaux*, p. 151) points out that the word *cul*, having no ready
    substitute in the medieval language, never became taboo except in courtly
    literature.

CHAPTER VI

1   I dwell perhaps heavily on this point here and in chapter 3, above, because focusing on plot, and thus on narrative art, tends to muffle one's sense of the meaning of the genre as cultural history. We can obviously appreciate the art—the exquisite plotting—of such fabliaux as *Le Bouchier d'Abeville* or *La Borgoise d'Orliens* without needing to implicate ourselves too deeply in what they are saying about cultural values. From focusing on narrative art *in* fabliaux, it is an easy and perfectly natural step to focusing on fabliau *as* narrative art, and thus to viewing all elements of texture as subservient to plotting. This cutting off of the fabliau from time, place, and finally from history is well illustrated by Theiner's "Fabliau Settings." Fabliaux can also escape historical examination by too great emphasis on the origin and persistence of their plots in oral tradition. The question then becomes, for any given piece, "Is this a great *telling* of a familiar story?" rather than "What causes this familiar story to be remembered and written up in this time and place?"

2   Bédier, *Fabliaux,* p. 385; see above, p. 26.

3   Nykrog, *Fabliaux,* pp. 239–241.

4   A recent extreme formulation of the contrastive view, with inevitable emphasis on fabliau as parody, is Charmaine Lee, "I *Fabliaux* e le convenzioni della parodia," in Alberto Limentani, ed., *Prospettive sui fabliaux* (Padua: Liviana, 1976), pp. 3–41. Pierre Bec, in his recent edition of the corpus of "counter-texts"—the self-consciously contrastive texts— in troubadour poetry, takes the opposite view of the fabliaux (*Burlesque et obscénité*, p. 13): "Le contre-texte est donc, par définition, un texte minoritaire et marginalisé, une sorte d'infra-littérature *(underground)*. Sa référence paradigmatique reste le texte, dont il se démarque, et son récepteur, inévitablement, le même que celui du texte. Car sa réception et son impact sont étroitement liés aux modalités du code textuel majoritaire. De ce point du vue, son outrance me semble assez différente de celle, par exemple, du fabliau français. Certes, le fabliau peut être vu comme une sorte de contre-texte réaliste et burlesque (voire scatologique et obscène) de la nouvelle courtoise, en l'occurrence le lai. On y retrouve en effet les mêmes procédés narratifs, le même moule prosodique (octosyllabes à rimes plates), mais tout cela dans le cadre d'une parodie voulue et joviale du monde courtois. Pourtant, le fabliau, malgré

son caractère de rupture sociologique, me paraît être néanmoins un genre constitué, plus ou moins défini certes, mais bien un texte et reçu comme tel. L'abondance de ses attestations (quelque cent soixante pièces) plaiderait dans ce sens, et il est clair d'autre part que les fabliaux, malgré leur caractère scabreux, n'ont vraisemblablement pas circulé sous le manteau. Si contretexte il y a (au sens où nous l'entendons), il n'apparaît que par intervalles dans le tissu même du texte narratif: paraphrases isolées, parodies burlesques, scatologiques ou littéraires, dispersées de-ci, de-là dans le récit."

5 *Rich,* pp. 222–224 (vv. 945ff.).

6 See, for instance, the pseudo-Breton lai *Le Lecheor,* ed. Gaston Paris, *Rom* 8 (1879), 64–66; two pieces by Gautier le Leu: *Du C.,* in *Liv,* pp. 233–249, and *Des C.,* in *Liv,* pp. 251–253; and related passages in *Le Debat du c. et du c.,* II, 133–136.

7 Mikhail Bakhtin, *Rabelais and His World,* trans. Helene Iswolsky (Cambridge, Mass.: MIT Press, 1968). For passages involving the fabliaux, see particularly pp. 7–15, 24–27, 73–96, 239–242.

8 An enthusiastic application of Bakhtin's notion of the "carnivalesque" to the fabliaux will be found in Lee, "Fabliaux e convenzioni" pp. 26–31.

9 Romantic views of folk tradition such as Bakhtin's find a useful correction in the sensible historical perspective of Jacques Heers, *Fêtes des fous et Carnavals* (Paris: Fayard, 1983).

10 Suzanne K. Langer, *Feeling and Form* (New York: Scribner's, 1953), p. 331.

11 From the mid-1950s through the 1970s social psychology paid considerable attention to a theory that inconsistency, or "cognitive dissonance," is virtually always uncomfortable, and that the mind tries to keep internal beliefs consistent with each other. See, e.g., Leon Festinger, *A Theory of Cognitive Dissonance* (Stanford: Stanford University Press, 1957): "The existence of dissonance . . . will motivate the person to try to reduce the dissonance and achieve consonance" (p. 3). The early formulation of the theory was modified by considerations of ego satisfaction and self-esteem as affecting motivation, but the theory still rested on the importance of reducing dissonance. An early expression of moderate scepticism was that of Jonathan L. Freedman, "How Important is Cognitive Consistency?", in Robert P. Abelson et al., *Theories of Cognitive Consistency: A Sourcebook* (Chicago: Rand-McNally, 1968): "People are not particularly on the look-out for inconsistencies among

their cognitions, they are not aware of most such inconsistencies, and they do not spend much time trying to find them. In addition, once they find them, it generally does not bother them terribly and therefore does not activate very strong processes of reducing or minimizing the inconsistencies" (p. 499). The theory has lately been abandoned as research on cognition has turned in the direction of information-processing. In sociology, on the contrary, there has recently emerged an interest in "sociological ambivalence" or "normative dissonance" as a constructive social phenomenon. See, e.g., Robert K. Merton, "Sociological Ambivalence" [1963], in *Sociological Ambivalence and Other Essays* (New York: The Free Press, 1976), 3–31; Edgar W. Mills, Jr., "Sociological Ambivalence and Social Order: The Constructive Uses of Normative Dissonance," *Sociology and Social Research,* 67 (1983), 279–287. Mills comments (p. 281) that some prior researchers on neurosis were "so focused on a rational model of decision-making and upon self-consistency as essential to mental health that they did not see the utility of normative dissonance for retaining personal autonomy." He concludes: "At the level of the individual, the presence of contrasting sets of norms and values allows a degree of autonomy and develops skill in weighing alternatives, charting one's own among them, and managing inner dissonance arising from multiple reference orientations. Members of groups may legitimately behave inconsistently, invoking different standards at different times" (p. 284). In these terms, we might infer that comedy is one of the occasions and humor one of the signals by which people recognize and sanction normatively dissonant experience.

12 See Faral, *Manuscrit 19152.*

13 Emmanuel Le Roy Ladurie, *Montaillou, village occitan de 1294 à 1324* (Paris: Gallimard, 1975), p. 236; see also chap. 10.

A List and Index of the Fabliaux

Listed below alphabetically is each work that has been classified a fabliau in at least one of the four principal lists made in the last century. Each entry contains the following information:

1. Title (with English translation as necessary) and author (if known). Generally, the spelling is that adopted by NRCF.

2. Classed a fabliau by:
   B   Joseph Bédier, *Les Fabliaux* (1894)
   N   Per Nykrog, *Les Fabliaux* (1957)
   J   Omer Jodogne, *Le Fabliau* (1975)
   R   Willem Noomen and Nico van den Boogaard, eds., *Nouveau recueil complet des fabliaux (NRCF)* (1983–)
   **   Indicates that the work was previously undiscovered

3. The most recent edition(s). For collections the following abbreviations are used:

Chr   Hans Helmut Christmann, *Zwei altfranzösische Fablels* (Tübingen: Niemeyer, 1963)

DC   A. Hilka and W. Söderhjelm, *Petri Alphonsi Disciplina Clericalis*, III *Französische Versbearbeitungen*, Acta Societatis Scientarum Fennicae, 49, no. 4 (Helsingfors, 1922)

DE   John Duval, trans., and Raymond Eichmann, ed., *Cuckolds, Clerics, & Countrymen, Medieval French Fabliaux* (Fayetteville: University of Arkansas Press, 1982)

ED   Raymond Eichmann and John Duval, ed. and trans., *The French Fabliau, B.N. MS. 837*, 2 vols. (New York: Garland, 1984–). In progress; * indicates work projected for volume 2.

FB   Edmond Faral and Julia Bastin, *Oeuvres complètes de Rutebeuf*, II (Paris: J. Picard, 1960)

JO   R. C. Johnston and D. D. R. Owen, *Fabliaux* (Oxford: Blackwell, 1957)

Lång   Arthur Långfors, *Huon le Roi, Le Vair Palefroi, avec deux versions de La Male Honte par Huon de Cambrai et par Guillaume*, 2d ed., CFMA (Paris: Champion, 1957)

Liv	Charles H. Livingston, *Le Jongleur Gautier le Leu* (Cambridge: Harvard University Press, 1951)
LP	B. J. Levy and C. E. Pickford, *Selected Fabliaux* (Hull: Hull [University] French Texts, 1978)
Man	Annalisa Landolfi Manfellotto, *I "Fabliaux" di Jean de Condé* (L'Aquila: Japadre, 1981)
Mén	Philippe Ménard, *Fabliaux français du Moyen Age,* I (Geneva: Droz, 1979)
MR	(by volume and first page) A. de Montaigon and G. Raynaud, *Recueil général et complet des fabliaux,* 6 vols. (Paris, 1872–90)
Nar	Pierre Nardin, *Jean Bodel, Fabliaux,* 2d ed. (Paris: Nizet, 1965)
NRCF	(by volume and first page) W. Noomen and N. van den Boogaard, *Nouveau recueil complet des fabliaux (NRCF),* 10 vols. (Assen: Van Gorcum, 1983–). In progress; * indicates projected location.
OG	Richard O'Gorman, *Les Braies au Cordelier,* (Birmingham, Ala.: Summa, 1983)
Reid	T. B. W. Reid, *Twelve Fabliaux* (Manchester: University Press, 1958)
Rohlfs	Gerhard Rohlfs, *Sechs altfranzösische Fablels* (Halle: Niemeyer, 1925)
Rych	Jean Rychner, *Contribution à l'étude des fabliaux,* II (Neuchâtel: Faculté des Lettres, and Geneva: Droz, 1960)
Thom	Patrick A. Thomas, *L'Oeuvre de Jacques de Baisieux,* Studies in French Literature, 3 (The Hague: Mouton, 1973)
Warnke	Karl Warnke, *Die Fabeln der Marie de France* (Halle: Niemeyer, 1898)
WG	Martha Walters-Gehrig, *Trois fabliaux* (Tübingen: Niemeyer, 1961)

4. Translation(s) into English (the aim is convenience rather than completeness). For collections, the following abbreviations are used:

BA	Larry D. Benson and Theodore M. Andersson, *The Literary Context of Chaucer's Fabliaux* (Indianapolis: Bobbs-Merrill, 1971)
But	Isabel Butler, *Tales from the Old French* (Boston: Houghton Mifflin, 1910)

Brians   Paul Brians, *Bawdy Tales from the Courts of Medieval France*
                  (New York: Harper and Row, 1972)

DE   John Duval, trans., and Raymond Eichmann, ed., *Cuckolds,
                  Clerics, and Countrymen, Medieval French Fabliaux* (Fayette-
                  ville: University of Arkansas Press, 1982)

ED   Raymond Eichmann and John Duval, ed. and trans., *The
                  French Fabliau, B.N. MS. 837*, 2 vols. (New York: Garland,
                  1984–   ). In progress; * indicates work projected for vol-
                  ume 2.

Har   Robert Harrison, *Gallic Salt* (Berkeley: University of Cal-
                  ifornia Press, 1974)

HO   Robert Hellman and Richard O'Gorman, *Fabliaux, Ribald
                  Tales from the Old French* (New York: Crowell, 1965)

Mason   Eugene Mason, *Aucassin and Nicolette, and Other Medieval
                  Romances and Legends* (New York: Dutton, 1958)

MS   Margaret Schlauch, *Medieval Narrative: A Book of Translations*
                  (New York: Prentice-Hall, 1934)

Rick   Peter Rickard et al., *Medieval Comic Tales* (Totowa, N. J.:
                  Rowman and Littlefield, 1973)

5. Reference to the work in the pages of this book.

For information about fabliau manuscripts, see Nykrog, *Fabliaux*, pp. 309–
25; Van den Boogaard, "*NRCF;*" and the successive volumes of the *NRCF*.

Aloul BNJR; ed. MR I, 255;
ED; NRCF *3; trans. Brians;
ED. Ref. pp. 40, 49, 61, 65,
116, 125, 181, 190, 193

L'Anel qui fesoit les vis grans et
roids (The Ring That Made
Cocks Big and Stiff), by
Haiseau BNJR; ed. MR III,
51; NRCF *8. Ref. pp. 59,
114, 191

[Le Lai d'] Aristote (The Tale of
Aristotle), by Henri d'Andeli
BN; ed. MR V, 243; M. Del-
bouille, Bibliothèque de la Fa-
culté de Philosophie et Lettres
de l'Université de Liège, 123
(Paris: Belles Lettres, 1951);
ED; Reid; trans. ED; Har; HO;
S. G. Nichols, in Angel Flores,
ed., *Medieval Age* (New York:
Dell, 1963). Ref. pp. 9, 14,
66, 86, 135–36, 182

Auberee, by Jehan(?) BNJR; ed.
MR V, 1; Chr; Charmaine Lee,
Les Remaniements d'Auberee, Ro-
manica Neapolitana, 11 (Na-
ples: Liguori, 1983); LP; Reid;
NRCF 1, 161; trans. Brians.
Ref. pp. 4, 30, 31, 41, 48, 60,
75, 112, 185, 190

Baillet. *see* Le Prestre qui fu mis
au lardier
Barat et Haimet, by Jean Bodel
BNJR; ed. MR IV, 93; Nar;
WG; NRCF 2, 27; trans. Mason (as The Three Thieves). Ref.
pp. 20, 60, 62, 96–98, 159,
182, 184
Berengier au lonc cul I (Berengier
of the Long Ass), by Guerin
BNJR; ed. MR III, 252; DE;
Rych; NRCF *4; trans. BA;
DE; Har; HO. Ref. pp. 16,
44–45, 59, 73, 118, 191
Berengier au lonc cul II   BNJR;
ed. MR IV, 57; Rych; NRCF
*4. Ref. pp. 16, 44, 59, 118,
191
Boivin de Provins, by "him-
self"   BNJR; ed. MR V, 52;
ED; Mén; Rych; NRCF 2, 77;
trans. Brians; ED. Ref. pp. 7,
40, 48, 60, 67, 75, 83–86, 94,
115, 121, 185, 193–94
La Borgoise d'Orliens (The Towns-
woman of Orleans)   BNJR; ed.
MR I, 117; DE; *ED; JO; LP;
Mén; Richard O'Gorman (St.
Louis: Washington University
Press, 1957); Rohlfs; Rych;
NRCF *3; trans. DE; *ED;
Har; HO; Rick. Ref. pp.
48, 60, 79, 95, 185, 190,
197
Le Bouchier d'Abeville (The
Butcher of Abeville), by Eus-
tache D'Amiens   BNJR; ed.
MR III, 227; DE; *ED; John
Orr (London: Oliver and Boyd,

1947); Jean Rychner (Geneva:
Droz, 1975); NRCF *3; trans.
BA; DE; *ED; HO; Orr (in ed.
above). Ref. pp. 48, 66, 70,
76–77, 93, 159, 197
La Bourse pleine de sens (The
Purse Full of Sense), by Jean le
Galois d'Aubepierre   BJR; ed.
MR III, 88; NRCF 2, 109.
Ref. pp. 22, 184
Les Braies au Cordelier (The Friar's
Breeches)   BNJR; ed. MR III,
275; ED; OG; NRCF *3; trans.
ED. Ref. pp. 59, 190
Les Braies le prestre (The Priest's
Breeches), by Jean de Condé
BNJR; ed. MR VI, 257; Man;
OG; NRCF *10; trans. HO.
Ref. p. 32
Brifaut   BNJR; ed. MR IV, 150;
JO; NRCF *6. Ref. pp. 49,
93, 159
Brunain, la vache au prestre
(Browny, the Priest's Cow), by
Jean Bodel   NRCF; ed. MR I,
132; DE; *ED; JO; Nar; NRCF
*5; trans. DE; *ED; Har; HO;
Rick. Ref. pp. 59, 103
Cele qui fu foutue et desfoutue
(She Who Was Fucked and De-
Fucked): *see* La Grue *and* Le
Heron
Cele qui se fist foutre sur la fosse
de son mari (She Who Had
Herself Fucked on Her Hus-
band's Grave)   BNJR; ed. MR
III, 118; LP; NRCF *3; trans.
Playboy (March, 1958). Ref. pp.
21, 22, 122, 184

Celui qui bota la pierre I (He
Who Kicked the Stone)
BNJR; ed. MR IV, 147; Rych;
NRCF *6. Ref. p. 192

Celui qui bota la pierre II
BNJR; ed. MR VI, 147; Rych;
NRCF *6. Ref. pp. 116, 131

Le Chapelain (The Chaplain) [Le
Sagretaig IV] BNJR; ed. MR
VI, 243; NRCF *6. Ref. pp. 4,
103

Charlot le juif (Charley the Jew),
by Rutebeuf BNJR; ed. MR
III, 222; FB; NRCF *9. Ref. p.
129

Le Chevalier a la corbeille (The
Knight with the Basket)
BNJR; ed. MR II, 183; NRCF
*9. Ref. pp. 30, 32, 59, 190

Le Chevalier a la robe vermeille
(The Knight with the Red
Robe) BNJR; ed. MR III, 35;
ED; Rohlfs; NRCF 2, 241;
trans. ED. Ref. pp. 43, 59,
190

Un Chivalier et sa dame et un
clerk (A Knight and His Lady
and a Clerk) BNJR; ed. MR
II, 215; NRCF *10. Ref. pp.
10, 48, 123, 184, 190

Le Chevalier qui fist parler les cons
I (The Knight Who Made
Cunts Speak), by Garin
BNJR; ed. MR VI, 68; Rych;
NRCF *3; trans. Har; HO.
Ref. pp. 4, 43, 48, 65, 89–91,
190, 191

Le Chevalier qui fist parler les cons
II, by Gwaryn BNJR; ed. MR

VI, 198; Rych; NRCF *3. Ref.
pp. 4, 191

Le Chevalier qui fist sa fame confesse (The Knight Who Heard
His Wife's Confession) BNJR;
ed. MR I, 178; *ED; NRCF
*4; trans. *ED; Ref. pp. 50,
123–24

Le Chevalier qui recovra l'amour
de sa dame (The Knight Who
Regained His Lady's Love)
BNJR; ed. MR VI, 138; JO:
NRCF *7; trans. HO; MS (as
The Ghost-Knight); Rick

Les Chevaliers, les clers et les vilains (The Knights, the Clerks,
and the Peasants) BNJ; ed. E.
Barbazan and M. Méon, Fa-
bliaux et contes des poëtes françois,
III (Paris, 1808; *ED; trans.
*ED. Ref. p. 39

Le Clerc qui fu repus derriere l'escrin (The Clerk Who Was Hidden behind the Chest) by Jean
de Condé BNJR; ed. MR
IV, 47; Man; NRCF *10;
trans. MS. Ref. pp. 51, 184,
190

Du Con qui fu fait a la besche (Of
the Cunt That Was Made with
a Spade) BNR; ed. *ED; M.
Roques, Le Roman de Renart, V
(branches XII–XVII), pp. v–vii;
NRCF *4; trans. *ED. Ref. pp.
118, 193

Connebert, by Gautier le Leu
BNJR; ed. MR V, 160; Liv;
NRCF *7. Ref. pp. 50, 52, 62,
126–27, 128, 139, 160, 189

Constant du Hamel BNJR; ed.
MR IV, 166; M. Nasra, thèse
3ᵉ cycle, Univ. de Paris IV,
1977; C. Rostaing (Gap: Louis-
Jean, 1953); NRCF I, 29. Ref.
pp. 32, 41, 127, 128, 192

La Contrarieuse (The Contrary
Woman), by Marie de France
N; ed. Warnke

La Couille noir (The Black
Balls) BNJR; ed. MR VI, 90;
NRCF *5. Ref. pp. 4, 40, 49,
129–30

Le Couvoiteus et l'envieus (The
Covetous Man and the Envious
One), by Jean Bodel BNR;
ed. MR V, 211; LP; Nar; Reid;
NRCF *6; trans. Har; HO; Ma-
son

La Crote (The Turd) BNJR; ed.
MR III, 46; *ED; NRCF *6;
trans. *ED. Ref. pp. 39, 49,
129

Le Cuvier (The Tub) BNJR; ed.
MR I, 126; *ED; NRCF *5;
trans. *ED. Ref. p. 49

La Dame escoillee (The Lady Who
Was Castrated) BNJR; ed.
MR VI, 95; NRCF *8; trans.
Brians. Ref. pp. 4, 75, 127,
128

Dame Jouenne **NJ; ed. A.
Långfors, Romania, 45 (1918–
19), 99–107. Ref. pp. 60, 70,
181, 182

La Dame qui aveine demandoit
pour Morel sa provende avoir
(The Lady Who Asked for

Blackie to Be Fed His
Oats) BNJR; ed. MR I, 318;
NRCF *9. Ref. pp. 32, 120,
122, 140, 189, 192, 193

La Dame qui fist batre son mari
(The Lady Who Had Her Husband Beaten) BNJR; ed. MR
IV, 133; NRCF *3 (La Borgoise
d'Orliens). Ref. pp. 31, 49, 61,
190

La Dame qui fist entendant son
mari qu'il sonjoit (The Lady
Who Made Her Husband Think
He Was Dreaming), by
Garin BNJR; ed. MR V 132;
(as Les Tresces:) Rych; NRCF
*6; trans. MS (as Tale of the
Tresses). Ref. pp. 49, 125

La Dame qui fist trois tors entor le
moustier (The Lady Who Did
Three Turns around the
Church), by Rutebeuf BNJR;
ed. MR III, 192; *ED; FB;
NRCF *5; trans. *ED. Ref. pp.
50, 61, 190, 193

La Dame qui se venja du chevalier (The Lady Who Took Revenge on the Knight) BNJR;
ed. MR VI, 24; NRCF *7.
Ref. pp. 51, 121, 139–40,
184

La Damoisele qui ne pooit oïr par-
ler de foutre I (The Damsel
Who Couldn't Stand Hearing
Talk of Fucking) BNJR; ed.
MR III, 81; Rych; NRCF *4.
Ref. pp. 7, 32, 132, 141–42,
158

La Damoiselle qui ne pooit oïr parler de foutre II BNJR; ed. MR V, 24; Rych; NRCF *4. Ref. pp. 32, 33, 141–43

La Damoiselle qui sonjoit (The Damsel Who Was Dreaming) BNJR; ed. MR V, 208; NRCF *4. Ref. p. 120

Les Deus Anglois et l'anel (The Two Englishmen and the Ring) BNJR; ed. MR II, 178; Reid; NRCF *8; trans. Keith Busby, *Interlanguage Studies Bulletin, Utrecht*, 3 (1978), 118–26. Ref. p. 115

Les Deus Changeors (The Two Exchangers) BNJR; ed. MR I, 245; *ED; NRCF *5. Ref. p. 94

Les Deus Chevaus (The Two Horses), by Jean Bodel BNJR; ed. MR I, 153; *ED; Nar; NRCF *5; trans. *ED. Ref. pp. 54, 175

Les Deus Vilains (The Two Peasants), by Gautier le Leu **NJR; ed. Liv; NRCF *9. Ref. pp. 5, 50, 160, 191, 193

L'Enfant qui fu remis au soleil (The Child Who Was Melted by the Sun) BNJR; ed. MR I, 162; *ED; O. de Rudder, *Médiévales*, 1 (1982), 104–10; NRCF *5; trans. *ED; Har; HO. Ref. pp. 52, 190

L'Espee (The Sword) N; ed. DC

L'Espervier (The Sparrowhawk) BN; ed. MR V, 43. Ref. pp. 30, 66

L'Esquiriel (The Squirrel) BNJR; ed. MR V, 101; NRCF *6. Ref. pp. 32, 112, 113, 114, 142, 144–46, 158, 188, 189, 190, 192, 196

Estormi, by Hues Piaucele BNJR; ed. MR I, 198; ED; Men; NRCF 1, 3; trans. ED. Ref. pp. 40, 50, 52, 60

Estula BNJR; ed. MR IV, 87; JO; WG; NRCF *4. Ref. p. 184

L'Evesque qui beneï le con (The Bishop Who Blessed the Cunt) BNJR; ed. MR III, 178; NRCF *6. Ref. pp. 83, 131

La Femme qui charma son mari (The Woman Who Recited a Charm for Her Husband) N; ed. DC

La Fame qui cunquia son baron (The Woman Who Tricked Her Husband) BNJR; ed. Bedier, *Fabliaux*, pp. 344–45; NRCF *9

La Femme qui fist pendre son mari (The Woman Who Had Her Husband Hanged), by Marie de France N; ed. Warnke (no. 25); trans. HO. Ref. p. 21

Le Fevre de Creil (The Blacksmith of Creil) BNJR; ed. MR I, 231; *ED; NRCF *5; trans. *ED. Ref. pp. 32, 54, 116, 118–19, 122, 139, 189, 195–96

Fole Larguesce (Foolish Largesse), by Philippe de Beaumanoir

BN; ed. MR VI, 53. Ref. pp. 22, 86, 101

Le Fol vilain (The Peasant Fool), by Gautier le Leu **NJR; ed. Liv; NRCF *9. Ref. pp. 74, 99, 189

Le Foteor (The Fucker) BNJR; ed. MR I, 304; NRCF *6. Ref. pp. 30, 31, 66, 70–71, 83, 139, 186

Frere Denise (Brother Denise), by Rutebeuf BNR; ed. MR III, 263; *ED; FB; NRCF *6; trans. *ED; HO. Ref. p. 50

La Gageure (The Wager) BNJR; ed. MR II, 193; NRCF *10. Ref. pp. 30, 45, 48, 79, 120, 191

Gauteron et Marion BNJR; ed. MR III, 49; NRCF *8. Ref. p. 128

Gombert et les deus clers (Gombert and the Two Clerks), by Jean Bodel BNJR; ed. MR I, 238; Nar; NRCF *4; trans. BA. Ref. pp. 20, 116, 120, 181

Gonbaut **R; [In Troyes, Bibliothèque Municipale, MS 1511] ed. NRCF *10

La Grue (The Crane), by Garin BNJR; ed. MR V, 151; Rych; NRCF *4 (Cele qui fu foutue et desfoutue). Ref. pp. 12, 73, 76, 184

Guillaume au faucon (William and the Falcon) BNJR; ed. MR II, 92; DE; Reid; NRCF *8; trans. DE, HO. Ref. pp. 30, 65, 115, 139, 182, 190

Le Heron (The Heron) **NJR; ed. Paul Meyer, Romania, 26 (1897), 85–91; Rych; NRCF *4 (Cele qui fu foutue et desfoutue). Ref. pp. 73, 76, 184

L'Home qui avoit feme tencheresse (The Man Who Had a Quarrelsome Wife), by Marie de France N; ed. Warnke (no. 95); trans. HO

La Housse partie I (The Divided Horse-Cloth), by Bernier BR; ed. MR I, 82; NRCF *3; trans. But; Mason. Ref. pp. 22, 101, 184

La Housse partie II BR; ed. MR II, 1; NRCF *3. Ref. pp. 22, 101, 184

Jouglet, by Colin Malet BNJR; ed. MR IV, 112; ED; NRCF 2, 187; trans. ED. Ref. pp. 40, 61, 99, 129

Le Jugement (The Judging) NR; ed. MR VI, 154; NRCF *10. Ref. p. 140

Le Jugement des cons (The Judging of the Cunts) BNJR; ed. MR V, 109; *ED; NRCF *4; trans. *ED

Le Maignien qui foti la dame (The Tinker Who Fucked the Lady) BNJR; ed. MR V, 179; NRCF *6. Ref. p. 60

La Male Honte I (Honte's Bag), by Guillaume BNJR; ed. MR IV, 41; Lång; JO; Rych; NRCF *5. Ref. pp. 41, 100

La Male Honte II, by Hues de Cambrai BNJR; ed. MR V,

95; Lång; Rych; NRCF *5.
Ref. pp. 41, 100 ,185
Le Mantel mautaillée (The Ill-Fit-
ting Cloak) B; ed. MR III. Ref.
p. 13
Le Meunier d'Arleux (The Miller
of Arleux), by Engerran
d'Oisi BNJR; ed. MR II, 31;
NRCF *9. Ref. pp. 9, 13, 52,
75
Le Meunier et les deux clers (The
Miller and the Two Clerks)
BNJR; ed. MR V, 83; W. M.
Hart in *Sources and Analogues of
Chaucer's Canterbury Tales,* ed.
W. F. Bryan and G. Dempster
(Chicago: University of Chicago
Press, 1941); Rych; Men;
NRCF *7; trans. BA; Har; HO
Le Moigne (The Monk) **NJR;
ed. A. Långfors, *Romania,* 45
(1915–17), 559–74; NRCF
*10. Ref. pp. 61, 113, 117–
18, 131
La Nonete I (The Little Nun), by
Jean de Condé BNJR; ed. MR
VI, 263; Man; NRCF *10. Ref.
pp. 60, 131–32
La Nonete II **N; ed. G. Ray-
naud, *Romania,* 34 (1905),
279–83. Ref. pp. 60, 190
L'Oue au chapelain (The Chap-
lain's Goose) BNJR; ed. MR
VI, 46; NRCF *8. Ref. pp. 50,
54, 61, 73, 77
Les Perdris (The Partridges)
BNJR; ed. MR I, 188; *ED;
LP; NRCF *4; trans. *ED;
HO. Ref. pp. 77, 100, 181

Le Pescheor de Pont seur Saine
(The Fisherman of Pont-seur-
Saine) BNJR; ed. MR III, 68;
*ED; NRCF *4; trans. *ED.
Ref. pp. 49, 113, 116, 121,
122, 188
Le Pet au vilain (The Peasant's
Fart), by Rutebeuf BNJR; ed.
MR III, 103; FB; NRCF *5;
trans. *ED. Ref. pp. 39, 193
La Piere au puis (The Stone in the
Well) N; ed. DC
La Plantez (The Abundance)
BNJR; ed. MR III, 170; NRCF
*7; trans. HO. Ref. p. 41
Le Pliçon (The Fur Cloak), by Jean
de Condé BNJR; ed. MR VI,
260; Man; NRCF *10; trans.
HO (as The Petticoat). Ref. pp.
51, 173
Porcelet (Piggy) BNJR; ed. MR
IV, 144; NRCF *6. Ref. pp.
32, 189, 191, 193
Le Povre Clerc (The Poor Clerk)
BNJR; ed. MR V, 192 NRCF
*7; trans. HO; MS. Ref. pp.
10, 103
Le Povre Mercier (The Poor Ped-
dler) BNJR; ed. MR II, 114;
JO; NRCF *8. Ref. p. 9
Le Prestre comporté [Le Prestre
qu'on porte] (The Transported
Priest) BNJR; ed. MR IV, 1;
A. Stepphuhn (Koenigsberg,
1913); NRCF *9. Ref. pp. 31,
74, 76, 79, 125, 176, 180,
192
Le Prestre crucefié (The Crucified
Priest) BNJR; ed. MR I, 194;

*ED; LP; NRCF *4; trans.
*ED. Ref. pp. 125–26

Le Prestre et Alison (The Priest
and Alison), by Guillaume le
Normand   BNJR; ed. MR II,
8; Mén; NRCF *8. Ref. pp.
52, 54, 61, 118, 131, 161

Le Prestre et la dame (The Priest
and the Lady)   BNJR; ed. MR
II, 235; NRCF *8; trans. BA.
Ref. pp. 173, 192

Le Prestre et le chevalier (The
Priest and the Knight), by
Milles d'Amiens   BNJR; ed.
MR II, 46; NRCF *9. Ref. pp.
38, 43, 52, 63–65, 66, 77–79,
83, 93, 125, 159, 190

Le Prestre et le leu (The Priest and
the Wolf)   BNJR; ed. MR VI,
51; LP; NRCF *8. Ref. p. 125

Le Prestre et le mouton (The
Priest and the Sheep), by Haiseau
BNJR; ed. MR VI, 50; NRCF
8; trans. HO, p. 186n.; above,
p. 176, n. 29. Ref. p. 176

Le Prestre et les deux ribaus (The
Priest and the Two Rascals)
BNJR; ed. MR, III, 58; *ED;
NRCF *5; trans. *ED. Ref. pp.
54, 67–68, 94

Le Prestre pelé (The Priest Made
Bald), by Gautier de Coincy
**N; ed. J. Morawski, Roman-
ia, 55 (1929), 542–48. Ref.
pp. 31, 181

Le Prestre qui abevete (The Spying
Priest), by Garin   BNJR; ed.
MR III, 54; DE; NRCF *8;
trans. BA; DE. Ref. pp. 47–48

Le Prestre qui dist la Passion (The
Priest Who Recited the Pas-
sion)   BNJR; ed. MR V, 80;
NRCF *8. Ref. p. 54

Le prestre qui fu mis au lardier
(The Priest Who Was Put in
the Larder); also known as
Baillet   BN; ed. MR II, 24;
JO; trans. Har

Le Prestre qui manja mores I (The
Priest Who Ate Mulberries), by
Guerin   BNJR; ed. MR IV,
53; JO; Reid; Rych; NRCF *7;
trans. Mason. Ref. p. 73

Le Prestre qui manja mores,
II   BNJR; ed. MR V, 37;
Rych; NRCF *7. Ref. p. 180

Le Prestre qui ot mere a force (The
Priest Who Had a Mother in
Spite of Himself)   BNJR; ed.
MR V, 143; *ED; Reid; Rohlfs;
NRCF *5; trans. *ED. Ref. pp.
93–100

Le Prestre qu'on porte: see Le
Prestre comporté

Le Prestre teint (The Dyed Priest),
by Gautier le Leu   BNJR; ed.
MR VI, 8; Liv; NRCF *7. Ref.
pp. 49, 87, 181

Le Pré tondu (The Mowed Mead-
ow)   BNJ; ed. MR IV, 154;
trans. MS (final third, as The
Reaped Field)

Le Preudome qui rescolt son compere de noier (The Good Man
Who Saved His Fellow from
Drowning)   BNR; ed. MR I,
301; JO; Reid; NRCF *8;
trans. Rick. Ref. p. 22

Le Provost a l'aumuche (The Provost with the Hood) BNJR; ed. MR I, 112; *ED; NRCF *4; trans. *ED. Ref. pp. 41, 54, 60, 73

La Pucele qui abevra le polain (The Girl Who Watered the Pony) BNJR; ed. MR IV, 199; (as La Damoisele qui ne pooit oïr parler de foutre:) Rych; NRCF *4. Ref. pp. 142, 143–44

La Pucele qui voloit voler (The Girl Who Wanted to Fly) BNJR; ed. MR IV, 208; NRCF *6. Ref. pp. 120, 122

Les Putains et les lecheors (The Whores and the Lechers) BNR; ed. MR III, 175; NRCF *6. Ref. pp. 37, 54–55, 180

Les Quatre Prestres (The Four Priests), by Haiseau BNJR; ed. MR VI, 42; LP; Rohlfs; NRCF *8

Les Quatre Sohais Saint Martin (The Four Wishes of St. Martin) BNJR; ed. MR V, 201; LP; Rych; NRCF *4; trans. Har. Ref. pp. 115, 185, 188

Richeut B; ed. I. C. Lecompte, Romanic Review, 4 (1913), 261–305; ed. and trans. Donald E. Ker (Ann Arbor: University Microfilms, 1978). Ref. pp. 18–19, 25, 121, 161–62, 174–75

Le Roy d'Angleterre et le jongleur d'Ely (The King of England and the Minstrel of Ely) BN; ed.

MR II, 242. Ref. pp. 54, 83, 99–100, 180, 192

Le Sacristain I (The Sacristan) BNJR; ed. MR V, 115; NRCF *7. Ref. pp. 4, 17, 61, 87, 190

Le Sacristain II BNJR; ed. MR V, 215; LP; Reid; V. Väänänen (Helsinki, 1949); NRCF *7; trans. Brians; Har. Ref. pp. 4, 48, 62, 75, 76, 93

Le Sacristain III, by Jean le Chapelain BNJR; ed. MR VI, 117; NRCF *7. Ref. pp. 4, 9, 40

Le Sacristain IV [Le Sagretaig IV]: see Le Chapelain

La Saineresse (The Lady Doctor) BN; ed. MR I, 289; DE; *ED; NRCF *4; trans. BA; DE; *ED. Ref. pp. 54, 139, 184

Saint Pierre et le jongleur (St. Peter and the Minstrel) BNJR; ed. MR V, 65; ED; JO; WG; NRCF 1, 129; trans. ED; Rick. Ref. pp. 48, 158, 182

Le Sentier battu (The Beaten Track), by Jean de Condé BNJR; ed. MR III, 247; Man; NRCF *10; trans. Har; HO. Ref. pp. 33, 51, 94, 184

Une Seule Fame qui a son con servoit cent chevaliers de tous poins (A Woman Who by Herself Fully Served with Her Cunt a Hundred Knights) BNR; ed. MR I, 294; NRCF *9. Ref. pp. 14, 190, 191, 192

Sire Hain et Dame Anieuse (Mr.
Hate and Mrs. Scold), by Hu-
gues Piaucele   BNJR; ed. MR
I, 97; ED; Rohlfs; NRCF 2, 3;
trans. DE. Ref. pp. 53, 74–75
Les Sohais (The Wishes), by Gau-
tier le Leu   **NJR; ed. Liv;
NRCF *9. Ref. p. 87
Le Sohait desvé (The Wild Desire),
by Jean Bodel   BNJR; ed.
MR. V, 184; Nar; NRCF *6.
Ref. pp. 12, 80–81, 119, 123,
159
La Sorisete des estopes (The Mouse
in the Tow)   BNJR; ed. MR
IV, 158; NRCF *6. Ref. pp.
71, 99
Le Sot chevalier (The Fool
Knight), by Gautier le Leu
BNJR; ed. MR I, 220; *ED;
Liv; NRCF *5; trans. *ED;
Har. Ref. pp. 75, 99, 118,
160, 184, 192, 194
Le Testament de l'asne (The Don-
key's Last Will), by Rutebeuf
BNJR; ed. MR III, 215; FB;
JO; NRCF *9; trans. Rick
Les Tresces (The Tresses)   BNJR;
ed. MR IV, 67; DE; Mén;
Reid; Rych; NRCF *6; trans.
DE; Ref. pp. 49, 127, 190
Les Trois Aveugles de Compiegne
(The Three Blind Men of Com-
piègne), by Cortebarbe   BNJR;
ed. MR I, 70; ED; G. Gougen-
heim, CFMA (Paris: Champion,
1932); Mén; NRCF 2, 153;
trans. ED. Ref. pp. 79, 96,
159, 184

Les Trois boçus (The Three
Hunchbacks), by Durand
BNJR; ed. MR I, 13; DE;
*ED; JO; NRCF *5; trans. DE;
*ED; Rick. Ref. pp. 42, 75,
91–92, 181, 184
Les Trois Chanoinesses de Cou-
loigne (The Three Canonesses of
Cologne), by Watriquet de
Couvin   BNJR; ed. MR III,
137; NRCF *10. Ref. pp. 8,
54, 82–83, 141
Les Trois Chevaliers et le chainse
(The Three Knights and the
Chemise), by Jakes de Ba[i]siu
B; ed. MR III, 123; Thom
Les Trois Dames de Paris (The
Three Ladies of Paris), by Wa-
triquet de Couvin   BNR; ed.
MR III, 145; Albert Henry,
Chrestomathie . . . (Berne:
Francke, 1953); Men; NRCF
*10; trans. Har. Ref. pp. 54,
81–82, 182
Le Trois Dames qui troverent
l'anel I (The Three Ladies Who
Found the Ring)   BNJR; ed.
MR I, 168; ED; NRCF 2, 217;
trans. ED. Ref. pp. 9, 47, 76,
94–95
Le Trois Dames qui troverent
l'anel II, by Haiseau   BNJR;
ed. MR VI, 1; NRCF 2,
217
Les Trois Dames qui troverent un
vit I (The Three Ladies Who
Found a Cock)   BNJR; ed. MR
IV, 128; NRCF *8. Ref. pp.
113, 185

Les Trois Dames qui troverent un vit II   BNJR; ed. MR V, 32; NRCF *8. Ref. pp. 9, 113, 185

Les Trois Meschines (The Three Girls)   BNJR; ed. MR III, 76; *ED; NRCF *4; trans. *ED. Ref. pp. 60, 128, 173

Les Trois Orements (The Three Wishes), by Marie de France   N; ed. Warnke (no. 57)

Trubert, by Douin de Lavesne   BJR; ed. J. Ulrich (Dresden, 1904); G. Raynaud de Lage (Geneva, 1974); NRCF *10. Ref. pp. 18, 19, 41, 174, 193

Le Vair Palefroi (The Grey Palfrey), by Huon le Roi   B; ed. MR I, 24; Lång; trans. But; Mason. Ref. pp. 87–89, 183

Le Vallet aus douze fames (The Young Man and the Twelve Wives)   BNJR; ed. MR III, 186; *ED; NRCF *4; trans. *ED. Ref. pp. 122, 181

Le Vallet qui d'aise a malaise se met (The Young Man Who Went from Comfort to Misery)   BNJR; ed. MR II, 157; NRCF *8. Ref. pp. 41, 54, 71, 180, 181, 193

Le Velous (The Bedspread)   N; ed. DC

Le Vescie a prestre (The Priest's Bladder), by Jakes de Baisiu   BNJR; ed. MR III, 106; Thom; NRCF *10; trans. BA; Har. Ref. pp. 79, 184

La Veuve (The Widow), by Gautier le Leu   BN; ed. MR II, 197; Liv; trans. Har; HO. Ref. pp. 30, 54, 62–63, 70, 75, 110, 180, 192

La Vieille et la lisette (The Old Woman and the Little Dog)   N; ed. DC

La Vieille qui oint la palme au chevalier (The Old Woman Who Greased the Knight's Palm)   BNJR; ed. MR V, 157; NRCF *6. Ref. pp. 39, 41, 184

La Vieille truande (The Old Beggar Woman)   BNJR; ed. MR V, 171; *ED; NRCF *4; trans. *ED. Ref. pp. 42, 68

Le Vilain asnier (The Peasant Donkey-Driver)   BNJR; ed. MR V, 40; DE; JO; LP; Mén; Reid; NRCF *8; trans. DE; Rick. Ref. p. 39

Le Vilain au buffet (The Peasant and the Blow)   BNJR; ed. MR III, 199; *ED; NRCF *5; trans. Jeremy du Q. Adams, Patterns of Medieval Society, (Englewood Cliffs, N. J.: Prentice-Hall, 1969); *ED. Ref. pp. 7, 41, 68, 73–74, 180, 181, 184

Le Vilain de Bailluel (The Peasant of Bailluel), by Jean Bodel   BNJR; ed. MR IV, 212; Nar; NRCF *5; trans. Har. Ref. pp. 20, 61, 98

Le Vilain de Farbu (The Peasant of Farbu), by Jean Bodel   BNJR; ed. MR IV, 82; Nar; NRCF

*6. Ref. pp. 20, 60, 73, 76, 181

Le Vilain mire (The Peasant Doctor) BNJR; ed. MR III, 156; Chr; JO; Mén; NRCF 2, 311; trans. Har; HO; Rick. Ref. pp. 12, 31, 40, 43

Le Vilain qui conquist paradis par plait (The Peasant Who Argued His Way into Paradise) BNJR; ed. MR III, 209; LP; Reid; Rohlfs; Rych; NRCF *5; trans. But; [I. Butler in] *The Portable Medieval Reader*, ed. James Bruce Ross and Mary M. McLaughlin (New York: Viking, 1949), pp. 512–15. Ref. pp. 39, 94, 98

Le Vilain qui n'iert pas de son hostel sire (The Peasant Who Was Not Master of His Own House) **N; ed. L.-F. Flutre, *Romania* 62 (1936), 2–5. Ref. pp. 39, 54

Le Vilain qui od sa fame vit aler son dru (The Peasant Who Saw His Wife's Lover Go Off with Her), by Marie de France N; ed. Warnke (no. 45); trans. BA

Le Vilain qui vit un autre home od sa feme (The Peasant Who Saw Another Man with His Wife), by Marie de France N; ed. Warnke (no. 44); trans. BA. Ref. pp. 93, 190

.W., by "the young magistrate of Hamel" BNR; ed. W. Förster, *Jahrbuch für romanische und englische Sprache und Literatur*, 13 (1874), 288; NRCF *8. Ref. p. 9

General Index

Adam de la Halle, 25
Adams, N., 190, 195
Alda, 195
Anticlericalism, 17, 93, 132, 162, 185
Antifeminism, 104, 121–22, 127, 192
Aquinas, St. Thomas, 130, 192
Aristocratic class and literature. *See*
Courtly culture
Aristotle, 192
Audience, 46, 55, 104, 109, 124, 132,
152, 155, 177
Audigier, 14
Auerbach, E., 173
Augustine, St., 138, 195
Aulularia, 14

Badel, P.-Y., 174
Bakhtin, M., 164, 166, 198
Bandello, M., 27
Barth, B., 186, 187
Bataille de Caresme et de Charnage, Le, 182
Bate, K., 173
Bec, P., 194, 197
Becker, P., 175
Bédier, J.: definition of fabliau, 23, 47,
54; on social origins of fabliaux, 24–
29, 155; *Les Fabliaux,* 2, 12, 20, 71,
72, 105, 171–86 passim, 192, 197
Bergerfurth, W., 175
Beyer, Jürgen: *Schwank und Moral,* 107,
173–87 passim; "Morality of the Amor-
al," 186
Bloch, Marc, 133, 194
Boccaccio, G., 195
Bodel, Jean, 4, 20, 25, 80, 123, 159,
175
Bonnin, T., 193
Boogaard, N. van den: "Le Nouveau Re-
cueil," 171, 172; ed. *NRCF,* 171;
"NRCF," 180
Bossuat, R., 26, 176
Bourgeoisie and "bourgeois" literature,
24–46, 156, 176–77

Boy Bishop, 164
Brennan, M., 173
Brown, S., 193
Burger, G., 186
Burlesque, 18, 29, 106, 139, 158, 195,
197–98
Butler, H., 195

Caplan, H., 180
Caricature and the grotesque, 68, 72, 164
Carnival, 164, 198
Cercamon, 195
Chanson de geste, 14, 134
Characters: animal, 16–17, type, 17, 68
Characterization, 68–72, 73–75
Chaucer, Geoffrey, 136, 195
Chevalier à l'espee, Le, 13
Chrétien de Troyes, 13, 173
Christianity: morality and doctrine, 3,
87, 92, 93–94, 102–03, 104, 106,
109, 130–31 (on sexual intercourse),
137–38, (on obscene language), 151,
160, 163, 166–68, 183; as subculture,
155
Chronology, 4, 136
Cicero, 195
Clergy, treatment of in fabliau, 93, 125–
27, 128, 131–32, 140–41, 162, 184,
193
Clericis et Rustico, De, 15
Clerks: as characters, 9; as authors, 9, 15
Cleverness *(engin). See* Wit
Cognitive Dissonance, 198
Cohen, G., 173, 195
Coilles (term), 113, 116, 144, 146–50,
188, 196
Colby, A., 181
Comedy: verbal, 99–101; pleasure char-
acteristic of, 152; theory of, 166, 199.
See also Humor
Comedy (glure): medieval Latin, 14–15,
26, 152, 156, 173–74, 184; ancient,
14, 156

Composition, 5–10
Con (term): 113, 133, 134, 150, 163,
    189, 196; variations on: 113–14; puns
    on: 115, 189, 190, 194
Con, Du, 160, 198
Cons, Des, 198
Consistency, moral, 167
Cooke-Honeycutt collection, 107, 172
Cooke, T.: *Old French and Chaucerian Fa-*
    bliaux, 48, 179, 180; ed. *Humor,* 172,
    181, 183, 186; "Pornography," 107;
    "Two Ozark Analogues," 172–73
Cor, Lai du, 13
Courtly culture, literature, and style, 24–
    29, 34–39, 42–46, 62, 65–66, 87,
    89, 133–38, 151, 156, 157, 167, 196
Cremonesi, C., 173
Cul (term), 134, 191–192, 196

Debat du cul et du con, Le, 198
de' Negri, E., 174
Description, 62, 65–69, 117–19
Deux Bordeors ribauz, Les, 5–6
Dialogue, 70–71
Diction, 70
Dieu et le pescour, 160
Disciplina Clericalis, 21
Double entendre, 33, 54, 99–100. *See*
    also Puns
Dronke, P., 174
Dubuis, R., 180, 182
Duby, G., 178

Epic, 17
"Edward," 195
Eichmann, R., 172
Eneas, 133, 134, 194
Engerran d'Oisi, 13
Engin (term). *See* Wit
Ethos: fabliau, 72–104, 107, 124, 153–
    69; Judaeo-Christian, 166. *See also*
    Christianity
Euphemisms, 106, 107, 110–16 passim,
    132–33, 138, 140, 144, 146–50 pas-
    sim, 184, 190, 191, 196
Evergates, T., 178
"Exegetical" criticism, 3, 168–69

Fable, 19–22
Fabliau: as genre, 3–23, 152, 169, 197–
    98; definition of, 3, 23, 47, 54. *See*
    also specific topics, such as Audience,
    Composition, Geographical origins,
    etc.
Fabliau (term), 22–23, 171–72, 176
Fantasy, sexual, 118
Faral, E.: On social background, 26–27,
    28–29, 156–57; *Les Jongleurs,* 26, 172;
    Vie Quotidienne, 104, 185, 193; *MS*
    19152, 172, 199; "Fabliau latin," 173;
    ed. *Babione,* 173; "Fabliaux," 177;
    "Conte de Richeut," 175; *Arts Poé-*
    tiques, 180, 181, 185
Feast of Fools, 164
Festinger, L., 198
Flinn, J., 174
Flutre, L.-F., 172, 177
Foerster, W., 172
Food and eating, 73–78, 182
Fools, 98–99, 129
Fossier, R., 178, 179
Foulet, L.: *Roman de Renard,* 174; "Poème
    de Richeut," 175; ed. *Galeran,* 194
Fourquin, G., 178
Fourrier, A., 173
Foutre (term): 110, 115–16, 133, 134,
    142–44, 158, 191; variations on, 110–
    12, 140; pun on, 115
Freedman, J., 198–99

Galeran de Bretagne, 135
Garbaty, T., 173
Garin, 12
Gautier d'Arras, 13
Gautier le Leu, 5, 49–50, 52, 54, 74,
    111, 112, 113, 115, 126–27, 160,
    188, 194, 198
Genicot, L., 178, 179
Geoffroy of Vinsauf: *Documentum,* 15, 56–
    57, 180–81; *Poetria,* 58–59, 181, 185
Geographical origins, 25, 31, 179
Gesture, 69
Geta, 14
Gougenheim, G., 96
Green, D. H., 173
Guiette, R., 176

Guillaume de Blois, 195
Guillaume de Lorris, 134, 150, 194

Hanning, R., 183
Harrison, R., 189
Hedonistic materialism, 73, 124, 153
Heers, J., 198
Henri d'Andeli, 9, 66, 135
Hellman, R., 172
Helsinger, H., 183
Henderson, J., 190
Heptameron (Marguerite of Navarre), 27
Holden, A., 194
Holmes, U., 183
Homosexuality, 125, 160, 194
Honeycutt, B., 107, 172
Horace, 180–81
Hue de Rotelande, 13, 134
Humor: clerical, 15–19, 174; sexual,
   107, 108, 159–60, 163; monastic,
   163; as signal of dissonance. *See also*
   Comedy

Ignaurès, Lai d', 13
Imagery, 30–34, 59–69, 110–14 (sexual), 152
Ipomedon, 134, 183, (ed.) 194
Irony, 27, 52, 101, 104, 153, 158, 160

Jauss, H., 172, 174
Jay, T., 187, 189
Jean de Condé, 4, 51, 101, 173
Jean de Meun, 24, 113, 146–50, 194,
   195, 196
Jeanroy, A., 195
Jehan le Chapelain, 9
Jodogne, O.: "Considérations," 171, 176,
   180, 189; *Le Fabliau*, 171, 175, 184
John of Garland, *Poetria*, 57–58, 181
Johnston, R., 175
Jongleurs, 5–6
Joris, A., 177
Justice, 93, 183

Ker, D., 174–75
Kiesow, R., 171, 176

La Barre, W., 186
Ladurie, E., 168, 199
La Fontaine, Jean de, 27
Lai (genre), 13
Langer, S., 166, 198
Långfors, A., 183
Langlois, E., 194
Language, obscene: 105–51 passim; use
   by women, 112, 113, 116, 132–33,
   144–46, 158, 160, 189; in ancient
   world, 117, 137. *See also* individual
   terms
Lawler, T., 181
Le Bras, G., 193
Lecheor, Lai du, 14, 160, 198
Lecompte, I., 174
Lee, C., 197, 198
Le Gentil, P., 23, 176
Le Goff, J., 179
Lestocqoy, J., 177
Lian, A., 190
Limentani, A., 197
Little, L., 179
Livingston, C., 187, 188. *See also* Abbreviations section
Lorein, M.-T., 179
Lou et de l'ove, Dou, 20
Lozinski, G., 182

Mantel mautaillée, Le, 13. *See also* List and
   Index of Fabliaux
Manuscripts: of fabliaux 4, 11, 168, 172,
   183–85, 193–94; comic drawings in,
   164
Marcheans, Le Dit des, 181
Marcus, S., 107
Marie de France, 19, 21, 92, 175
Martin, E., 163, 171, 172, 174
Matron of Ephesus story, 21
Matthew of Vendôme, 15
Médecin malgré lui, 12
Ménard, P.: *Fabliaux*, 107–08, 175, 176,
   177, 179, 180 (on plot), 182 (on morality), 186, 192, 193, 196; *Rire et
   Sourire*, 133–34, 173, 177, 194, 196
Mercator, 174
Merton, R., 199
Merveilles de Rigomer, Les, 8, 172

Metaphor: and simile, 30–34; animal, 143; sexual, 110–14
Mills, E., 199
Milo, 15
"Modus Liebinc," 174
Molière, 12
Money, 83–92, 154, 183
Monier, R., 178
Monologues, 69–70, 182
Montaiglon, A. de, 181. *See also* Abbreviations section
Montaillou, 168
Moralization, 19–22, 40, 91–92, 96, 98, 101–04, 154, 184–85. *See also* Proverbs
Muscatine, C.: *Chaucer*, 173, 177; "Canterbury Tales," 177

Nardin, P., 175
Noomen, W.: "Qu'est-ce qu'un fabliau?," 171; ed. *NRCF*, 171
Noonan, John, 130, 193
Normative Dissonance, 199
NRCF, 171, 172, 180, 183, 184. *See also* Abbreviations section
Nykrog, Per: critique of Bédier, 2, 24, 27–29; on fabliau and fable, 20, 175; on definition of fabliau, 23; on fabliau as courtly genre, 27–29, 37–38, 156–57, 158; on obscenity, 105–06, 107, 111, 115, 141, 149; on courtly burlesque, 139; *Les Fabliaux*, 9, 57, 65, 66, 71, 171–91 passim, 195, 196, 197; "Courtliness," 195

Obscene marketplace (motif), 12, 119, 159
Obscenity. *See* Language, obscene
O'Gorman, R., 172
Olschki, L., 27, 29, 177
Olson, G., 184
Ombre, Lai de l', 135
Oral tradition, 11–13, 155, 197
Orr, J., 194
O'Sullivan, J., 193
Oustillement au villain, L', 181
Owen, D., 175
Owst, G., 174

Paden, W., 194
Pamphilus, 15
Paris, G., 198
Parody, 17, 28, 65, 91, 158, 160, 174, 194, 197
Parsons, H., 195
Pasero, N., 194
Paul, St., 102, 138
Pauphilet, A., 177
Pearcy, R.: "Obscene Diction," 107, 108, 116, 187; "Investigations," 179–80, 373
Peasants (social class), 34–40 passim
Petrus Alphonsus, 21, 175
Pfeffer, P., 183
Philippe de Beaumanoir, 9
Pierre de Saint-Cloud, 16
Pilz, O., 176
Plautus, 14
Plot, 47–55, 59–60, 101, 153, 179–80, 197
Poirion, D., 196
Pornography, 105, 107, 117
Portraits, 65–68, 181
Pregnancy, 131, 164, 193
Propp, V., 180
Provençal poetry, 133, 136, 194–95, 197
Proverbs and proverbial expressions, 30, 33, 40, 101–04, 130; *See also* Moralization
Psychoanalytic Theory, 168
Puns, 33, 114–15, 138–39, 184, 189, 190. *See also* Double entendre

Quintilian, 137, 195

Raby, F., 173, 174
Raynaud, G., 181
Raynaud de Lage, G., 174
Realism: in romance, 13; fabliau, 23, 45, 55–72, 153, 156, 176; of Rabelais, 164; tradition of in sermons and saints' lives, 15
Recitation and performance, 5–11, 51, 59
Reid, T., 20, 175, 189
Renart, Jean: *Ombre*, 135, 194; *Galeran*, 194

Renart, Roman de, 15–18, 19, 20, 24, 162–63, 171–72, 191
Revard, C., 185
Rhetorica ad Herennium, 56, 180, 195
Rhetorical theory, medieval, 55–59, 102, 185
Richeut, 18–19, 25, 121, 161–62, 174–75, 192. See also List and Index of Fabliaux
Roman de la Rose, 24, 113, 134, 146–50, (ed.) 194, 195, 196
Romance, Old French, 13, 24–25, 60, 91, 117, 133–34, 152, 169, 183
Roques, M., 172, 174
Rossi, L., 174
Rutebeuf, 50–51, 190
Rychner, J.: "Les Fabliaux," 171, 175, 176; Contribution, 172, 180, 194

Sadism, 125–28, 162, 190
Sapori, A., 178
Satire, 17, 42, 106, 122, 158
Scatology, 14, 122, 128–30, 134, 160
Schaar, C., 181
Schenck, M., 180, 183
Schneider, J.: Metz, 177, 178; Thiebaut de Heu, 178
Schulze-Busacker, E., 175, 184
Settings, 30, 60, 62, 181
Sexual activity, treatment of, 117–21, 124–28, 161–62, 189–92 passim
Sexuality: in fabliau, 83, 105–51, 159–63; female, 121–24, 192; language of, 32–33, 105–51 passim. See also Language, obscene, and individual terms
Siciliano, I., 194
Snow baby theme, 174
Social background, 24–46, 152. See also Bourgeoisie; Courtly culture; Peasants
Sociological Ambivalence, 199
Speech and dialogue, 69–71
Spencer, R., 192
Stempel, W.-D., 106, 186
Style: fabliau, 55–72; courtly, 62, 65–66, 69, 182. See also Realism, Rhetorical theory
Subrenat, J., 196

Suchomski, J.: "Delectatio und Utilitas," 173, 174, 184, 185; Lateinische Comediae, 173

Taboo, verbal, 108–10, 112, 113, 133–50 passim, 187, 188, 189, 196
Taylor, J., 175
Texture, 52–55, 59–65
Theiner, P., 181, 197
Thomson, I., 173
Tiemann, H., 171
Togeby, K., 171, 173
Toussaert, J., 179, 193
Transmission, 4–5
Trubert, 18, 19, 41, 174, 193. See also List and Index of Fabliaux

Ungureanu, M., 178

Vair Palefroi, Le, 87–89, 183. See also List and Index of Fabliaux
Varvaro, A.: "Società," 38, 39, 177, 178; "Segretaine Moine," 72, 176, 182, 185; "Richeut," 175
Vinay, G., 173
Virgil, 58
Vit (term): 112–16, 134, 145–46, 147, 148, 158, 160, 188, 189, 190; variations on, 112–13, 116, 144–45; puns on, 114–15, 190
Vital de Blois, 14

Waddell, H., 174
Wailes, S., 172, 174
Warnke, K., 175
Watriquet de Couvin, 81–83, 101, 141
Wenzel, S., 174
Whicher, G., 174
William IX of Aquitaine, 133, 194
Wine, 79–83
Wit, cleverness, 92–99, 154, 158–59, 183
Women, presentation of, 104, 121–24. See also Language, obscene

Ysengrinus (Nivard), 17

Zeydel, E., 174